Revenue Statistics in Latin America

1990-2012

Estadísticas tributarias en América Latina

1990-2012

INTER-AMERICAN CENTER OF TAX ADMINISTRATIONS CIAT ESTABLISHED IN 1967
OECD BETTER POLICIES FOR BETTER LIVES
UNITED NATIONS ECLAC

Please cite this publication as:
OECD/Economic Commission for Latin America and the Caribbean/Inter-American Center of Tax Administrations (2014), *Revenue Statistics in Latin America*, OECD Publishing.
http://dx.doi.org/10.1787/9789264207943-en-fr

Por favor, cite esta publicación de la siguiente manera:
OCDE/CEPAL/CIAT (2014), *Estadísticas tributarias en América Latina*, OECD Publishing.
http://dx.doi.org/10.1787/9789264207943-en-fr

ISBN 978-92-64-20793-6 (print/*impresa*)
ISBN 978-92-64-20794-3 (PDF)

The statistical data for Israel are supplied by and under the responsibility of the relevant Israeli authorities. The use of such data by the OECD is without prejudice to the status of the Golan Heights, East Jerusalem and Israeli settlements in the West Bank under the terms of international law.

Los datos estadísticos para Israel son suministrados por y bajo la responsabilidad de las autoridades israelíes competentes. El uso de estos datos por la OCDE es sin perjuicio del estatuto de los Altos del Golán, Jerusalén Este y los asentamientos israelíes en Cisjordania bajo los términos del derecho internacional.

Corrigenda to OECD publications may be found on line at: *www.oecd.org/publishing/corrigenda*.
Las erratas de las publicaciones de la OCDE se encuentran en línea en *www.oecd.org/publishing/corrigenda*.

Foreword

Revenue Statistics in Latin America is a joint publication by the OECD Centre for Tax Policy and Administration, the OECD Development Centre, the United Nations Economic Commission for Latin America and the Caribbean (ECLAC) and the Inter-American Centre of Tax Administrations (CIAT). It presents detailed, internationally comparable data on tax revenues for 18 Latin American economies, 2 of which are OECD members. Its approach is based on the well-established methodology of the OECD Revenue Statistics database (OECD, 2013), which has become an essential reference source for OECD member countries. Comparisons are also made with the average for OECD economies.

The term "taxes" in this publication is confined to compulsory, unrequited payments to general government. As outlined in the Interpretative guide to the Revenue Statistics, taxes are "unrequited" in the sense that benefits provided by government to taxpayers are not normally in proportion to their payments. The OECD methodology classifies a tax according to its base: income, profits and capital gains (classified under heading 1000), payroll (heading 3000), property (heading 4000), goods and services (heading 5000) and other taxes (heading 6000). Compulsory social security contributions paid to general government are treated as taxes, and classified under heading 2000. Much greater detail on the tax concept, the classification of taxes and the accrual basis of reporting is set out in the Interpretative Guide in Annex A.

Extending the OECD methodology to Latin America enables comparisons of tax systems on a consistent basis both across Latin America and between OECD and Latin American countries. However, in a few cases this methodology is different from the approach used by ECLAC and CIAT. In these cases the differences are noted in the text and in the tables, either with a footnote or an extra row.

The report provides an overview of the main taxation trends in Latin America. It examines changes in both the level and the composition of taxation plus the attribution of tax collection by sub-level of government between 1990 and 2012.

Presentación

La publicación *Estadísticas tributarias en América Latina* ha sido elaborada conjuntamente por el Centro de Política y Administración Tributaria de la OCDE, el Centro de Desarrollo de la OCDE, la Comisión Económica de las Naciones Unidas para América Latina y el Caribe (CEPAL) y el Centro Interamericano de Administraciones Tributarias (CIAT). Esta publicación presenta datos detallados comparables a escala internacional sobre los ingresos tributarios de 18 economías latinoamericanas, 2 de las cuales son miembros de la OCDE. Su enfoque se basa en la metodología consagrada de la base de datos Revenue Statistics de la OCDE (OCDE, 2013), que se ha convertido en un referente esencial para los países miembros de la OCDE. Se presentan también comparaciones con la media de la OCDE.

En la presente publicación, el término "impuestos" se circunscribe exclusivamente a los pagos obligatorios sin contraprestación efectuados al gobierno general. Tal y como lo subraya la Guía de interpretación de Revenue Statistics, los impuestos carecen de contraprestación en el sentido en que, normalmente, las prestaciones proporcionadas por el gobierno a los contribuyentes no guardan relación directa con los pagos realizados por estos. La metodología de la OCDE clasifica los impuestos según la base sobre la que recaen: renta, utilidades y ganancias del capital (categoría 1000); nómina (categoría 3000); propiedad (categoría 4000); bienes y servicios (categoría 5000); y otros impuestos (categoría 6000). Las contribuciones obligatorias a la seguridad social abonadas al gobierno general se tratan aquí como impuestos (categoría 2000). Para mayor detalle sobre el concepto de impuesto, su clasificación y su registro según el criterio de devengo, véase la Guía de interpretación que figura en el Anexo A.

Aplicar la metodología de la OCDE a América Latina posibilita la comparación de sistemas tributarios a partir de una base coherente tanto entre países latinoamericanos como entre estos y los países de la OCDE. Sin embargo, en contadas ocasiones, esta metodología difiere de la empleada por la CEPAL y el CIAT; en esos casos, las diferencias se han indicado en el texto y los cuadros, sea con una nota a pie de página, o en una línea adicional.

El informe ofrece un panorama general de las principales tendencias en materia tributaria en América Latina. A tal efecto, examina los cambios registrados entre 1990 y 2012 en el nivel y la composición de la tributación, así como en la atribución de la recaudación tributaria a los diversos subsectores de gobierno.

Acknowledgements

This edition of *Revenue Statistics in Latin America* has been jointly produced by the Organisation for Economic Co-operation and Development (OECD) Centre for Tax Policy and Administration, the OECD Development Centre, the United Nations Economic Commission for Latin America and the Caribbean (ECLAC) and the Inter-American Centre of Tax Administrations (CIAT). The staff from these organisations with responsibility for producing the publication were: Daniel Adshead of the OECD Development Centre under the supervision of Director Mario Pezzini; Maurice Nettley of the OECD Centre for Tax Policy and Administration under the supervision of Director Pascal Saint-Amans; Ricardo Martner, Michael Hanni and Andrea Podestá from the Economic Development Division of UN-ECLAC, under the supervision of Juan Alberto Fuentes; and Julio Alberto López from the CIAT Tax Studies and Research Directorate, under the supervision of Director, Miguel Eduardo Pecho.

The authors would like to thank other staff at the OECD Development Centre and the Centre for Tax Policy and Administration for their invaluable help in completing this third edition of the publication. Christian Daude, Head of the Americas Desk, provided substantial support and feedback throughout the whole process. Delphine Grandrieux and Elizabeth Nash from the OECD Development Centre's Communications and Publications team ensured the production of the publication, in both paper and electronic form. The publication has also greatly benefited from several individuals and institutions. Special mention is due to Alberto Barreix from the Inter-American Development Bank (IDB) and CIAT Network of Tax Studies Units.

The Centre for Tax Policy and Administration and the Development Centre gratefully acknowledge financial support from the Agencia Española de Cooperación Internacional para el Desarrollo (AECID) to the LAC Initiative, under the fiscal pillar of which this publication has been produced. Finally, we are also very grateful to our colleagues working in national entities with whom we have consulted regularly. These institutions include the finance ministries and national tax agencies of Argentina, Bolivia, Brazil, Chile, Colombia, Costa Rica, Dominican Republic, Ecuador, El Salvador, Guatemala, Honduras, Mexico, Nicaragua, Panamá, Paraguay, Peru, Uruguay and Venezuela, the Ministry of Economy and Production of Argentina and the Central Reserve Bank of Peru.

Agradecimientos

Esta edición de la publicación *Estadísticas tributarias en América Latina* ha sido elaborada conjuntamente por el Centro de Política y Administración Tributaria de la Organización para la Cooperación y el Desarrollo Económicos (OCDE), el Centro de Desarrollo de la OCDE, la Comisión Económica de las Naciones Unidas para América Latina y el Caribe (CEPAL) y el Centro Interamericano de Administraciones Tributarias (CIAT). Las personas de esas organizaciones responsables de redactar la presente publicación han sido: Daniel Adshead del Centro de Desarrollo de la OCDE, bajo la supervisión del director, Mario Pezzini; Maurice Nettley del Centro de Política y Administración Tributaria de la OCDE, bajo la supervisión del director, Pascal Saint-Amans; Ricardo Martner, Michael Hanni y Andrea Podestá de la División de Desarrollo Económico de la CEPAL, bajo la supervisión del director, Juan Alberto Fuentes; y Julio Alberto López de la Dirección de Estudios e Investigaciones Tributarias del CIAT, bajo la supervisión del Director, Miguel Eduardo Pecho.

Los autores desean agradecer a otras personas del Centro de Desarrollo y del Centro de Política y Administración Tributaria de la OCDE su incalculable contribución a la finalización de la tercera edición de esta publicación. En particular, Christian Daude, Jefe de la Oficina de las Américas del Centro de Desarrollo, que ha aportado un respaldo y una orientación sustanciales a lo largo de todo el proceso; y Delphine Grandrieux y Elizabeth Nash, del equipo de Comunicaciones y Publicaciones del Centro de Desarrollo de la OCDE, que aseguró la producción de la publicación, tanto en papel como en formato electrónico. La publicación ha contado igualmente con la inestimable colaboración de varias personas e instituciones. Mención especial merece Alberto Barreix del Banco Interamericano de Desarrollo (BID) y a la Red de Áreas de Estudios del CIAT.

El Centro de Política y Administración Tributaria y el Centro de Desarrollo de la OCDE desean también expresar su agradecimiento a la Agencia Española de Cooperación Internacional para el Desarrollo (AECID) por su apoyo económico a la Iniciativa LAC, bajo cuyo pilar fiscal se ha elaborado la presente publicación. Por último, hacemos partícipes de nuestro agradecimiento a nuestros colegas de entidades nacionales, a los que hemos consultado con frecuencia. Entre esas instituciones, se cuentan los ministerios de finanzas y las agencias tributarias nacionales de Argentina, Bolivia, Brasil, Chile, Colombia, Costa Rica, Ecuador, El Salvador, Guatemala, Honduras, México, Nicaragua, Panamá, Paraguay, Perú, República Dominicana, Uruguay y Venezuela, así como el Ministerio de Economía y Producción de Argentina, y el Banco Central de Reserva del Perú.

Table of Contents

Índice de Materias

List of Tables/Índice de cuadros

Part I/Parte I

Tax Revenue Trends 1990-2012/Tendencias tributarias, 1990-2012

Part II/Parte II

Tax Levels and Tax Structures, 1990-2012/Niveles impositivos y estructuras tributarias, 1990-2012

Part III/Parte III

Country Tables 1990-2012 - Tax Revenues/Cuadros país, 1990-2012 - Ingresos tributarios

Part IV/Parte IV

Tax Revenues by Sub-sectors of General Government/Ingresos tributaries por sub-sector de gobierno general

List of Charts/ Índice de gráficos

Part II/Parte II

Part IV/Parte IV

Executive summary

Tax revenues as a proportion of national incomes are rising in Latin American countries but they are still lower than in most OECD countries. In the group of 18 Latin American and Caribbean (LAC) countries covered by the Report the average tax to GDP ratio increased to 20.7% in 2012 compared with 20.1% in 2011 and 19.3% in 2010. Between 1990 and 2012, this average rose more quickly than the OECD equivalent. However it is still well below the corresponding OECD figure of 34.6%.

There are wide national variations in the tax ratio across both OECD and Latin American countries. In 2012, the LAC countries covered by the report range from 37.6% in Argentina (above the OECD average) to 12.3% in Guatemala. The corresponding range amongst OECD countries was from 48.0% in Denmark to 19.6% in Mexico.

The Report provides internationally comparable data on tax levels and tax structures for the group of 18 Latin American and Caribbean (LAC) countries. It is a joint publication by the Inter-American Centre for Tax Administrations (CIAT), the Economic Commission for Latin America and the Caribbean (ECLAC) and the OECD. Using the same methodology as the *OECD Revenue Statistics* database, it presents cross-country comparisons between LAC economies and between LAC and OECD economies. The LAC countries covered are Argentina, Bolivia, Brazil, Chile, Colombia, Costa Rica, Dominican Republic, Ecuador, El Salvador, Guatemala, Honduras, Mexico, Nicaragua, Panama, Paraguay, Peru, Uruguay and Venezuela. Bolivia, Honduras and Nicaragua have been added since the second edition. The Revenue Statistics in Latin America figure for the tax to GDP ratio in Mexico is different from those presented in ECLAC and CIAT publications because the former includes fees levied on hydrocarbon production as tax revenues.

The term "taxes" in this publication refers to compulsory, unrequited payments to general government. Taxes are "unrequited" in the sense that the benefits provided by governments to taxpayers are not normally allocated in proportion to their payments, as outlined in the Interpretative guide to the Revenue Statistics. The OECD methodology classifies a tax according to its base: income, profits and capital gains; payroll; property; goods and services; and other taxes. Compulsory social security contributions paid to general government are also treated as taxes, and are classified under a separate heading. Detailed information on the tax concept, the classification of taxes and the accrual basis of reporting is set out in the Interpretative Guide in Annex A of this report. The Report also analyses the share of tax revenue attributed to the various levels of government; federal or central; state (regional); local and social security funds.

It also includes a special chapter describing the trends in revenues from non-renewable natural resources in Latin American countries and discusses the drivers of the increases that have been observed since the year 2000.

Key findings

Tax to GDP ratios

- The average tax burden in the group of 18 LAC countries increased by 0.6 percentage points to 20.7% in 2012. This followed rises of 0.8 and 0.4 percentage points in 2010 and 2011, reversing the decline from 19.5% to 18.9% between 2008 and 2009.

- In 2012, the ratio of tax revenues to GDP compared to 2011 rose in 13 of the LAC countries and fell in 4.

- The difference between the OECD average tax to GDP ratio and that for the 18 LAC countries fell from 19 to 14 percentage points between 1990 and 2012.

- Increases in revenue from taxes on income and profits and taxes on goods and services were the main contributors to the recovery in tax-to-GDP ratios between 2010 and 2012.

- The largest increases in tax to GDP ratios in 2012 were in Argentina (2.6 percentage points), Ecuador (2.3 points), Bolivia (1.8) and Brazil (1.4).

- The largest falls in 2012 were in Uruguay (1.0 percentage points) and Chile (0.4) points

- There is considerable variation in trends over time for individual LAC countries. The countries with the largest increases between 1990 and 2012 were Argentina (21.2 percentage points) Bolivia (18.8), Ecuador (13.1), Paraguay (12.2) and Colombia (10.6). The lowest increase of 1.3 percentage points was in Honduras and there was a decline of 5 percentage points in Venezuela.

Tax structures

- Following strong growth over the past twenty years, general consumption taxes (mainly VAT and sales taxes accounted for 33.8% of tax revenues in the LAC countries in 2011 compared with 20.3% in OECD countries) whereas the share of specific consumption taxes (such as excises and taxes on international trade) declined to 17.7% (in OECD it's 10.7%)

- Taxes on income and profits accounted for 25.4% of revenues on average in the Latin American countries and social security contributions represented 16.9% (in OECD the corresponding figures are 33.5% and 26.2% respectively).

Tax revenues attributed to local governments

The share of tax revenues collected by local governments in Latin America is small in most countries and has not increased, reflecting the relatively narrow range of taxes under their jurisdictions compared with OECD countries.

Resumen ejecutivo

Los ingresos tributarios como proporción del PIB están aumentando en los países de América Latina, pero aún son inferiores a los de la mayoría de los países de la OCDE. En el grupo de 18 países de América Latina y el Caribe (LAC) objeto del informe, el ratio medio de recaudación tributaria sobre PIB se elevó hasta un 20.7% en 2012, frente al 20.1% de 2011 y el 19.3% de 2010. Entre 1990 y 2012, dicho ratio medio subió más rápidamente que su homólogo de la OCDE. Sin embargo, se sitúa aún muy por debajo del 34.6%, que es el último dato disponible de la OCDE.

Existen amplias diferencias nacionales entre los ratios de ingresos tributarios correspondientes tanto a los países latinoamericanos como a los de la OCDE. En 2012, en los países de América Latina y el Caribe incluidos en el informe, dichos ratios oscilan entre el 37.6% de Argentina (por encima de la media de la OCDE) y el 12.3% de Guatemala. Entre los países de la OCDE, ese mismo rango varía entre el 48.0% de Dinamarca y el 19.6% en México.

El informe presenta datos internacionalmente comparables sobre los niveles y estructuras tributarios para el grupo de 18 países de América Latina y el Caribe (LAC). Es una publicación elaborada conjuntamente por el Centro Interamericano de Administraciones Tributarias (CIAT), la Comisión Económica para América Latina y el Caribe (CEPAL) y la OCDE. Utilizando la misma metodología que la base de datos *Revenue Statistics* de la OCDE, ofrece comparaciones por países entre las economías de América Latina y el Caribe, y las economías de la OCDE. Los países de América Latina y el Caribe objeto de examen son Argentina, Bolivia, Brasil, Chile, Colombia, Costa Rica, República Dominicana, Ecuador, El Salvador, Guatemala, Honduras, México, Nicaragua, Panamá, Paraguay, Perú, Uruguay y Venezuela. En esta tercera edición, se han añadido Bolivia, Honduras y Nicaragua. En las Estadísticas Tributarias en América Latina, el dato de recaudación tributaria como porcentaje del PIB de México difiere del presentado en las publicaciones de la CEPAL y el CIAT, dado que las citadas Estadísticas Tributarias incluyen los derechos sobre la producción de hidrocarburos como ingresos tributarios.

En la presente publicación, el término "impuestos" se refiere a pagos obligatorios sin contraprestación efectuados al gobierno general. Los impuestos carecen de contraprestación en el sentido de que, normalmente, las prestaciones que los gobiernos proporcionan a los contribuyentes no guardan relación directa con los pagos realizados por estos, tal como se señala en la Guía de Interpretación de las Estadísticas Tributarias. La metodología de la OCDE clasifica los impuestos según la base sobre la que recaen: renta, utilidades y ganancias del capital; nóminas; propiedad; bienes y servicios; y otros impuestos. Las contribuciones obligatorias a la seguridad social abonadas al gobierno general se tratan también como impuestos y se clasifican dentro de una categoría distinta. Para obtener información más pormenorizada sobre el concepto de impuesto, y su clasificación y registro según el criterio de devengo, véase la Guía de Interpretación que figura en el Anexo A de este informe. El informe también analiza la parte de ingresos tributarios que se atribuye a los distintos niveles de gobierno; federal o central; estatal (regional); local y fondos de seguridad social.

Incluye asimismo un capítulo especial en el que se exponen las tendencias de los ingresos procedentes de recursos naturales no renovables en países latinoamericanos y se estudian los factores que han impulsado su crecimiento desde el año 2000.

Principales conclusiones

Recaudación tributaria como porcentaje del PIB

- La carga fiscal media en el grupo de los 18 países de América Latina y el Caribe se incrementó en 0.6 puntos porcentuales hasta un 20.7% en 2012. Esto tuvo lugar después de los incrementos de 0.8 y 0.4 puntos porcentuales de 2010 y 2011, que revirtieron el descenso del 19.5% al 18.9% producido entre 2008 y 2009.

- En 2012, el ratio de recaudación tributaria sobre PIB subió, con respecto a 2011, en 13 países de América Latina y el Caribe, reduciéndose en cuatro.

- La diferencia entre el ratio medio de recaudación tributaria sobre PIB de la OCDE y el correspondiente a los 18 países de América Latina y el Caribe se redujo de 19 a 14 puntos porcentuales entre 1990 y 2012.

- Los aumentos de recaudación de los impuestos sobre la renta y las utilidades y los impuestos sobre bienes y servicios fueron los que más contribuyeron a la recuperación de los ratios de recaudación tributaria sobre PIB entre 2010 y 2012.

- En 2012, los mayores incrementos de estos ratios de recaudación tributaria sobre PIB correspondieron a Argentina (2.6 puntos porcentuales), Ecuador (2.3 puntos porcentuales), Bolivia (1.8) y Brasil (1.4).

- Las mayores caídas se produjeron en Uruguay (1.0 puntos porcentuales) y Chile (0.4) puntos porcentuales.

- Existe una considerable disparidad entre las tendencias descritas a lo largo del tiempo para cada uno de los países de América Latina y el Caribe. Entre 1990 y 2012, los países que experimentaron mayores incrementos fueron Argentina (21.2 puntos porcentuales), Bolivia (18.8), Ecuador (13.1), Paraguay (12.2) y Colombia (10.6). Honduras registró el menor incremento (1.3 puntos porcentuales) y Venezuela sufrió un descenso de 5 puntos porcentuales.

Estructuras tributarias

- Luego del sólido crecimiento de los últimos veinte años, los impuestos generales sobre el consumo (principalmente el IVA y los impuestos sobre las ventas) representan un 33.8% de los ingresos tributarios de los países de América Latina y el Caribe en 2011, frente al 20.3% de los países de la OCDE, mientras que el peso de los impuestos específicos sobre el consumo (como los impuestos selectivos o los impuestos sobre el comercio internacional) se ha reducido hasta un 17.7% (en la OCDE es de un 10.7%).

- Por su parte, en los países latinoamericanos los impuestos sobre la renta y las utilidades representan, en promedio, un 25.4% de la recaudación, mientras que las contribuciones a la seguridad social suponen un 16.9% (en la OCDE, dichos porcentajes son de un 33.5% y 26.2% respectivamente).

Ingresos tributarios atribuidos a gobiernos locales

- La parte de los ingresos tributarios recaudada por los gobiernos locales es pequeña y no se ha elevado en la mayoría de los países de América Latina, debido al reducido abanico de impuestos sobre el que tienen competencia en contraste con los países de la OCDE.

PART 1

Tax Revenue Trends 1990-2012

PARTE 1

Tendencias tributarias, 1990-2012

PART I

Tax Revenue Trends 1990-2012

A. Tax ratios

Tax revenues as a proportion of gross domestic product (GDP) have increased considerably in Latin America during the last two decades. Both Chart A and Table A show how revenues, including social security contributions, for these Latin American countries have, with the exception of 2009, risen almost continuously from 13.6% of GDP in 1990 to 20.7% of GDP (unweighted averages) in 2012. This growth in the relative importance of tax revenues is a reflection of favourable macroeconomic conditions, changes in the tax systems design and strengthening of tax administrations.

This trend contrasts with that in the OECD area where the ratio has been relatively stable – in 2011 it stood at 34.1% – just over one percentage point above its level in 1990. As a result, the gap between the averages for the two areas started to narrow after 2000. This difference was around 19 percentage points in both 1990 and 2000 but had fallen to 14 percentage points by 2011.

Tax to GDP ratios in Latin America increased in each year from 2010 to 2012 following the interruption of the long-term rising trend in 2009, as a result of the fall in economic activity and commodity prices due to the international financial crisis. The average tax ratio was 20.7% in 2012 compared with 20.1% one year earlier and 19.3% in 2010. In 2012, the tax ratio rose in 13 of 18 countries and fell in 4 compared with 2011, while it remained the same in Costa Rica. The corresponding figures for 2011 compared with 2010 were for an increase in 15 countries and a fall in 1. The average in OECD countries, however, rose by 0.3 percentage points in 2011 to 34.1% but still remained 0.4 percentage points below the pre-crisis tax-to-GDP level of 34.5% in 2008.

The average tax to GDP ratio in OECD countries is much higher than the one for Latin American countries in the sample (34.1% compared with 20.1% in 2011, respectively). However, there is a wide range between the highest and lowest tax to GDP ratios across countries in Latin America. Amongst the sample countries the highest levels in 2012 were in Argentina and Brazil (37.3% and 36.3% respectively) whereas the lowest levels were observed in Guatemala (12.3%) and Venezuela (13.7%). In the same way, the characteristics of the OECD economies show a wide variation. In 2012, the OECD tax to GDP ratios ranged from 48.0% in Denmark down to 19.6% in Mexico (this figure is different from the ones presented in ECLAC and CIAT publications because of the inclusion of fees levied on hydrocarbon production as tax revenues). The implications of these wide ranges are that differences in tax to GDP ratios between OECD and Latin America should be interpreted with caution given that they include economies that are widely different in character.

There are many factors that determine what should be the appropriate ratio for an individual country, but one of them is the extent of goods and services provided by the State. From the 1980s onwards many Latin American countries to greater or lesser degrees privatised healthcare, education and social security (ECLAC, 2010). This regional position stands in contrast to the substantial public provision of these services, and the corresponding need for revenue receipts, in many OECD countries, particularly in Europe. There are also high levels of informality that exclude many from paying taxes in Latin American countries (OECD, 2008 and Gómez Sabaini *et al.* 2010), something which has a particular incidence in the case of SMEs. However the issue of non-payment of taxes generally has a significant impact on tax revenues in all countries.

Table A shows considerable variation in trends over time for individual countries. Irrespective of the wide range of tax levels, widespread strengthening of public revenues can be observed since 1990. The countries with the largest increases between 1990 and 2012 were Argentina (21.2. percentage points) Bolivia (18.8), Ecuador (13.1), Paraguay (12.2) and Colombia (10.6). The majority of the countries showed increases of between 3 and 8 percentage points. The exceptions were Honduras with an increase of 1.3 percentage points and Venezuela, where a decline of 5 percentage points was observed over the same period.

Chart A. **Total tax revenues as percentage of GDP in Latin America and OECD, 1990-2012**

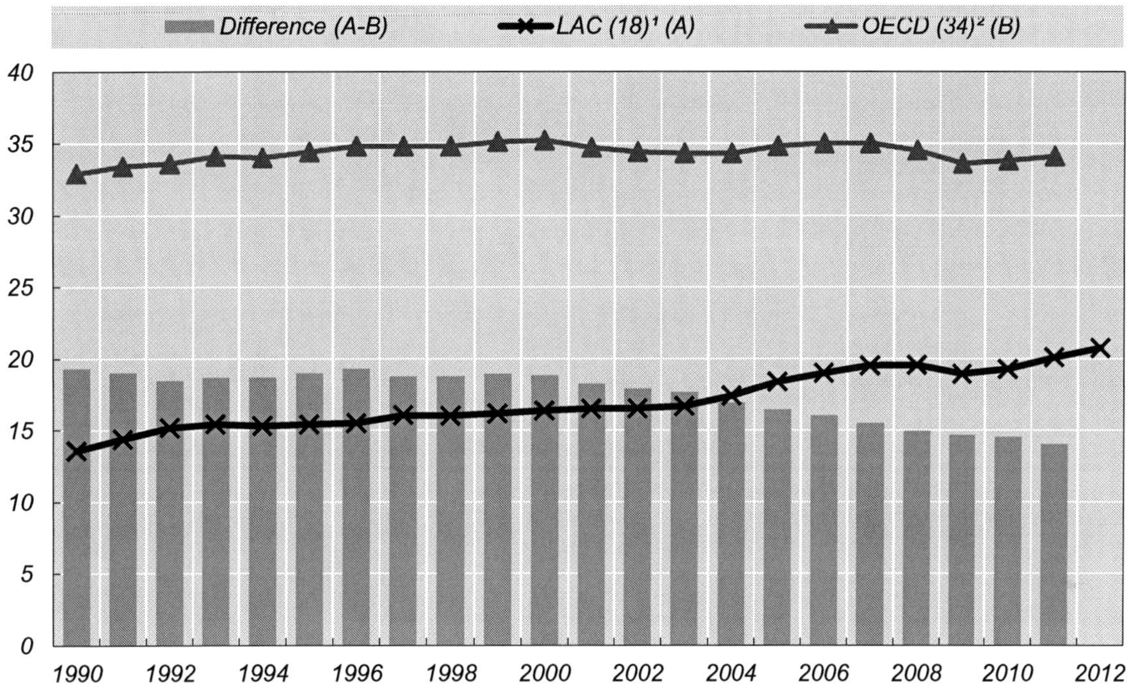

1. Represents a group of 18 Latin American countries. These are Argentina, Bolivia, Brazil, Chile, Colombia, Costa Rica, Dominican Republic, Ecuador, El Salvador, Guatemala, Honduras, Mexico, Nicaragua, Panama, Paraguay, Peru, Uruguay and Venezuela. Chile and Mexico are also part of the OECD (34) group.

2. Represents the unweighted average for OECD member countries.

Source: Table 1 in Part II.A.

StatLink http://dx.doi.org/10.1787/888932970418

The background to the rise in tax revenues that started in the early 1990s was the period of macroeconomic instability occurring in Latin American countries during the previous decade. During the 1980s, countries ran large fiscal imbalances and at the same time some recoursed to alternative ways to finance their spending (borrowing or printing money). This caused rapid inflation across the region, which eroded the real value of their tax revenues. As a result, the reforms in the 1990s focused on fighting this inflation and imposing fiscal discipline.

Table A. **Total tax revenue as percentage of GDP**[1]

	1990	2000	2007	2008	2009	2010	2011	2012
Argentina	16.1	21.5	29.1	30.8	31.5	33.5	34.7	37.3
Bolivia[2,3]	7.2	14.7	22.6	20.5	22.7	20.7	24.2	26.0
Brazil	28.2	30.1	33.8	34.0	32.6	33.2	34.9	36.3
Chile	17.0	18.8	22.8	21.4	17.2	19.5	21.2	20.8
Colombia	9.0	14.6	19.1	18.8	18.6	18.0	18.8	19.6
Costa Rica	16.1	18.2	21.7	22.4	20.8	20.5	21.0	21.0
Dominican Republic	8.3	12.4	16.0	15.0	13.1	12.8	12.9	13.5
Ecuador	7.1	10.1	12.8	14.0	14.9	16.8	17.9	20.2
El Salvador	10.5	12.2	15.2	15.1	14.4	14.8	14.8	15.7
Guatemala	9.0	12.4	13.9	12.9	12.2	12.3	12.6	12.3
Honduras	16.2	15.3	19.0	18.9	17.1	17.3	16.9	17.5
Mexico[4,5]	15.8	16.9	17.7	20.9	17.4	18.9	19.7	19.6
Nicaragua	n.a.	16.9	17.4	17.3	17.4	18.3	19.1	19.5
Panama	14.7	16.7	16.7	16.9	17.4	18.1	18.1	18.5
Paraguay[2]	5.4	14.5	13.9	14.6	16.1	16.5	17.0	17.6
Peru	11.8	13.9	17.8	18.2	16.3	17.4	17.8	18.1
Uruguay	19.6	21.6	25.0	26.1	27.1	27.0	27.3	26.3
Venezuela[2]	18.7	13.6	16.8	14.1	14.3	11.4	12.9	13.7
Unweighted average:								
LAC (18)[6]	13.6	16.4	19.5	19.5	18.9	19.3	20.1	20.7
OECD (34)[7]	32.9	35.2	35.0	34.5	33.6	33.8	34.1	n.a

1. The figures exclude local government revenues for Argentina (but include provincial revenues), Bolivia, Costa Rica (up to 1997), Dominican Republic, Ecuador, El Salvador, Honduras, Nicaragua, Panama (up to 1998), Paraguay (up to 2004, 2011 and 2012), Peru (up to 2004), Uruguay and Venezuela as the data are not available.

2. Estimated figures for 2011 and 2012.

3. In ECLAC data, the excise tax on hydrocarbons is treated as non tax revenue.

4. In ECLAC and CIAT data, fees levied on hydrocarbon production are treated as non tax revenues.

5. Estimated figure for 2012 including expected revenues for state and local governments.

6. Represents a group of 18 Latin American countries. Chile and Mexico are also part of the OECD (34) group.

7. Represents the unweighted average for OECD member countries.

StatLink http://dx.doi.org/10.1787/888932970855

Most Latin American governments responded by both cutting public expenditure and implementing policies aimed at increasing tax revenues with budget management and fiscal balance improving considerably. On the revenue side of the equation, tax policy and administration reforms contributed considerably in achieving this goal. As part of that, the impact of inflation on revenues forced policy makers to find ways to render tax systems less vulnerable to inflationary episodes by shortening collection lags and indexing tax liabilities.

The tax burden in the group of 18 Latin American countries increased by 7.1 percentage points of GDP between 1990 and 2012. The introduction of VAT was the most significant tax reform in Latin America in the 1980s and early 1990s. Subsequent reforms relating to the tax have concentrated on extending and strengthening it by increasing the tax rate and widening the tax base. In the 1990s the VAT to GDP ratio increased by 2.1 percentage points and then by a further 1.4 points up to 2012 (see Table B).

Between 2000 and 2012, the increase in revenue from income taxes – mainly corporate income tax – (by 2.0 percentage points of GDP) became a more important contributor than VAT to the rise in tax revenues. One of the elements that contributed to this result was the commodity prices' boom period following 2003, which was very important for some countries in the region (see the Special Feature for more information). Other tax reforms also included the introduction or development of simplified regimes for small taxpayers and the taxation of property based on presumed incomes. In addition, during the past half-decade various income tax reforms were introduced in Latin America and the Caribbean, which have included rate hikes and increases in the tax base. These measures have had a positive effect thanks to the expansion of taxation to all labour and capital income, including dividends (Colombia, Dominican Republic, Guatemala, El Salvador, Nicaragua, Panama, Peru). Additionally, they have also included the establishment of minimum taxes, reductions in exemptions, a tightening of deductible expenses, the gradual reduction in the real income level taxed at the top marginal rate and additional controls on transfer prices (ECLAC, 2013).

Table B. **Value added taxes as percentages of GDP**

	1990	2000	2007	2008	2009	2010	2011	2012
Argentina	2.5	6.5	7.5	7.5	7.4	7.9	8.1	8.7
Bolivia	3.2	5.1	6.5	7.0	6.3	6.7	7.3	7.6
Brazil	10.4	8.6	7.8	8.1	7.6	7.8	7.8	8.5
Chile	6.3	7.9	7.5	8.4	7.3	7.6	7.8	8.0
Colombia	2.0	4.1	5.4	5.6	5.1	5.3	5.6	5.5
Costa Rica	3.2	4.5	5.9	6.0	4.9	4.8	5.0	5.0
Dominican Republic	1.3	2.6	4.9	4.7	4.2	4.3	4.2	4.0
Ecuador	2.0	4.6	4.9	4.6	4.8	5.8	5.5	6.4
El Salvador	-	5.4	6.9	6.8	6.1	6.7	6.8	7.0
Guatemala	2.4	4.7	5.9	5.5	4.9	5.1	5.2	5.3
Honduras	2.7	4.8	6.1	6.3	5.2	5.4	5.7	5.6
Mexico	3.3	3.1	3.6	3.8	3.4	3.9	3.7	3.8
Nicaragua	n.a.	5.9	5.8	5.6	5.3	5.6	6.0	6.1
Panama	1.3	0.6	1.0	2.3	2.3	2.9	3.3	3.3
Paraguay	-	4.7	5.0	5.5	5.6	6.3	6.5	6.5
Peru	1.4	5.1	5.9	6.8	6.0	6.6	6.5	6.4
Uruguay	5.5	6.5	9.3	9.2	9.0	8.9	8.9	8.7
Venezuela	-	4.1	5.6	4.6	5.9	5.5	6.2	6.8
Unweighted average:								
LAC (18)[1]	2.8	4.9	5.9	6.0	5.6	5.9	6.1	6.3
OECD (34)[2]	5.3	6.6	6.7	6.5	6.4	6.7	6.6	n.a.

n.a.: indicates not available.

1. Represents a group of 18 Latin American countries. Chile and Mexico are also part of the OECD (34) group.
2. Represents the unweighted average for OECD member countries.

StatLink http://dx.doi.org/10.1787/888932970874

Changes in revenue from taxes on goods and services and taxes on income and profits are the main contributors to the recovery in tax-to-GDP ratios since 2010. These increases in tax revenues are partly due to the recovery of Latin American economic activity and to some extent due to the temporal recovery of commodity prices (ECLAC-OECD, 2012).

B. Tax structures

At the same time that tax levels have been rising in Latin America, the tax structure (defined as the share of major taxes in total tax revenue) also changed significantly between 1990 and 2012. Table C illustrates the several trends on "tax mix" that emerge from the data. The most important trends are those related to consumption taxes and taxes on income and profits.

The overall share of consumption taxes remained fairly stable over the period but within the total, the share of general consumption taxes increased considerably by 11 percentage points between 1990 and 2012, while specific consumption taxes saw their share decline by 14 percentage points over the same period.

Table C. **Tax structures in a group of Latin American countries**[1]

	1990	2000	2009	2010	2011	2012
Taxes on income and profits	21	20	26	25	25	26
Social security contributions	16	17	17	17	17	17
Payroll taxes	1	1	1	1	1	1
Property taxes	6	4	4	4	4	4
General consumption taxes	23	32	33	34	34	34
Specific consumption taxes	31	24	18	18	18	17
Other taxes[2]	4	2	2	2	2	2
Total	100	100	100	100	100	100

1. Represents the percentage shares of major tax categories in total tax revenue. The group of 18 countries is listed in Table A.
2. Including certain taxes on goods and services (heading 5200) and stamp taxes.

StatLink http://dx.doi.org/10.1787/888932970893

These two opposing trends within consumption taxes are due to the rising importance of VAT and the diminishing role of specific consumption taxes, such as excises and taxes on international trade. Although VAT was adopted early by the economies of the region (most countries had already introduced it in some form by the late 1970s), its expansion in revenue terms has been relatively recent. From the early 1990s, it has represented a growing source of revenue for Latin American countries and has been consolidated by the implementation of cumulative adjustments to the tax base and statutory rates, as well as strengthening of tax administrations. The reforms also focused on the simplification of tax systems, with most countries reducing the number of items with zero or reduced rates, moving towards single-rate VAT schemes in several cases.

In contrast, the decline in the share of specific consumption taxes is associated with the processes of trade liberalisation generating a consequent reduction in import tariffs and the elimination of taxes on exports in a considerable number of Latin American countries (one important exception being Argentina where taxes on exports were re-established in 2002). Additionally, the range of goods and services subject to excises has been narrowed to focus mainly on products and services with a relatively inelastic demand, such as alcoholic beverages, fuel and derivatives and tobacco.

At the same time, revenues from incomes and profits grew from 21% to 26% of total tax revenues from 1990 to 2012, mainly as a result of much higher collection levels in the late 2000s. Corporate income tax shares are generally larger than those from personal income tax in Latin American countries and this growth reflects the sizeable increase in revenues from the former category, especially from companies in the natural–resources sector. The income and profits share actually peaked over the years from 2008 to 2009 at a level of 26% before declining to 25% in 2010, probably due to the impact of the global crisis on the generation of income and profits. It has subsequently risen back to 26% in 2012 (Table 3b).

On average the revenues from social security contributions as a percentage of GDP increased from 2.4% in 1990 to 3.8% in 2012 (Table 4A), while their share in total tax revenues increased from 15.6% to 17.2% in this period (Table 4B). This reflects two major factors working simultaneously. Firstly, rising personal incomes have had an upward impact on the amounts collected. But this is partially counter-balanced, and sometimes more than off-set, by the varying processes of full or partial privatisation that occurred in many countries in the region. There has been a wide variation in the ways that countries have implemented and reformed their social-security schemes. Some countries like Chile, Mexico and Peru rely heavily on private, personally funded schemes, explaining the relatively low levels of tax revenues used to finance social security. In countries with public or mixed schemes, including Brazil, Costa Rica Ecuador, Nicaragua, Panama, Paraguay and Uruguay, social-security contributions still have a significant weight (more than 20% of total tax revenues). In Argentina, the figures reflect the introduction of funded schemes in 1994 and their subsequent nationalisation in 2008.

Turning to the comparison between OECD and Latin American countries, the main difference between the tax-structures of the two groups is immediately apparent. Relative to the OECD, Latin America exhibits a relatively low direct-tax take counterbalanced by high indirect-tax receipts (see Chart B). In particular, Latin America relies heavily on taxes on goods and services, which make up about half of overall tax revenues compared with around 30% in OECD economies. By comparison around 40% of revenues in Latin America come from the combination of taxes on income and profits and social security contributions compared with 60% in OECD economies. This greater reliance on indirect taxes may imply a more regressive tax system.

In 2011, the average ratio of the combined tax revenue from income and profits and social security contributions to GDP in the selected Latin American countries was 8.5% compared with 20.5% in OECD countries. As a result, these taxes play a secondary role as a source of revenue in Latin America compared with the OECD area. The share of social security contributions in total tax revenues was a full 9 percentage points lower in Latin America than in the OECD (16.9% compared with 26.2%). As noted above, the tendency towards privately-oriented provision of social security in many countries in the Latin American region explains some of the differences for this category. The corresponding figures for taxes on income and profits were 8 percentage points lower (25.4% compared with 33.5%).

Revenues from personal income taxes contributed as much as to 24% of the aggregate tax collection in the OECD area in 2011, while this category has a considerably lower share in Latin American countries. Previous OECD studies (OECD, 2008 and Daude *et al.*, 2010) suggest that this has two main drivers: the share of labour income in GDP is substantially lower in Latin America than in OECD countries; and its distribution means that there are relatively fewer taxpayers, given the concentration of income earners at low income levels. Moreover, several ECLAC studies (ECLAC, 2010 and Gómez Sabaini *et al.,* 2010) mention two additional factors: the high income tax gap in Latin American countries and a more limited taxable base that is comprised primarily of wages, given the tax privileges granted to returns on capital.

Chart B. **Tax structures in Latin America and OECD, 2011**

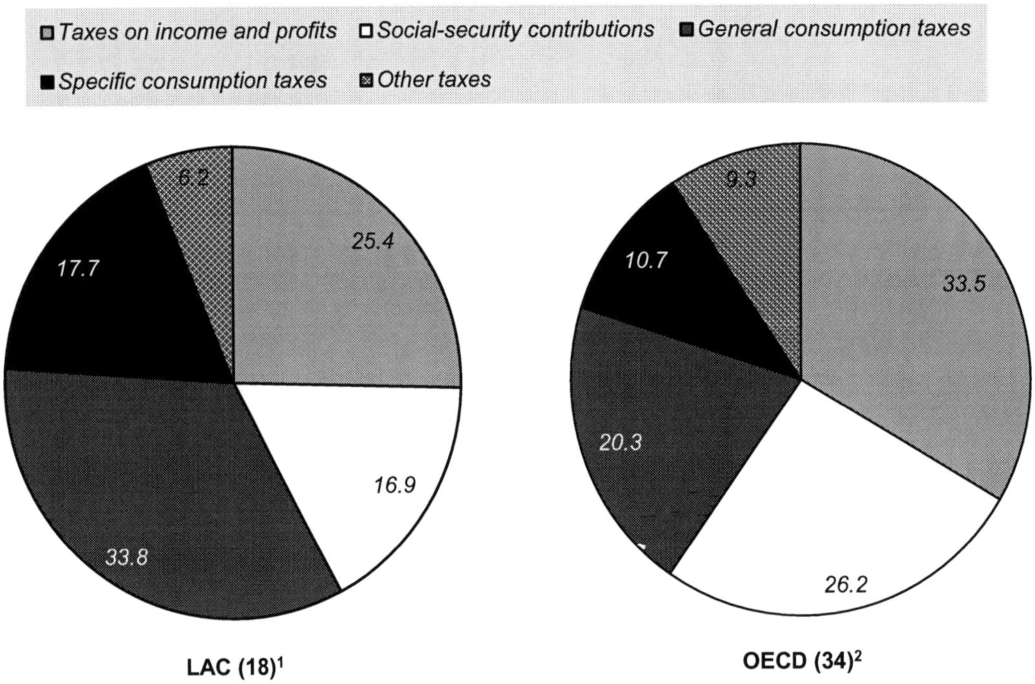

1. Represents a group of 18 Latin American countries listed in Table A. Chile and Mexico are also part of the OECD (34) group.
2. Represents the unweighted average for OECD member countries.

Source: Table 2B in Part II.A.

StatLink http://dx.doi.org/10.1787/888932970437

As a counterpart of a lower share of direct taxes, general consumption taxes represent a significant portion of total tax collection. In 2011, this category accounted for 34% of the total tax revenues in the region whereas the corresponding figure in the OECD area is only 20%. However, the ratio of general consumption taxes to GDP in the countries of Latin America is similar to that of OECD (6.7% of GDP compared with 6.9%).

Finally, taxes on immovable property and payroll (comprised within the category "Other taxes" in Chart B) are not important sources of revenues for Latin American countries. The difficulties that sub-national governments have in collecting their own taxes are exemplified by the weak revenue-generating capacity of property taxes, which are usually the main source of revenue for local governments in the region (Brossio and Jiménez, 2012). The share of payroll taxes has been negligible over the whole period, partly because these types of schemes are not very well developed in Latin America. Nevertheless, it must be pointed out that missing data at the sub-national level makes the analysis of this category difficult. The shares of property and payroll taxes as a proportion of total tax revenue in the Latin American countries are similar on average to those in OECD countries.

C. Taxes by level of government

Since the mid-1980s the Latin American region has generally experienced reforms involving the transfer of government functions from the central government to sub-national entities. In the first stage, this wave of decentralisation mainly focused on strengthening the democratic role of local authorities. This has been followed by a gradually increasing trend towards a higher share of public expenditure being executed at sub-national level.

In contrast, the scope of the sub-national tax policies in the region has been relatively modest and focuses on a limited number of taxes. The available data suggests that most Latin American countries have not been concentrated on the strengthening of the revenues received by the sub-national entities. Between 1995 and 2011, the share of revenue raised by sub-national levels of government declined by between 1 and 4 percentage points in Argentina, Brazil and Uruguay and rose by 2 percentage points in Colombia. In the other countries where trends in sub-national revenue data are available, the share changed by less than one percentage point. At the same time the share of social security funds has fallen in 10 of the 18 Latin American countries sometimes due to full or partial privatisation. The largest changes were in Colombia and Uruguay (by around 14 and 6 percentage points, respectively) (see Table D).

There are two statistical issues to be taken into account when comparing the attribution of revenues for these Latin American countries with that of OECD members. First, the revenues of both groups have been attributed to the different levels of government according to the revised guidelines set out in to the final version of the 2008 System of National Accounts (SNA). This means that revenues are generally attributed to the level of government that exercises the authority to impose the tax or has the final discretion to set and vary the tax rate. This has implications for situations where one level of government collects tax revenues and transfers them in whole or in part to other levels. Regional examples of this type of mechanism are the Co-participation Law in Argentina, federal participations in Mexico mandated in the Fiscal Co-ordination Law, and participation funds in Brazil defined in Article 159 of the Constitution. The second issue is that the data for some of the Latin American countries are affected by the lack of tax-revenue statistics at sub-national level.

Not-withstanding these points, the attribution of tax revenues appears to be highly skewed towards central or federal entities with sub-national activities relying more heavily on a system of transfers from upper to lower levels of administration compared with OECD members. In all but one of the Latin American countries, receipts by central governments accounted for about two thirds or more of the total collected whereas the corresponding figure for OECD countries was about 60%. Brazil is a notable exception with less than 50% of revenues attributed to the Federal administration, and where a large part of the VAT (ICMS – *imposto sobre operações relativas à circulação de mercadorias e prestação de serviços de transporte interestadual e intermunicipal e de comunicação*) is collected at the sub-national state level. To a lesser extent, Argentina has a significant collection at state level, which is explained in part by the provincial sales tax (*impuesto sobre los ingresos brutos*).

These figures reflect the fact that sub-national governments in Latin America tend to have a relatively narrow range of taxes under their jurisdiction. The taxes most frequently assigned to sub-national entities are property taxes, motor-vehicle licenses, taxes on specific services and municipal fees and the revenue generation potential of these instruments is relatively limited compared with the tax bases under central jurisdiction, such as VAT and income taxes. In OECD member countries, sub-national entities on average tend to have much broader potential tax bases. A substantial proportion of the revenue collection for sub-national governments in OECD countries is through income taxes (representing more than a third of the total collected amount). In contrast, none of the Latin American countries with available data recorded any collection of income taxes by sub-national governments.

Table D. **Attribution of tax revenues to sub-sectors of general government as percentage of total tax revenue**[1]

	Central government			State or regional government			Local government			Social Security funds		
	1995	2000	2011	1995	2000	2011	1995	2000	2011	1995	2000	2011
Federal countries												
Argentina	59.0	66.4	64.0	17.5	17.8	14.5				23.4	15.8	21.5
Brazil	44.7	47.8	45.9	26.8	25.3	23.8	3.7	3.4	5.2	24.8	23.5	25.2
Mexico	80.1	80.7	81.9	2.1	2.0	2.5	1.1	0.8	1.1	16.6	16.5	14.5
Venezuela	94.6	94.6	96.6							5.4	5.4	3.4
OECD[2,3]	53.3	56.5	54.5	15.9	15.3	16.3	7.7	6.9	7.7	22.9	21.1	21.3
Regional countries												
Colombia[4]	58.9	64.4	71.7	5.5	5.6	4.7	8.6	9.4	11.0	27.0	20.6	12.6
OECD[5]	50.4	49.0	29.9	4.8	7.6	23.1	8.5	9.1	9.6	35.8	33.8	36.9
Unitary countries												
Bolivia	100.0	91.3	93.4								8.7	6.6
Chile	89.9	87.8	88.5				6.5	7.9	6.6	3.6	4.4	4.9
Costa Rica	66.2	65.3	63.3					2.1	2.9	33.8	32.6	33.8
Dominican Republic	99.3	99.0	99.5							0.7	1.0	0.5
Ecuador	73.9	87.7	71.1							26.1	12.3	28.9
El Salvador	85.9	83.6	88.8							14.1	16.4	11.2
Guatemala	83.8	83.6	83.7				0.6	0.9	1.4	15.6	15.5	15.0
Honduras	90.1	89.4	87.7							9.9	10.6	12.3
Nicaragua	84.1	80.1	77.1							15.9	19.9	22.9
Panama	62.0	59.6	62.4					2.2	1.5	38.0	38.2	36.0
Paraguay[6]	100.0	82.7	76.7								17.3	23.3
Peru	88.2	87.7	87.5						2.9	11.8	12.3	9.6
Uruguay	62.0	62.5	71.4				7.8	7.9	4.1	30.1	29.6	24.5
OECD[2,7]	65.8	66.4	63.0				10.7	11.0	12.0	23.2	22.3	24.7

1. The figures exclude local government revenues for Argentina (but include provincial revenues), Bolivia, Costa Rica (up to 1997), Dominican Republic, Ecuador, El Salvador, Honduras, Nicaragua, Panama (up to 1998), Paraguay, Peru (up to 2004) and Venezuela as the data are not available.

2. Chile and Mexico are also part of the OECD group.

3. Represents the unweighted average for OECD federal member countries.

4. Colombia is constitutionally a unitary country with high autonomy of its territorial entities.

5. Represents Spain, which is constitutionally a non-federal country with a highly decentralised political structure.

6. Data estimated for 2011.

7. Represents the unweighted average for OECD unitary countries.

StatLink http://dx.doi.org/10.1787/888932970912

D. Comparative charts

Chart C. **Total tax revenues as percentage of GDP, 2012**[1]
Gráfico C. **Total de recaudación tributaria como porcentaje del PIB, 2012**[1]

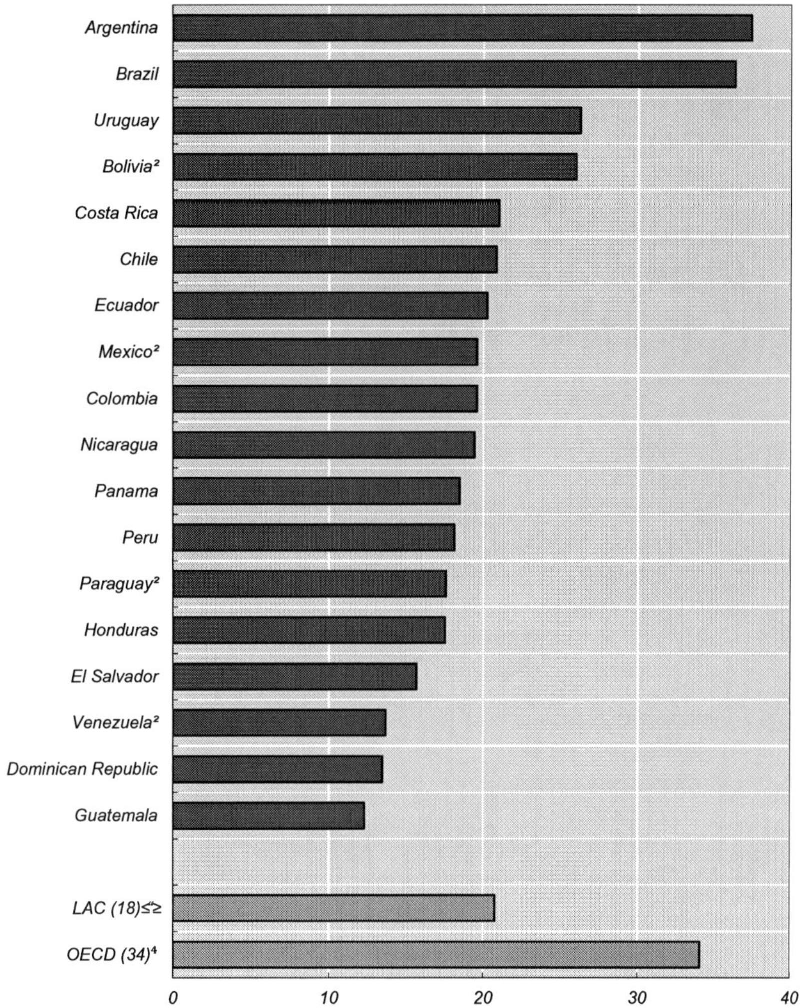

1. Countries have been ranked by their total tax revenue to GDP ratios.

1. Los países han sido ordenados según el ratio total de ingresos tributarios como porcentaje de PIB.

2. Estimated figures.

2. Datos estimados.

3. Represents the unweighted average for a group of 18 Latin American countries. Chile and Mexico are also part of the OECD (34) group.

3. Representa el promedio no ponderado para un grupo de 18 países de América Latina. Chile y México son también parte del grupo OCDE (34).

4. Represents the unweighted average for OECD member countries (2011).

4. Representa el promedio no ponderado para los países miembros de la OCDE (2011).

Source: Table 1 in Part II.A/Cuadro 1 en Parte II.A

StatLink http://dx.doi.org/10.1787/888932970456

Chart D. **Changes in tax to GDP ratios in selected Latin American countries, 1990-2012**[1]

Gráfico D. **Cambios en la recaudación tributaria como porcentaje del PIB en países seleccionados de América Latina, 1990-2012**[1]

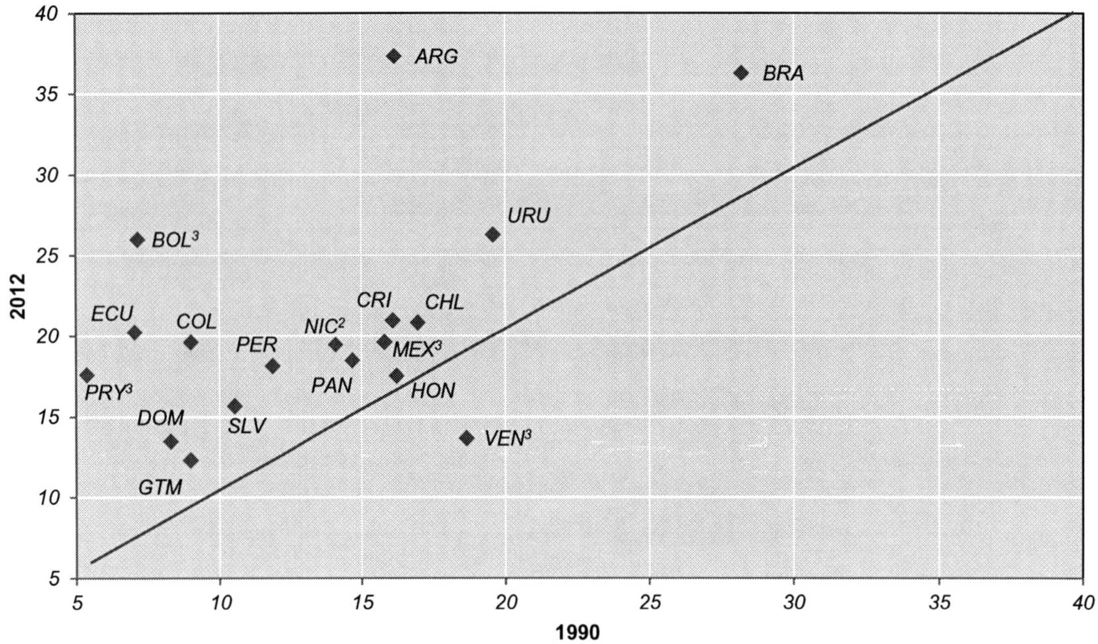

1. In ECLAC and CIAT data, fees levied on hydrocarbon production are treated as non tax revenues.

1. En los datos de CEPAL y CIAT, los derechos sobre la producción de hidrocarburos son tratados como ingresos no tributarios.

2. Figures for 1991 are used.

2. Se utilizan datos para el 1991.

3. Data estimated for 2012.

3. Datos estimados para el 2012.

Source: Table 1 in Section II.A/Cuadro 1 en sección II.A.

StatLink http://dx.doi.org/10.1787/888932970475

Chart E. **Changes in tax to GDP ratios in selected Latin American countries, 1990-2000**[1]
Gráfico E. **Cambios en la recaudación tributaria como porcentaje del PIB en países seleccionados de América Latina, 1990-2000**[1]

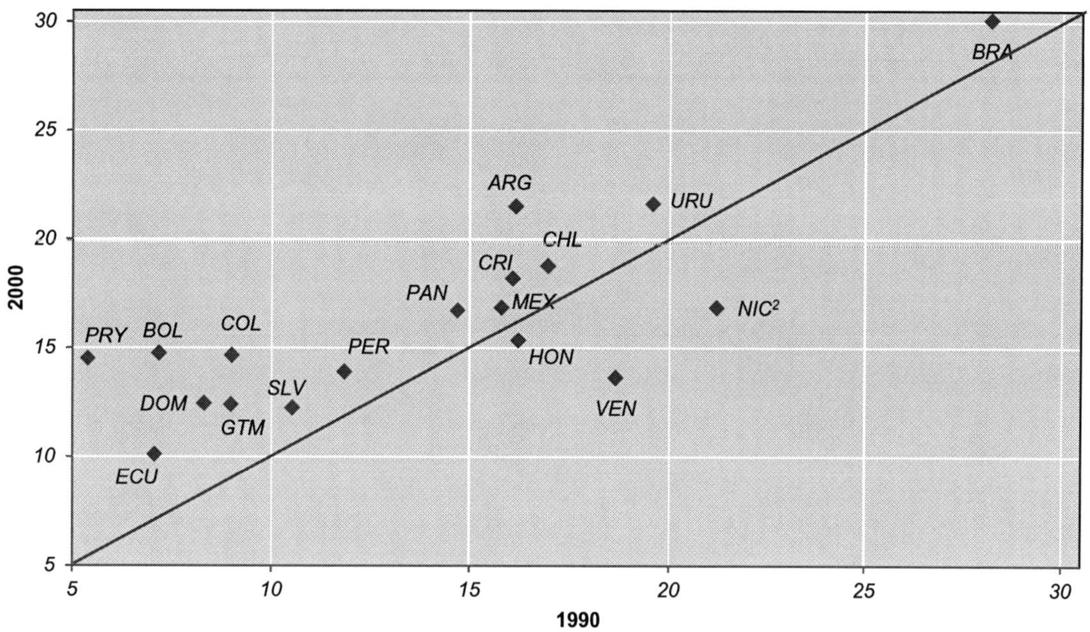

1. In ECLAC and CIAT data, fees levied on hydrocarbon production are treated as non tax revenues.

1. En los datos de CEPAL y CIAT, los derechos sobre la producción de hidrocarburos son tratados como ingresos no tributarios.

2. Figures for 1991 are used.

2. Se utilizan datos para el 1991.

Source: Table 1 in Part II.A/Cuadro 1 en Parte II.A.

StatLink http://dx.doi.org/10.1787/888932970494

Chart F. **Changes in tax to GDP ratios in selected Latin American countries, 2000-12**[1]

Gráfico F. **Cambios en la recaudación tributaria como porcentaje del PIB en países seleccionados de América Latina, 2000-12**[1]

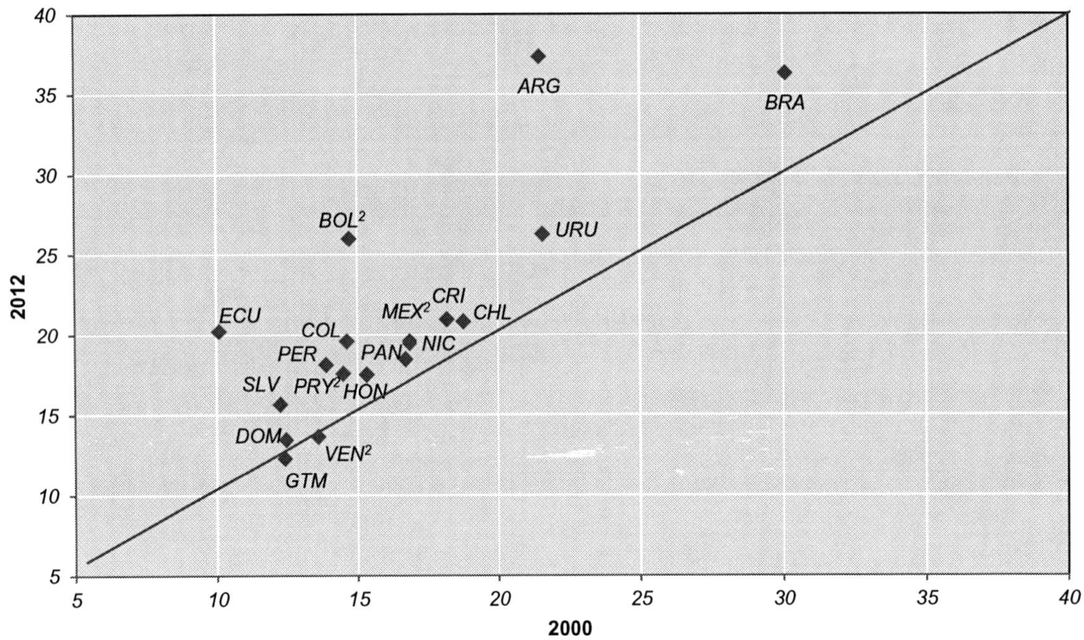

1. In ECLAC and CIAT data, fees levied on hydrocarbon production are treated as non tax revenues.

1. En los datos de CEPAL y CIAT, los derechos sobre la producción de hidrocarburos son tratados como ingresos no tributarios.

2. Data estimated for 2012.

2. Datos estimados para el 2012.

Source: Table 1 in Part II.A/Cuadro 1 en Parte II.A.

StatLink http://dx.doi.org/10.1787/888932970513

References

Brossio, G. and J.P. Jiménez (2012), *Decentralization and Reform in Latin America: Improving Intergovernmental Relations*, Edward Elgar, in press, Cheltenham, UK and Northampton, MA.

Daude, C., A. Melguizo and A. Neut (2010), "Fiscal Policy in Latin America: Countercyclical and Sustainable at Last?", *OECD Development Centre Working Paper* No. 291, OECD Development Centre, Paris.

ECLAC (2013), *Fiscal Panorama of Latin America and the Caribbean: tax reform and renewal of the fiscal covenant*, ECLAC, Santiago de Chile

ECLAC (2011), "Economic Survey of Latin America and the Caribbean 2010-2011", ECLAC, Santiago, Chile.

ECLAC (2010), "La Hora de la igualdad. Brechas por cerrar, caminos por abrir", (LC/G.2432(SES.33/3)), Santiago, Chile, ECLAC.

ECLAC-OECD (2012), *Latin American Economic Outlook 2013*, ECLAC and OECD Publishing.

Gómez Sabaini, J.C., J.P. Jiménez and A. Podestá (2010), "Evasión y equidad en América Latina", *Project documents*, No. 309 (LC/W.309/ Rev.1), Santiago, Chile, ECLAC.

OECD (2013), *Revenue Statistics 1965-2012*, OECD Publishing, Paris.

OECD (2008), *Latin American Economic Outlook 2009*, OECD Publishing, Paris.

SPECIAL FEATURE
Fiscal revenues from non-renewable natural resources in Latin America

Rapid global growth between 2003 and 2008, especially in developing regions, supported a boom in the international demand for many of the commodities exported by Latin America. This increased demand, and associated higher prices, in turn helped drive stronger growth in the region and a significant strengthening of the region's fiscal position, especially in commodity exporting countries. While these revenues have declined somewhat as a share of GDP after the crisis, they remain considerable, reaching an estimated USD 237 billion in 2012 (Figure S.1). This special section reviews the trends in non-renewable natural resource revenues in the region during the period 2000-12, as well as the drivers that underpinned these trends.

Figure S.1. **Fiscal revenues from non-renewable natural resources, 2012**

(USD billions and percentage of GDP

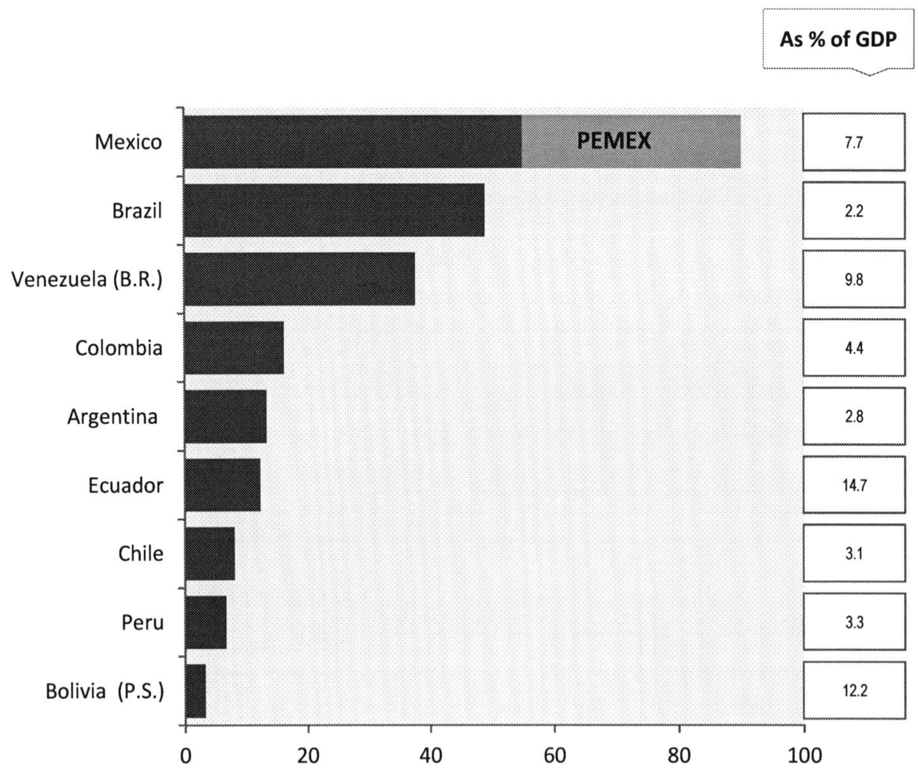

Source: ECLAC.

StatLink http://dx.doi.org/10.1787/888932970532

Drivers of rising non-renewable natural resource revenues

Much of the rapid increase in fiscal revenues associated with non-renewable natural resources has been due to fluctuations in prices as opposed to changes in the volume produced. Between 2000 and 2012, commodity prices worldwide rose sharply as increased demand faced a fairly inelastic supply. Prices for crude oil and copper, two of the primary commodities produced in the region, more than tripled in value, with copper prices registering a near quintupling in 2011 compared to 2000 (Figure S.2). Iron ore prices skyrocketed, with a 1 297% increase between 2000 and 2011, though they eased somewhat in 2012. The global economic crisis tempered price increases in 2009, but in the aftermath many commodities prices have maintained a significantly elevated level.

Production has responded relatively more slowly than the changes in prices would suggest, due mainly to the large lag times associated with responding to changes in market prices and demand and realizing new investments (Figure S.2). Copper production between 2000 and 2011 jumped 31.9% in volume terms (metric tons), helped by a strong increase in Peru of 130%. Iron ore production in Brazil, the primary exporter, also rose, nearly doubling in volume terms. Production of crude oil, however, registered only a modest increase over the period, rising 4.9%. Of the region's primary crude producers, the Bolivarian Republic of Venezuela and Mexico saw their production levels decline, while those of Brazil rose sharply, registering a 57% increase. Of the smaller producers, Colombia (+38%) and Ecuador (+25%) also registered increases, while production in Argentina declined (-19%).

Figure S.2. **Production versus prices, copper and crude oil, 2000-12**

(Index 2000=100)

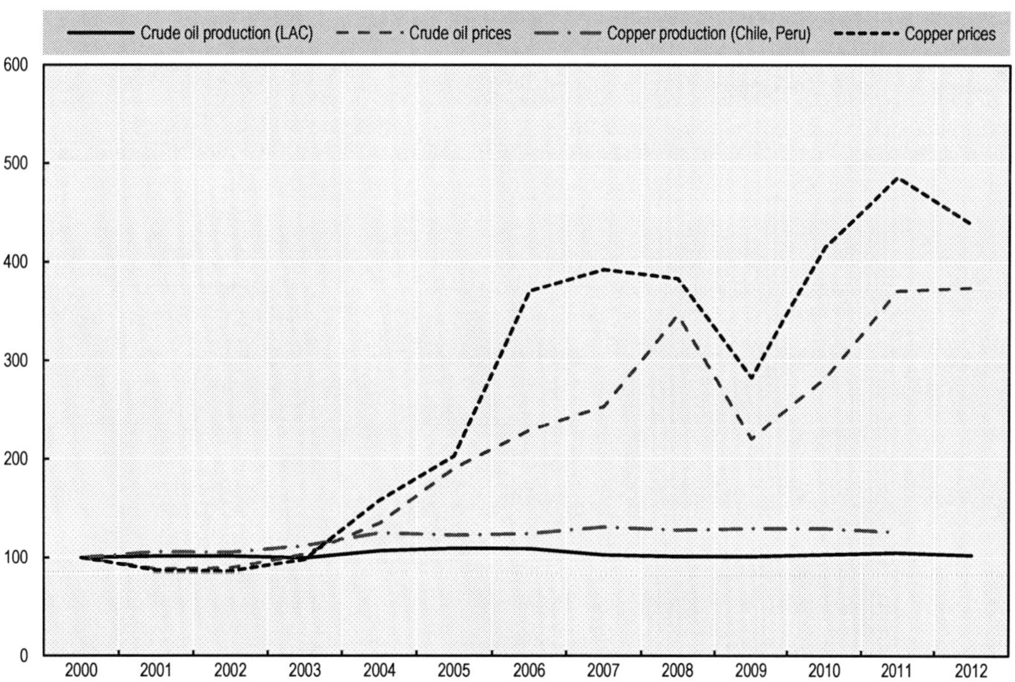

Source: ECLAC, based on data from USGS (copper production), IEA (crude oil production), and CEPALstat (prices).

StatLink http://dx.doi.org/10.1787/888932970551

While market factors may have played a predominate role, in a number of countries fiscal reforms have also increased the State's take of natural resource rents. Evidence suggests that the State took a larger share of the economic rents and relative fiscal contribution of sectors exporting non-renewable resources (minerals and hydrocarbons) during the latest boom period 2003-08, in contrast to the performance in the preceding period 1990-2003, which is suggestive of institutional frameworks becoming more effective (Aquatella, 2012).

As highlighted in ECLAC (2013), between 2005 and 2012, the most important legal reforms aimed at ensuring public control of non-renewable natural resources targeted the hydrocarbons sector. Measures included sector nationalization through firms of mixed ownership in the Bolivarian Republic of Venezuela (2005 and 2007); nationalization of hydrocarbons and re-nationalization of the Huanani tin mine in the Plurinational State of Bolivia (2006); renegotiation of oil contracts in Ecuador, under which the government receives 100% of any increases in oil prices (2010); expropriation of 51% of YPF shares in Argentina (2012); and nationalization of the Colquirí mine in Oruro, Bolivia (2012).

Governments have also used other state appropriation mechanisms, such as royalties, usually production-based, and specific taxes (Table S.1). This has been particularly important in the mining sector, where relatively smaller amounts of resources have been obtained through state participation in the respective enterprises. Royalties and specific taxes have made it possible to ensure a minimum payment is made for the resources both to national and subnational governments; and a growing number of countries have reformed their royalty systems for this purpose, including the Plurinational State of Bolivia (2005), Ecuador (2010), Colombia (2011) and Peru (2011). Moreover, most countries have also applied the traditional income tax with differential rates, in conjunction with other special taxes, often at progressive rates, levied on public or private enterprises engaged in the exploitation of non-renewable natural resources. This has been strengthened through reforms undertaken in Chile (2005), the Bolivarian Republic of Venezuela (2006, 2008 and 2011) and Peru (2011).

Table S.1. **Selected fiscal regimes related to the exploitation of non-renewable commodities in Latin America**

Country and product	Royalties	Income tax	Other taxes on incomes	Other levies	Public participation
Argentina (hydrocarbons and mining)	12%-15%; or 5% for marginal deposits (oil); 0%-3% (mining)	Corporate income tax: 35%		Export duties (25%-45% for hydrocarbons and 5%-10 for mining); Taxes on liquid fuels, natural gas, gas oil, liquefied gas, naphthas and compressed natural gas.	YPF (hydrocarbons)
Bolivia (P.S.) (hydrocarbons and mining)	Subnational royalties: 11% Compensatory national royalties: 1% National royalties (National Treasury): 6%	Corporate income tax: 25%	Tax on profits-beneficiaries abroad: 12.5%	Direct hydrocarbons tax (IDH): 32%; Special tax on hydrocarbons and derivatives (IEHD)	YPFB (hydrocarbons)
Brazil (hydrocarbons and mining)	10% of the value of production (can be reduced to 5%, depending on geological risk and other factors) (oil); 0.2%-3% (mining, CFEM)	Corporate income tax: 15%, plus a surcharge of 10% if profits are above BRL 240 000 per year	Special state participation: 10%-40%; Tax on profits-beneficiaries abroad: 15% (or 25% for payments to tax havens)	Social levy on net profit: 9%; CIDE: 10%; State level tax on tax on sale of oil and gas (ICMS combustiveis)	Petrobras (hydrocarbons)

Table S.1. **Selected fiscal regimes related to the exploitation of non-renewable commodities in Latin America (*cont*)**

Country and product	Royalties	Income tax	Other taxes on incomes	Other levies	Public participation
Chile (mining)		Corporate income tax: 20%	Tax on profit remittances 35%; Tax on interest remittances 4%; Special 40% tax on profits (for public enterprises)	Specific tax on the operating income of mining activity: progressive rates between 0.5% and 14%; Tax with revenue earmarked for the Armed Forces: 10% of foreign currency earnings from exports of CODELCO copper production	CODELCO (copper)
Colombia (hydrocarbons and mining)	8-25% (hydrocarbons); 1-12% (mining)	Corporate income tax: 25% Income tax for equity (CREE): 9% for 2013-15, 8% thereafter		Oil Pipeline Transport Tax; National Gasoline Tax and ACPM; ANH duties	Ecopetrol (hydrocarbons)
Ecuador (hydrocarbons)	12.5-18.5% (of gross crude oil production)	Corporate income tax: 23%	The State reserves for itself 25% of gross income from the contract area	Labour share of profits: the State receives 12% of profits (destined for decentralized autonomous governments)	Petroecuador (hydrocarbons)
Mexico (hydrocarbons and mining)		Oil Revenue Tax (PEMEX): 30%; Corporate income tax (certain subsidiary companies): 30%	Flat Rate Business Tax (IETU) (certain subsidiary companies): 17.5%	Mining duties; Hydrocarbons duties; Special Production and Services Tax (IEPS gasoline); Merchandise Import Duty	Pemex (hydrocarbons)
Peru (hydrocarbons and mining)	1-12% on operating profit (mining); 5-35%, depending on method used in contract (hydrocarbons)	Corporate income tax: 30%	Dividends and profit distribution: 4.1%	Special Mining Tax (IEM): 2% - 8.4%; Special Mining Levy (GEM): 4% - 13.12% (on operating profit); Excise tax on gasoline	
Venezuela (B.R.) (hydrocarbons)	Equivalent to 30% of the extracted crude	Petroleum corporate income tax (ISLR): 50%		Windfall Oil Price Tax; Extraction tax (33% of value); Export registration tax (0.1% of value exported)	PDVSA (hydrocarbons)

Source: ECLAC, based on ECLAC (2013).

New policy measures – announced or enacted – in 2013 suggest that while policymakers are keen to increase the fiscal contribution from non-renewable natural resources, they are also concerned with bolstering private investment. Mexico's recently announced energy sector reform includes, for the first time since the nationalization of the oil sector, a role for private sector investment through the use of profit-sharing contracts. A new mining regulation framework under debate in Brazil would see royalties capped at 4%, or double their current level for iron and coal. Ecuador's recently enacted mining reform attempts to both increase investment in the country, especially in small and medium-sized projects, while increasing the sector's fiscal contribution through minimum royalties and a windfall tax (which has been delayed).

As noted in Aquatella (2012), the region's countries have historically found it difficult to harness commodity-export boom periods to long-term economic development processes. Nonetheless, in recent years, Latin America has seen the benefits of having the capacity to deploy counter-cyclical policies to cushion the impact of the international crisis, through the management of fiscal savings made during the 2003-08 commodity-price boom. The instruments used to achieve this include stabilization funds – financed with surplus income from copper exports (Chile), or based on oil income (Colombia, Ecuador, Mexico and the Bolivarian Republic of Venezuela).

Trends in non-renewable natural resource revenues

The fiscal contribution from non-renewable natural resources grew strongly during the last decade (Figure S.3). Revenues rose from an average of 4.3% of GDP in the first half of the decade, to a high of 7.2% of GDP in 2008, or an increase of 3 percentage points in 3 years. While most countries followed this general trend, in some cases the increase was more pronounced, such as in Ecuador (increase of 8.2), Chile (increase of 6.8 in 2007), and the Plurinational State of Bolivia (increase of 6.2).

Figure S.3. **Latin America (9 countries): Total public revenues and revenues from non-renewable natural resources**

(percentage of GDP)

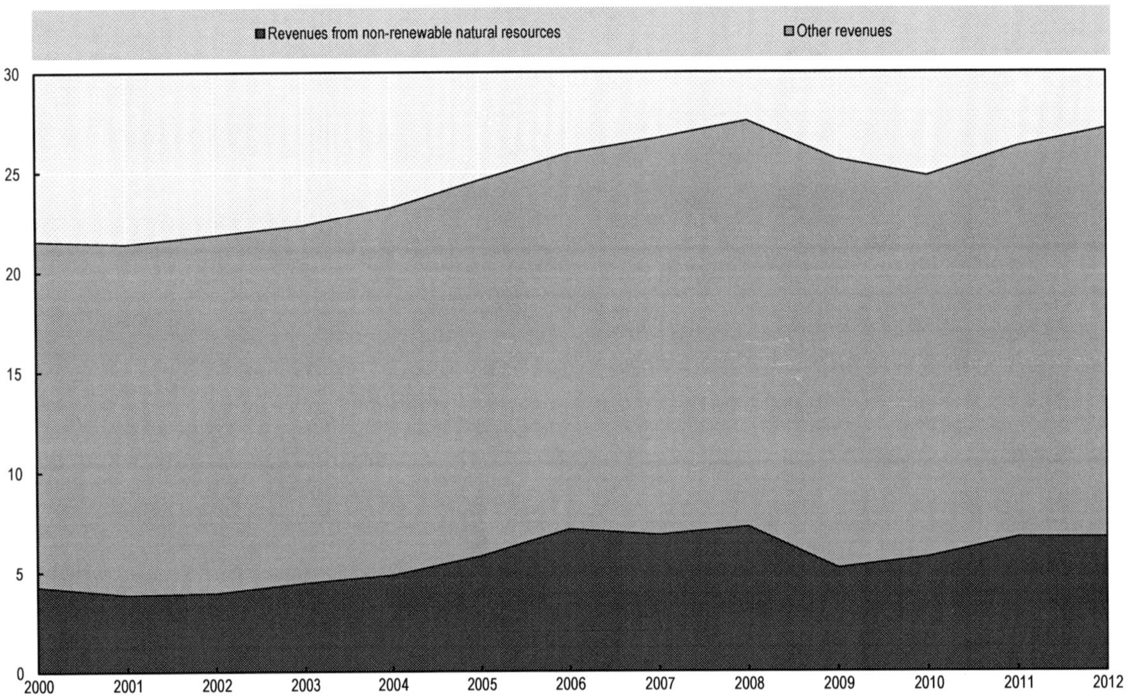

Note: Includes Argentina (NFNPS), Bolivia (P.S.) (GG), Brazil (GG), Chile (CC), Colombia (CG), Ecuador (NFPS), Mexico (PS), Peru (GG) and Venezuela (B.R.) (CG).

Source: ECLAC.

StatLink http://dx.doi.org/10.1787/888932970570

However, with the same speed with which these revenues rose, they fell in 2009 with the onset of the international financial and economic crisis, declining 2.1 percentage points of GDP between 2008 and 2009. Each country's experience, however, was different, and some experienced much more pronounced declines: Ecuador (decrease of

5.7 percentage points), Chile (decrease of 5.7, 2007 to 2009), and the Bolivarian Republic of Venezuela (decrease of 4.6). While these revenues increased at a faster rate than other government revenues before the crisis, their performance in the aftermath has been marked by its volatility: relatively strong growth in 2010 and 2011, before stalling in 2012.

These general trends belie a more differentiated dynamic when viewed by the performance of individual groups of commodities, such as hydrocarbons and minerals. Although revenues from both experienced sharp declines as a percentage of GDP in 2009 – with revenues from minerals already exhibiting a decrease in 2008 – in the aftermath of the crisis their performance has been strongly differentiated (Figure S.4). Revenues from hydrocarbons have registered a sustained recovery as a percentage of GDP, with a return to their 2006-08 levels as soon as 2011. In contrast, revenues from minerals have stagnated at levels lower than those registered during the "boom", even though prices remain relatively high and production steady. This result is largely explained by squeezed profit margins due to increased production costs in the principal exporting countries and, to a lesser extent, the appreciation of exchange rates which generates smaller local currency revenues. The case of CODELCO, the Chilean State-owned copper producer, is illustrative of these trends, with the company reporting sharply higher production costs between 2010 and 2012 as compared to during 2006-07 (Figure S.5).

Figure S.4. **Latin America (8 countries): Revenues from non-renewable natural resources, by product group, 2000-12**

(percentage of GDP)

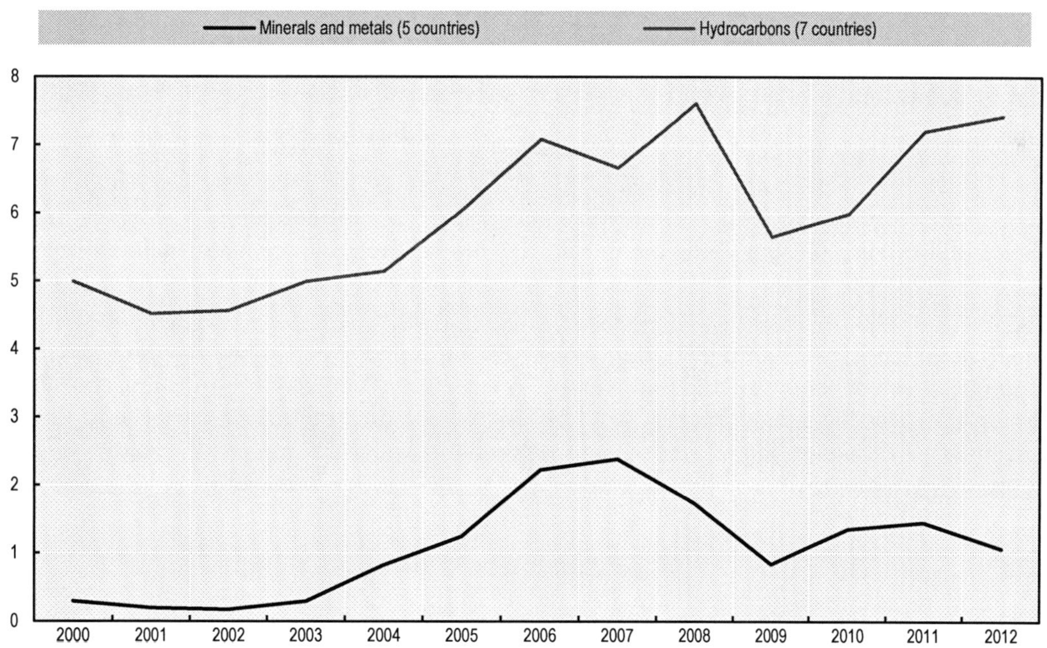

Note: Disaggregated data for Argentina was not available thus it is not included in this figure. For the Plurinational State of Bolivia, Brazil, Colombia and Peru data were separated by commodity group, thus the sum of the two commodities groups is greater than that of the countries covered.

Source: ECLAC.

StatLink http://dx.doi.org/10.1787/888932970589

Figure S.5. **Revenue and cost of revenue of CODELCO, 2000-12**

(USD billions)

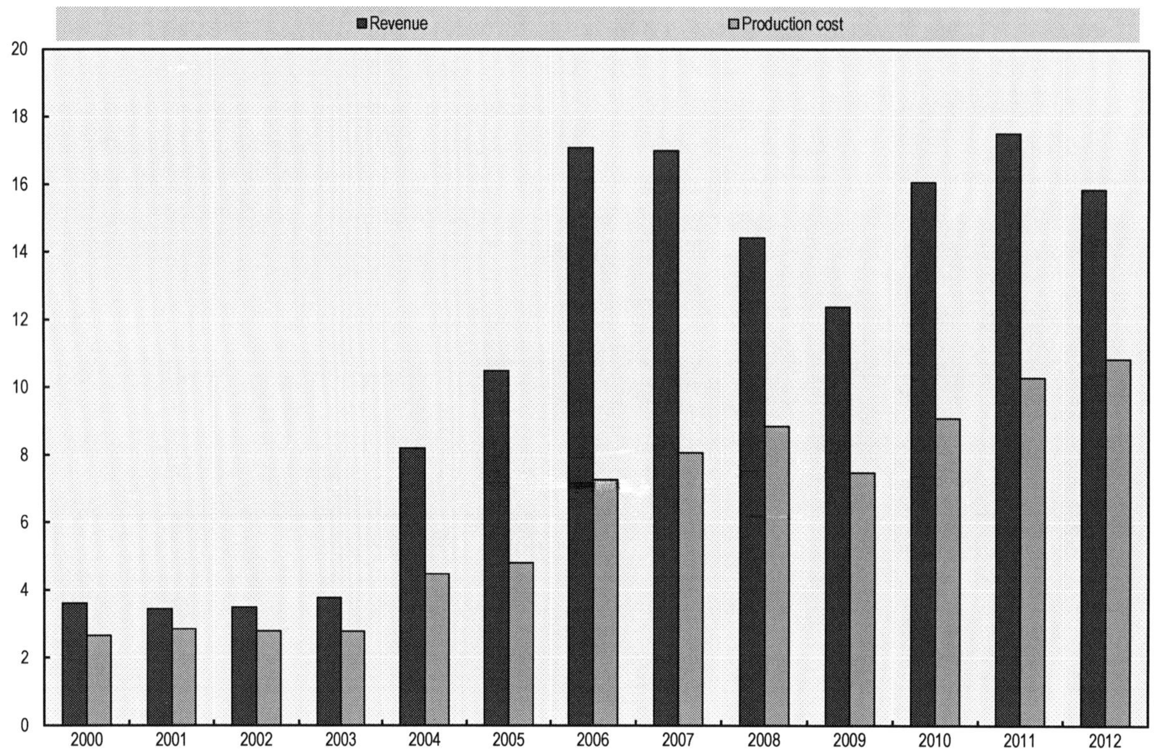

Source: ECLAC, based on data from Bloomberg.

StatLink http://dx.doi.org/10.1787/888932970608

Fiscal revenues from non-renewable natural resources continue to be very important as a percentage of the total revenues in many countries. In particular, the Plurinational State of Bolivia, Ecuador, Mexico and the Bolivarian Republic of Venezuela exhibit a high level of dependence, with commodity-based revenues accounting for more than 30% of the total (Figure S.6). For these countries, the high level of revenues from commodities implies both a greater participation in the rents they generate as well as a higher level of risk due to the dynamics of a global market. In those countries that don't form part of this group the crisis has not necessarily served to slow the increase in the importance of these revenues. Colombia and Ecuador, for example, exhibit a greater participation of commodity-based revenues in their total revenues after the crisis as compared to before.

Figure S.6. **Relative participation of revenues from non-renewable natural resources in total revenues**

(percentage)

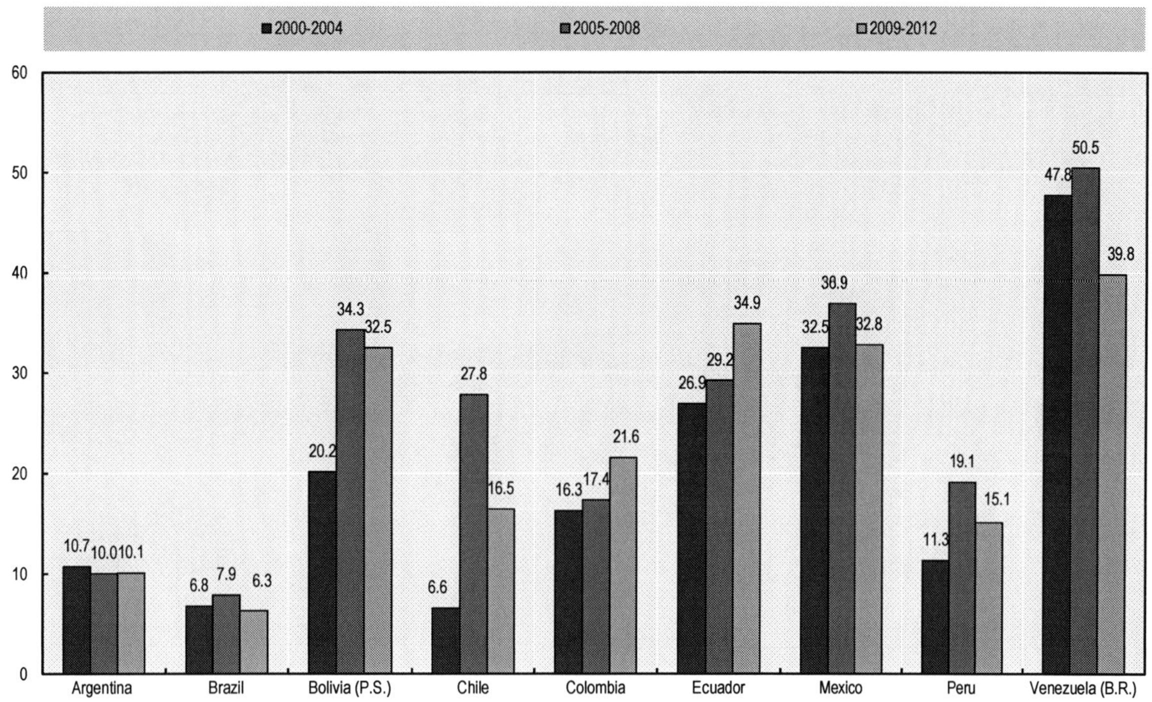

Note: See Figure S.3 for description of data coverage by country.

Source: ECLAC.

StatLink http://dx.doi.org/10.1787/888932970627

References

Aquatella, J. (2012); "Rentas de recursos naturales no-renovables en América Latina y el Caribe: Evolución 1990 -2010 y participación estatal", Seminario "Gobernanza de los Recursos Naturales en ALC", División de Recursos Naturales e Infraestructura, ECLAC, April.

ECLAC (Economic Commission for Latin America and the Caribbean) (2013), "Panorama fiscal de América Latina y el Caribe: reformas tributarias y renovación del pacto fiscal", Santiago de Chile, Chile.

PARTE I

Tendencias tributarias, 1990-2012

A. Niveles de recaudación

Los ingresos tributarios como proporción del producto interno bruto (PIB) han aumentado considerablemente en América Latina en los dos últimos decenios. Tanto el cuadro A como el gráfico A plasman cómo los ingresos de los países latinoamericanos objeto de este estudio, incluidas las contribuciones a la seguridad social, han venido incrementándose casi ininterrumpidamente, con excepción de 2009, y han pasado del 13.6% del PIB en 1990 al 20.7% del PIB (promedios no ponderados) en 2012. Este crecimiento de la importancia relativa de los ingresos tributarios es reflejo de unas condiciones macroeconómicas favorables, así como de los cambios en el diseño de los sistemas tributarios y del fortalecimiento de las administraciones tributarias.

Esta tendencia contrasta con la registrada en la zona de la OCDE, donde la proporción ha permanecido relativamente estable, ya que, en 2011, arrojaba un valor del 34.1% del PIB, menos de un punto porcentual por encima de su nivel de 1990. Como resultado, la brecha entre los promedios de las dos zonas comenzó a disminuir a partir del año 2000: si la diferencia era de unos 19 puntos porcentuales entre 1990 y 2000, para 2011 había caído a 14 puntos porcentuales.

Los ingresos tributarios como proporción del PIB en América Latina aumentaron cada año desde 2010 a 2012, continuando con una tendencia expansiva que se venía dando desde hace muchos años pero que se había visto interrumpida en 2009, como consecuencia de la caída del nivel de actividad y de los precios de los materias primas debido a la crisis financiera internacional. El ratio de ingresos tributarios sobre el PIB en 2012 representó un 20.7%, por encima del 20.1% registrado en 2011 y del 19.3% experimentado en 2010. En 2012 este ratio, comparado con 2011, creció en 13 de los 18 países analizados de la región, se mantuvo igual en Costa Rica, y cayó en los 4 países restantes. Si se compara el ratio de 2011 con el del 2010, sólo en 15 países se ha experimentado un crecimiento, mientras que solo en uno se ha registrado una caída. La media de los países OCDE creció en 0.3 puntos porcentuales en 2011, dejando el ratio en un nivel de 34.1%, todavía 0.4 puntos porcentuales por debajo del nivel precrisis de 2008 de 34.5%.

La proporción media de los impuestos en relación con el PIB es mucho mayor en los países de la OCDE que en los países latinoamericanos de la muestra (el 34.1% frente al 20.1%, respectivamente, en 2011). Sin embargo, cabe señalar que existe una amplia variación entre las proporciones más altas y más bajas de impuestos en relación con el PIB entre los países latinoamericanos. Entre los países de la muestra, las cifras más elevadas en 2012 correspondieron a Argentina y Brasil (37.3% y 36.3%, respectivamente), mientras que Guatemala (12.3%) República Dominicana (13.5%) y Venezuela (13.7%) registraron los niveles más bajos. Del mismo modo, las características de las economías de la OCDE muestran una gran disparidad. Así, en 2012, la proporción de los impuestos en el PIB en el seno de la OCDE oscilaba desde un 48.0% de Dinamarca al 19.6% en México (esta cifra difiere de las presentadas en las publicaciones de CEPAL y CIAT debido a la inclusión de derechos sobre la producción de hidrocarburos como ingresos tributarios). Estas amplias variaciones implican que la interpretación de las diferencias aparentes entre las proporciones de impuestos en relación con el PIB de la OCDE y América Latina debe realizarse con cautela, dado que en estas regiones se incluyen economías de naturaleza muy dispar.

Entre los numerosos factores que determinan cuál debería ser la proporción de impuestos adecuada para cada país, se encuentra el volumen de provisión de bienes y servicios por parte del Estado. De los años 1980 en adelante, muchos países latinoamericanos privatizaron, en mayor o menor medida, los servicios de atención sanitaria, educación y seguridad social (CEPAL, 2010). Esta característica regional contrasta con la provisión sustancialmente pública de esos servicios, y la consiguiente necesidad de ingresos fiscales, en múltiples países de la OCDE, en particular en Europa. Además, en los países latinoamericanos, los elevados niveles de informalidad hacen que muchas personas queden al margen de la imposición (OCDE, 2008; Gómez Sabaini et al., 2010), algo que además tiene especial importancia en el entorno de las pymes. Con todo, la cuestión del incumplimiento en el pago de impuestos suele tener un impacto significativo en los ingresos tributarios en todo tipo de países.

El cuadro A muestra una considerable disparidad entre las tendencias de los diversos países considerados a lo largo del tiempo. Pero, independientemente de la amplia variedad de niveles impositivos, se observa un reforzamiento de los ingresos tributarios desde el 1990. Los países que mayores incrementos registraron entre 1990 y 2012 fueron Argentina (21.4 puntos porcentuales), Bolivia (18.8), Ecuador (13.1), Paraguay (12.2) y Colombia (10.6). En el mismo periodo, en la mayoría de los países restantes los aumentos oscilaron entre 3 y 8 puntos porcentuales, con la excepción de Honduras, con un aumento de 1.3 puntos porcentuales y Venezuela, que sufrió un descenso de 5 puntos porcentuales.

Gráfico A. **Total de recaudacion tributaria como porcentaje de PIB en América Latina y la OCDE, 1990-2012**

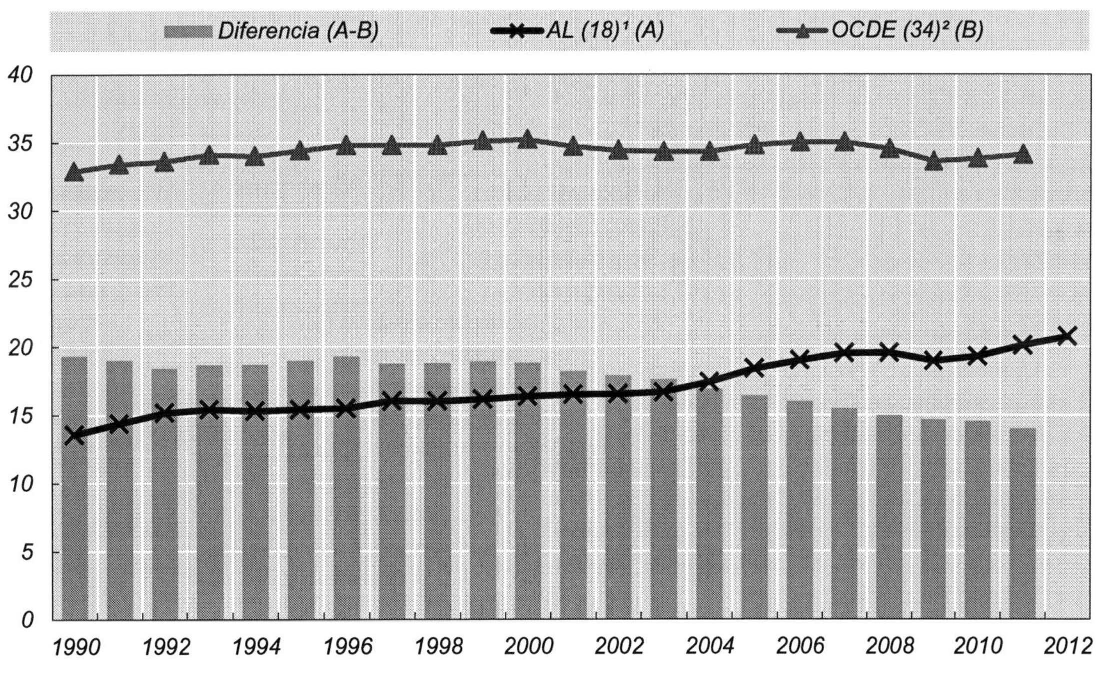

1. Representa un grupo de 18 países de América Latina. Estos son Argentina, Bolivia, Brasil, Chile, Colombia, Costa Rica, República Dominicana, Ecuador, El Salvador, Guatemala, Honduras, México, Nicaragua, Panamá, Paraguay, Perú, Uruguay y Venezuela. Chile y México son también parte del grupo OCDE (34).

2. Representa el promedio no ponderado de los países miembros de la OCDE.

Fuente: Cuadro 1 en Parte II.A.

StatLink http://dx.doi.org/10.1787/888932970646

El contexto en el que se produjo el incremento de los ingresos tributarios registrado a partir de los años 1990 fue el periodo de inestabilidad macroeconómica que vivieron los países latinoamericanos en la década anterior. Durante los años 1980, los países de la región padecieron fuertes desequilibrios fiscales y, al mismo tiempo, algunos recurrieron a vías alternativas para financiar su gasto (tomando préstamos o imprimiendo moneda), lo que generó una inflación que se extendió rápidamente por toda la región y erosionó el valor real de los ingresos tributarios. Como resultado de ello, las reformas de los años 1990 se centraron en controlar dicha inflación y en imponer disciplina fiscal.

Cuadro A. **Total de ingresos tributarios en porcentaje del PIB**[1]

	1990	2000	2007	2008	2009	2010	2011	2012
Argentina	16.1	21.5	29.1	30.8	31.5	33.5	34.7	37.3
Bolivia[2,3]	7.2	14.7	22.6	20.5	22.7	20.7	24.2	26.0
Brasil	28.2	30.1	33.8	34.0	32.6	33.2	34.9	36.3
Chile	17.0	18.8	22.8	21.4	17.2	19.5	21.2	20.8
Colombia	9.0	14.6	19.1	18.8	18.6	18.0	18.8	19.6
Costa Rica	16.1	18.2	21.7	22.4	20.8	20.5	21.0	21.0
Ecuador	7.1	10.1	12.8	14.0	14.9	16.8	17.9	20.2
El Salvador	10.5	12.2	15.2	15.1	14.4	14.8	14.8	15.7
Guatemala	9.0	12.4	13.9	12.9	12.2	12.3	12.6	12.3
Honduras	16.2	15.3	19.0	18.9	17.1	17.3	16.9	17.5
México[4,5]	15.8	16.9	17.7	20.9	17.4	18.9	19.7	19.6
Nicaragua	n.d.	16.9	17.4	17.3	17.4	18.3	19.1	19.5
Panamá	14.7	16.7	16.7	16.9	17.4	18.1	18.1	18.5
Paraguay[2]	5.4	14.5	13.9	14.6	16.1	16.5	17.0	17.6
Perú	11.8	13.9	17.8	18.2	16.3	17.4	17.8	18.1
República Dominicana	8.3	12.4	16.0	15.0	13.1	12.8	12.9	13.5
Uruguay	19.6	21.6	25.0	26.1	27.1	27.0	27.3	26.3
Venezuela[2]	18.7	13.6	16.8	14.1	14.3	11.4	12.9	13.7
Promedio no ponderado:								
AL (18)[6]	13.6	16.4	19.5	19.5	18.9	19.3	20.1	20.7
OCDE (34)[7]	32.9	35.2	35.0	34.5	33.6	33.8	34.1	n.a

1. Las cifras excluyen los ingresos de gobiernos locales en Argentina (pero incluye ingresos de las provincias), Bolivia, Costa Rica (hasta 1997), República Dominicana, Ecuador, El Salvador, Honduras, Nicaragua, Panamá (hasta 1998), Paraguay (hasta 2004, 2011 y 2012), Perú (hasta 2004), Uruguay y Venezuela dado que los datos no están disponibles.

2. Datos estimados para el 2011 y el 2012.

3. En los datos de CEPAL, el Impuesto Directo sobre Hidrocarburos (IDH) es considerado como regalía en los ingresos no tributarios.

4. En los datos de CEPAL y CIAT, los derechos sobre la producción de hidrocarburos son tratados como ingresos no tributarios.

5. La data estimada incluye ingresos esperados a nivel estatal y local para el 2012.

6. Representa un grupo de 18 países de América Latina. Chile y México son también parte del grupo OCDE (34).

7. Representa el promedio no ponderado para los países miembros de la OCDE.

StatLink http://dx.doi.org/10.1787/888932970931

La mayor parte de los gobiernos latinoamericanos reaccionaron tanto recortando el gasto público como instaurando políticas destinadas a incrementar la recaudación, obteniendo así una notable mejora de la gestión presupuestaria y el saldo fiscal. En la parte recaudatoria de la ecuación, las reformas fiscales y de las administraciones tributarias contribuyeron notablemente a alcanzar ese objetivo. Como parte de este proceso, el impacto de la inflación en los ingresos obligó a los responsables de dictar políticas (policy-makers) a hallar soluciones para hacer que el sistema fuera menos vulnerable a episodios inflacionistas, tales como disminuir los plazos para el pago de impuestos e indexar las obligaciones tributarias.

De esta forma, la carga fiscal del grupo de 18 países latinoamericanos aumentó cerca de 7.1 puntos porcentuales del PIB entre 1990 y 2012. Pero la reforma fiscal más significativa en América Latina en los años 1980 y principios de los 1990 vino constituida por la introducción del IVA. Las subsiguientes reformas relacionadas con este impuesto se han centrado en extenderlo y reforzarlo mediante la subida de la tasa impositiva y la ampliación dc la base tributaria. En los años 1990, el porcentaje del IVA en el PIB aumentó 2.1 puntos porcentuales y, posteriormente, 1.4 puntos más hasta 2012 (véase el cuadro B).

Cuadro B. **Impuesto al valor agregado en porcentaje del PIB**

	1990	2000	2007	2008	2009	2010	2011	2012
Argentina	2.5	6.5	7.5	7.5	7.4	7.9	8.1	8.7
Bolivia	3.2	5.1	6.5	7.0	6.3	6.7	7.3	7.6
Brasil	10.4	8.6	7.8	8.1	7.6	7.8	7.8	8.5
Chile	6.3	7.9	7.5	8.4	7.3	7.6	7.8	8.0
Colombia	2.0	4.1	5.4	5.6	5.1	5.3	5.6	5.5
Costa Rica	3.2	4.5	5.9	6.0	4.9	4.8	5.0	5.0
Ecuador	2.0	4.6	4.9	4.6	4.8	5.8	5.5	6.4
El Salvador	-	5.4	6.9	6.8	6.1	6.7	6.8	7.0
Guatemala	2.4	4.7	5.9	5.5	4.9	5.1	5.2	5.3
Honduras	2.7	4.8	6.1	6.3	5.2	5.4	5.7	5.6
México	3.3	3.1	3.6	3.8	3.4	3.9	3.7	3.8
Nicaragua	n.d.	5.9	5.8	5.6	5.3	5.6	6.0	6.1
Panamá	1.3	0.6	1.0	2.3	2.3	2.9	3.3	3.3
Paraguay	-	4.7	5.0	5.5	5.6	6.3	6.5	6.5
Perú	1.4	5.1	5.9	6.8	6.0	6.6	6.5	6.4
República Dominicana	1.3	2.6	4.9	4.7	4.2	4.3	4.2	4.0
Uruguay	5.5	6.5	9.3	9.2	9.0	8.9	8.9	8.7
Venezuela	-	4.1	5.6	4.6	5.9	5.5	6.2	6.8
Promedio no ponderado:								
AL (18)[1]	2.8	4.9	5.9	6.0	5.6	5.9	6.1	6.3
OCDE (34)[2]	5.3	6.6	6.7	6.5	6.4	6.7	6.6	n.d.

n.d. : indica no disponible

1. Representa un grupo de 18 países de América Latina. Chile y México son también parte del grupo OCDE (34).

2. Representa el promedio no ponderado para los países miembros de la OCDE.

StatLink http://dx.doi.org/10.1787/888932970950

Entre 2000 y 2012, el incremento de los ingresos procedentes de los impuestos sobre la renta (principalmente, el impuesto sobre la renta de las sociedades), cercano a 2 puntos porcentuales del PIB, hizo de este tipo de tributos el principal motor del aumento de los ingresos tributarios, por delante del IVA. Uno de los elementos que contribuyó a este resultado fue el periodo de auge de los precios de las materias primas que se inició tras 2003, que resultó particularmente importante para algunos países de la región (ver la

Sección especial para más información). Otras reformas fiscales incluyeron la introducción o el desarrollo de regímenes simplificados para pequeños contribuyentes y la imposición de la propiedad sobre la base de ingresos presuntos. Además, en el último quinquenio se han impulsado varias reformas del impuesto sobre la renta en América Latina y el Caribe, donde ha predominado el efecto positivo de ampliaciones de las bases imponibles del impuesto debido a la extensión de la tributación al conjunto de ingresos del trabajo y de las rentas de capital, incluida la aplicación de impuestos a dividendos (Colombia, Guatemala, El Salvador, Nicaragua, Panamá, Perú, República Dominicana), además de otras medidas que han incluido el establecimiento de impuestos mínimos, la reducción de exenciones, la precisión de gastos deducibles para acotarlos, la gradual reducción del nivel de ingreso real al cual es aplicada la máxima tasa marginal y cierto control de los precios de transferencia (CEPAL, 2013).

El cambio en la recaudación procedente de los impuestos sobre los bienes y servicios, y de los impuestos sobre la renta y las utilidades contribuyó principalmente a la recuperación de la participación de los ingresos tributarios en el PIB desde el 2010. Estos aumentos en los ingresos tributarios se debe parcialmente a la recuperación de la actividad económica en América Latina y, en cierta medida, también a la recuperación de los precios de las materias primas (CEPAL-OCDE, 2012).

B. Estructuras impositivas

A medida que los niveles impositivos han ido aumentando en América Latina, la estructura impositiva (esto es, la proporción de las principales categorías de impuestos respecto al total de ingresos tributarios) ha venido transformándose también significativamente entre 1990 y 2012. El cuadro C plasma las diversas tendencias registradas en la "combinación tributaria" (tax mix) que se desprenden de los datos. Las tendencias más destacadas se han observado en relación con los impuestos sobre el consumo y los impuestos sobre la renta y las utilidades.

Cuadro C. **Estructuras impositivas en un grupo de países de América Latina**[1]

	1990	2000	2009	2010	2011	2012
Impuestos sobre ingresos y utilidades	21	20	26	25	25	26
Contribuciones a la seguridad social	16	17	17	17	17	17
Impuesto sobre la nómina	1	1	1	1	1	1
Impuestos sobre la propiedad	6	4	4	4	4	4
Impuestos generales sobre el consumo	23	32	33	34	34	34
Impuestos específicos sobre el consumo	31	24	18	18	18	17
Otros impuestos[2]	4	2	2	2	2	2
Total	100	100	100	100	100	100

1. Representa la proporción de las principales categorías de impuesto en el total de ingresos tributarios. El grupo de 18 países está listado en el cuadro A.

2. Incluye algunos impuestos sobre bienes y servicios (partida 5200) e impuestos de timbres.

StatLink http://dx.doi.org/10.1787/888932970969

La proporción global de los impuestos (generales y específicos) sobre el consumo permaneció bastante estable durante el periodo de referencia, pero el peso de los impuestos generales sobre el consumo aumentó considerablemente, 11 puntos porcentuales, entre 1990 y 2012, mientras que la incidencia de los impuestos específicos sobre el consumo cayó 14 puntos en ese mismo periodo.

Estas dos tendencias antagónicas en el seno de los impuestos sobre el consumo se explican por la creciente incidencia del IVA y la pérdida de importancia de impuestos específicos sobre el consumo tales como los impuestos selectivos o los impuestos sobre el comercio internacional. Aunque el IVA fue introducido tempranamente en las economías de la región (la mayoría de los países ya lo habían adoptado de alguna forma a finales de los años 1970), su expansión en términos de ingresos tributarios es relativamente reciente. Desde principios de los años 1990, este impuesto ha venido constituyendo una fuente creciente de ingresos para los países latinoamericanos y se ha consolidado mediante sucesivas ampliaciones de la base tributaria y de las tasas impositivas oficiales así como también a través del fortalecimiento de las administraciones tributarias. Las reformas se han enfocado también en la simplificación de los sistemas tributarios, con la mayoría de los países reduciendo el número de bienes con tasa nula o reducida, encaminándose así a un sistema de tasa única para el IVA en muchos casos.

En contraste, el declive del peso de los impuestos específicos sobre el consumo tiene que ver con los procesos de liberalización del comercio, y la consiguiente reducción de los derechos de aduanas sobre las importaciones y supresión de los impuestos sobre las exportaciones en numerosos países latinoamericanos (con la destacable salvedad de Argentina, donde los impuestos sobre las exportaciones se reestablecieron en 2002). Además, se ha acotado el conjunto de bienes y servicios sujetos a impuestos selectivos, que hoy se limitan principalmente a productos y servicios con una demanda relativamente inelástica, tales como bebidas alcohólicas, combustible y derivados, y tabaco.

Al mismo tiempo, han crecido los ingresos procedentes de la renta y las utilidades, que han pasado del 21% al 26% del total de ingresos tributarios entre 2000 y 2012, esencialmente como resultado de niveles de recaudación mucho más elevados a finales de los años 2000. Por lo general, en los países latinoamericanos, la participación del impuesto sobre la renta de las sociedades es superior a la del impuesto sobre la renta personal, y el incremento general de esta categoría refleja el notorio aumento de los ingresos generados por la tributación de las sociedades, especialmente las empresas del sector de los recursos naturales. Sin embargo, el peso de los impuestos sobre la renta y utilidades en el total de la recaudación cayó entre 2009 y 2010, probablemente debido al impacto de la crisis sobre los ingresos y utilidades, para posteriormente crecer hasta 26% en 2012 (Cuadro C).

En cuanto a las contribuciones a la seguridad social, en promedio, la proporción de los ingresos procedentes de esta categoría en el PIB aumentó entre 1990 y 2012, pasando de un 2.4% a un 3.8% en ese periodo. Su peso en los ingresos tributarios totales pasó de un 15.6% a un 17.2% en ese mismo período (Cuadro C). Este resultado traduce en realidad la actuación de dos fuerzas contrapuestas. En primer lugar, el incremento de las rentas personales ha empujado al alza las cantidades recaudadas. Pero este efecto se ha visto contrarrestado y, a menudo, más que compensado, por los variados procesos de privatización total o parcial registrados en numerosos países de la región. En este sentido, ha habido gran heterogeneidad en la forma en que los países han instaurado y reformado sus regímenes de seguridad social. Algunos países, como Chile, México y Perú, se basan en gran medida en regímenes privados de capitalización individual, lo que explica los niveles relativamente bajos de la recaudación por contribuciones a la seguridad social. En los países con sistemas públicos o mixtos, tales como Brasil, Costa Rica, Ecuador, Nicaragua, Panama, Paraguay y Uruguay, las contribuciones a la seguridad social aún mantienen una significativa importancia (más del 20% del total de ingresos tributarios). En Argentina, las cifras reflejan la introducción de sistemas de capitalización en 1994 y su posterior nacionalización en 2008.

Si se comparan los países de la OCDE y de América Latina, salta a la vista la principal diferencia de estructura impositiva entre estos dos grupos: en relación con la OCDE, América Latina registra una incidencia de los impuestos directos relativamente baja, compensada por ingresos fiscales elevados en concepto de impuestos indirectos (véase el gráfico B). En concreto, América Latina depende acusadamente de los impuestos sobre los bienes y servicios, que representan aproximadamente la mitad de los ingresos tributarios totales, en comparación con el 30% en el caso de las economías de la OCDE. A título comparativo, obsérvese que, en América Latina, cerca del 40% de los ingresos tributarios procede de la suma de los impuestos sobre la renta y las utilidades y de las contribuciones a la seguridad social, frente al 60% en la OCDE. Esta mayor dependencia de los impuestos indirectos puede acarrear que el sistema tributario sea más regresivo.

Gráfico B. **Estructuras impositivas en América Latina y la OCDE, 2011**

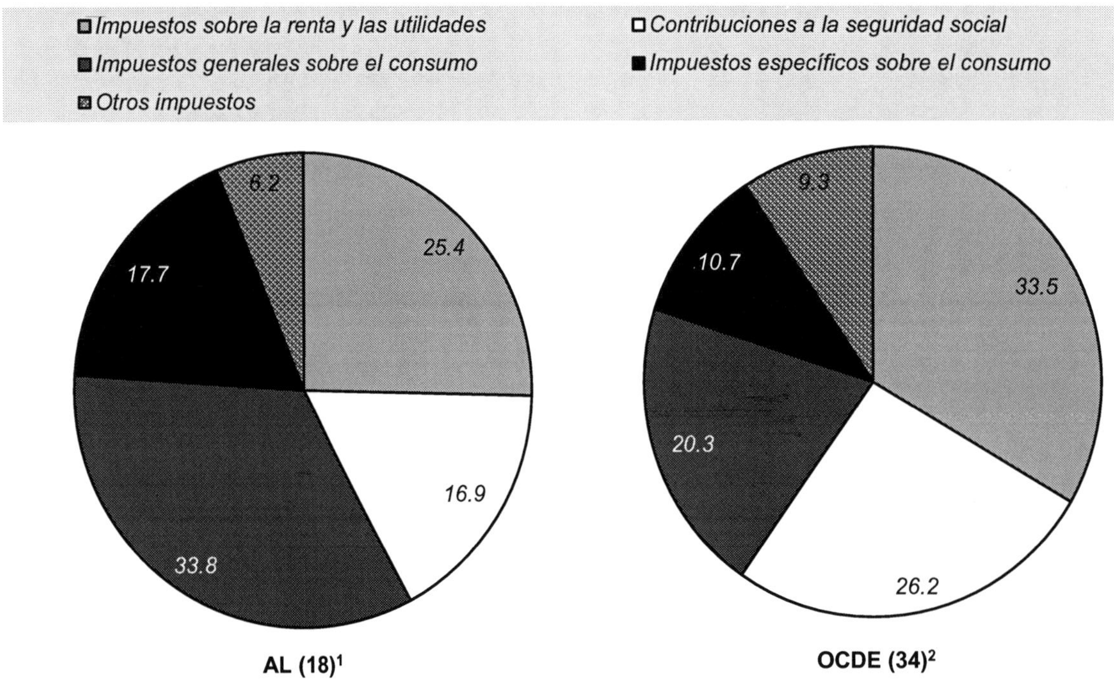

1. Representa un grupo de 18 países de América Latina listados en la Tabla A. Chile y México son también parte del grupo OCDE (34).

2. Representa el promedio no ponderado de los países miembros de la OCDE.

Fuente: Cuadro 2B en Parte II.A.

StatLink http://dx.doi.org/10.1787/888932970665

En 2011, la proporción media, en relación con el PIB, de los ingresos tributarios procedentes de la suma de los impuestos sobre la renta y las utilidades y de las contribuciones a la seguridad social era del 8.5% en el grupo seleccionado de países latinoamericanos, mientras alcanzaba el 20.5% en los países de la OCDE. Cabe pues inferir que, en América Latina, esos impuestos desempeñan una función secundaria como fuente de ingresos en comparación con la zona de la OCDE. La proporción de las contribuciones a la seguridad social sobre el total de ingresos tributarios era 9 puntos porcentuales menor en América Latina que en la OCDE (el 16.9% frente al 26.2%). Tal y como se ha apuntado anteriormente, la tendencia hacia una provisión privada de servicios de seguridad social en numerosos países latinoamericanos explica parte de las diferencias en esta categoría. Por su parte, la proporción de los impuestos sobre la renta y las utilidades era 8 puntos porcentuales inferior (25.4% frente al 33.5%).

Los ingresos procedentes de los impuestos sobre la renta personal contribuyeron en un 24% a la recaudación tributaria agregada de la zona de la OCDE en 2011, mientras que esta categoría representa una proporción considerablemente menor en los países latinoamericanos. Anteriores estudios de la OCDE (OCDE, 2008; Daude *et al.*, 2010) parecen sugerir que esto viene condicionado principalmente por dos factores: en primer lugar, la participación de la renta procedente del trabajo en el PIB es sustancialmente más débil en América Latina que en los países de la OCDE; y, en segundo lugar, su distribución implica que hay relativamente menos contribuyentes, dada la concentración de los perceptores en los niveles de renta inferiores. Además, varios estudios de la CEPAL (CEPAL, 2010; Gómez Sabaini et al., 2010) añaden dos factores: la elevada brecha de incumplimiento del impuesto sobre la renta en los países latinoamericanos y una base imponible más limitada, compuesta fundamentalmente por salarios, dados los privilegios fiscales otorgados a las ganancias del capital.

Como contrapartida de la menor importancia de los gravámenes directos, los impuestos generales sobre los bienes y servicios representan una significativa parte de la recaudación tributaria total. En 2011, esta subpartida supuso en la región el 34% del total de los ingresos tributarios mientras la cifra correspondiente en la zona de la OCDE fue sólo del 20%. Sin embargo, el peso de los impuestos generales sobre bienes y servicios como proporción del PIB es bastante similar tanto en América Latina como en la OCDE, con porcentajes en 2010 del 6.7% y del 6.9% respectivamente.

Por último, los impuestos sobre la propiedad inmueble y la nómina (incluidos en "Otros impuestos" en el gráfico B) no constituyen importantes fuentes de ingresos para los países latinoamericanos. Las dificultades que encuentran los gobiernos subnacionales para recaudar sus propios tributos quedan ejemplificadas por la escasa capacidad de generar ingresos que tienen los impuestos sobre la propiedad, que suelen ser la principal fuente de entradas de los gobiernos locales de la región (Brossio y Jiménez, 2012). Por su parte, los impuestos sobre la nómina han sido insignificantes durante todo el periodo, en parte porque este tipo de mecanismos no está muy desarrollado en América Latina. Sin embargo, conviene señalar que la falta de datos a escala subnacional dificulta el análisis de estas categorías. Las proporciones de los impuestos sobre la propiedad y la nómina en la recaudación tributaria total de los países latinoamericanos son similares, en promedio, a las de los países de la OCDE.

C. Impuestos por nivel de gobierno

Desde mediados de los años 1980, América Latina ha experimentado de forma generalizada reformas que implican la transferencia de funciones gubernamentales desde el gobierno central a entidades subnacionales. En su primera fase, la ola de descentralización se centró principalmente en reforzar el carácter democrático de las autoridades locales. A esto siguió una creciente tendencia a que, paulatinamente, una parte cada vez mayor del gasto público se ejecutase a escala subnacional.

Pese a ello, el alcance de las políticas tributarias subnacionales de la región ha permanecido relativamente modesto y se concentra en un reducido número de impuestos. Los datos disponibles parecen apuntar que la mayoría de los países latinoamericanos no se han ocupado de reforzar los ingresos que reciben las instancias subnacionales. Entre 1995 y 2011, la parte de ingresos recaudada por los niveles de gobierno subnacional descendió entre uno y cuatro puntos en Argentina, Brasil y Uruguay y aumentó en 2 puntos porcentuales en Colombia. En los otros países para los que se dispone de datos sobre las tendencias en los ingresos subnacionales, la proporción varió menos de un punto porcentual. Al mismo tiempo, la proporción de los fondos de seguridad social cayó en 10 de los 18 países latinoamericanos estudiados, a veces debido a su privatización total o parcial; los cambios más nítidos en este ámbito se registraron en Colombia y Uruguay (con descensos de casi 14 y 6 puntos porcentuales, respectivamente; véase el cuadro D).

A fin de comparar la atribución de los ingresos en los países latinoamericanos con la de los miembros de la OCDE, cabe tener en cuenta previamente dos cuestiones estadísticas. En primer lugar, los ingresos de ambos grupos se han atribuido a los diferentes niveles de gobierno de acuerdo con lo recogido en la versión final 2008 del Sistema de Cuentas Nacionales (SCN), según el cual, los ingresos se atribuyen por lo general al nivel de gobierno que ejerce la facultad de aplicar el impuesto o que puede a su discreción establecer y modificar la tasa del impuesto. Esto tiene claras implicaciones para aquellas situaciones en que un nivel de gobierno recauda los ingresos tributarios y los transfiere, en todo o en parte, a otros niveles. Ejemplos regionales de este tipo de mecanismos son la Ley de Coparticipación de Argentina; el Fondo General de Participación de México establecido en la Ley de Coordinación Fiscal; y los Fondos de Participación de Brasil definidos en el artículo 159 de la Constitución de este país. La segunda cuestión está relacionada con el hecho de que los datos para algunos países latinoamericanos se ven afectados por la falta de estadísticas de ingresos tributarios en la esfera subnacional.

Hechas pues las dos anteriores consideraciones, la atribución de los ingresos tributarios en América Latina, en comparación con la OCDE, parece estar muy orientada hacia las entidades centrales o federales, mientras que las actividades subnacionales dependen más claramente de las transferencias que reciben de niveles superiores de la Administración. En todos los países latinoamericanos, menos en uno, las entradas de los gobiernos centrales representaron cerca de dos tercios o más de la recaudación total, mientras los países de la OCDE arrojan un resultado aproximado del 60%. Brasil constituye la notable excepción a la regla, ya que atribuye menos del 50% a la Administración federal, entre otras, porque en este país una gran parte del IVA (ICMS – imposto sobre operações relativas à circulação de mercadorías e prestação de serviços de transporte interestadual e intermunicipal e de comunicação) se recauda en la esfera subnacional. Aunque en menor medida, Argentina cuenta también con una significativa recaudación a nivel estatal, que se explica en parte por la existencia del impuesto sobre los ingresos brutos, un impuesto provincial sobre las ventas.

Todo lo anterior pone de manifiesto que los gobiernos subnacionales latinoamericanos tienden a tener competencia sobre un abanico de impuestos restringido. Los impuestos que más frecuentemente se atribuyen a las instancias subnacionales son aquellos que gravan la propiedad, las licencias de vehículos automotores, las tasas por servicios específicos, así como ciertas tasas municipales, y no cabe duda de que el potencial de generación de ingresos de esos instrumentos es relativamente limitado en comparación con las bases tributarias atribuidas a los órganos centrales, tales como el IVA o los impuestos sobre la renta. En los países miembros de la OCDE, las entidades subnacionales tienden a disponer en promedio de bases tributarias potenciales mucho más amplias. De hecho, una proporción sustancial de la recaudación tributaria de los gobiernos subnacionales de los países de la OCDE se obtiene de los impuestos sobre la renta, que representan más de un tercio de la cantidad total recaudada. Por el contrario, ninguno de los países latinoamericanos para los que se dispone de datos registra recaudación alguna en concepto de impuestos sobre la renta por parte de los gobiernos subnacionales.

Cuadro D. **Atribución de los ingresos tributarios en los sub-sectores del gobierno general como porcentaje del ingreso tributario total**[1]

	Gobierno central			Gobierno estatal o regional			Gobierno local			Fondos de seguridad social		
	1995	2000	2011	1995	2000	2011	1995	2000	2011	1995	2000	2011
Países federales												
Argentina	59.0	66.4	64.0	17.5	17.8	14.5				23.4	15.8	21.5
Brasil	44.7	47.8	45.9	26.8	25.3	23.8	3.7	3.4	5.2	24.8	23.5	25.2
México	80.1	80.7	81.9	2.1	2.0	2.5	1.1	0.8	1.1	16.6	16.5	14.5
Venezuela	94.6	94.6	96.6							5.4	5.4	3.4
OCDE[2,3]	53.3	56.5	54.5	15.9	15.3	16.3	7.7	6.9	7.7	22.9	21.1	21.3
Países regionales												
Colombia[4]	58.9	64.4	71.7	5.5	5.6	4.7	8.6	9.4	11.0	27.0	20.6	12.6
OCDE[5]	50.4	49.0	29.9	4.8	7.6	23.1	8.5	9.1	9.6	35.8	33.8	36.9
Países unitarios												
Bolivia	100.0	91.3	93.4								8.7	6.6
Chile	89.9	87.8	88.5				6.5	7.9	6.6	3.6	4.4	4.9
Costa Rica	66.2	65.3	63.3					2.1	2.9	33.8	32.6	33.8
Ecuador	73.9	87.7	71.1							26.1	12.3	28.9
El Salvador	85.9	83.6	88.8							14.1	16.4	11.2
Guatemala	83.8	83.6	83.7				0.6	0.9	1.4	15.6	15.5	15.0
Honduras	90.1	89.4	87.7							9.9	10.6	12.3
Nicaragua	84.1	80.1	77.1							15.9	19.9	22.9
Panamá	62.0	59.6	62.4					2.2	1.5	38.0	38.2	36.0
Paraguay[6]	100.0	82.7	76.7								17.3	23.3
Perú	88.2	87.7	87.5						2.9	11.8	12.3	9.6
República Dominicana	99.3	99.0	99.5							0.7	1.0	0.5
Uruguay	62.0	62.5	71.4				7.8	7.9	4.1	30.1	29.6	24.5
OCDE[2,7]	65.8	66.4	63.0				10.7	11.0	12.0	23.2	22.3	24.7

1. Las cifras excluyen los ingresos de gobiernos locales en Argentina (pero incluye ingresos de las provincias), Bolivia, Costa Rica (hasta 1997), República Dominicana, Ecuador, El Salvador, Honduras, Nicaragua, Panamá (hasta 1998), Paraguay, Perú (hasta 2004) y Venezuela dado que los datos no están disponibles.

2. Chile y México son también parte del grupo OCDE.

3. Representa el promedio no ponderado para los países federales miembros de la OCDE;

4. Colombia es constitucionalmente un país unitario con una estructura política descentralizada.

5. Representa a España, que es constitucionalmente un país no federal con una estructura política altamente descentralizada.

6. Datos estimados para el 2011.

7. Representa el promedio no ponderado para los países unitarios miembros de la OCDE.

StatLink http://dx.doi.org/10.1787/888932970988

Referencias

Brossio, G. y J. P. Jiménez (2012), *Decentralization and Reform in Latin America: Improving Intergovernmental Relations*, Edward Elgar, próxima publicación, Cheltenham, UK y Northampton, MA.

CEPAL (Comisión Económica para América Latina y el Caribe) (2013), *Panorama fiscal de América Latina y el Caribe: reformas tributarias y renovación del pacto fiscal*, Santiago de Chile.

CEPAL (2011), "Estudio económico de América Latina y el Caribe 2010-2011", CEPAL, Santiago de Chile.

CEPAL (2010), "La Hora de la igualdad. Brechas por cerrar, caminos por abrir", (LC/G.2432(SES.33/3)), CEPAL, Santiago de Chile.

CEPAL-OCDE (2012), *Perspectivas Económicas de América Latina 2013*, CEPAL y OCDE.

Daude, C., A. Melguizo y A. Neut (2010), "Fiscal Policy in Latin America: Countercyclical and Sustainable at Last?", *Documentos de trabajo*, No. 291, Centro de Desarrollo de la OCDE, París.

Gómez Sabaini, J.C., J.P. Jiménez y A. Podestá (2010), "Evasión y equidad en América Latina", Documentos de proyectos, No. 309 (LC/W.309/ Rev.1), CEPAL, Santiago de Chile.

OCDE (2013), *Revenue Statistics 1965-2012*, OCDE, París.

OCDE (2008), *Perspectivas Económicas de América Latina 2009*, OCDE, París.

SECCIÓN ESPECIAL
Ingresos fiscales provenientes de recursos naturales no renovables en América Latina

El rápido crecimiento mundial entre 2003 y 2008, especialmente en las regiones en desarrollo, apoyó el auge en la demanda internacional de muchas de las materias primas exportadas por América Latina. Este aumento en la demanda y los precios más altos derivados de ello, a su vez impulsaron un crecimiento más fuerte en la región y un importante fortalecimiento en la posición fiscal, especialmente en los países exportadores de materias primas. Si bien después de la crisis estos ingresos disminuyeron como porcentaje del PIB, siguen siendo significativos y se estiman en 237.000 millones de USD en 2012 (Gráfico S.1). Esta sección especial examina las tendencias en los ingresos por recursos naturales no renovables en la región durante el período 2000-12, así como los factores clave que sustentaron estas tendencias.

Gráfico S.1. **Ingresos fiscales provenientes de recursos naturales no renovables, 2012**

(miles de millones de USD y porcentajes del PIB)

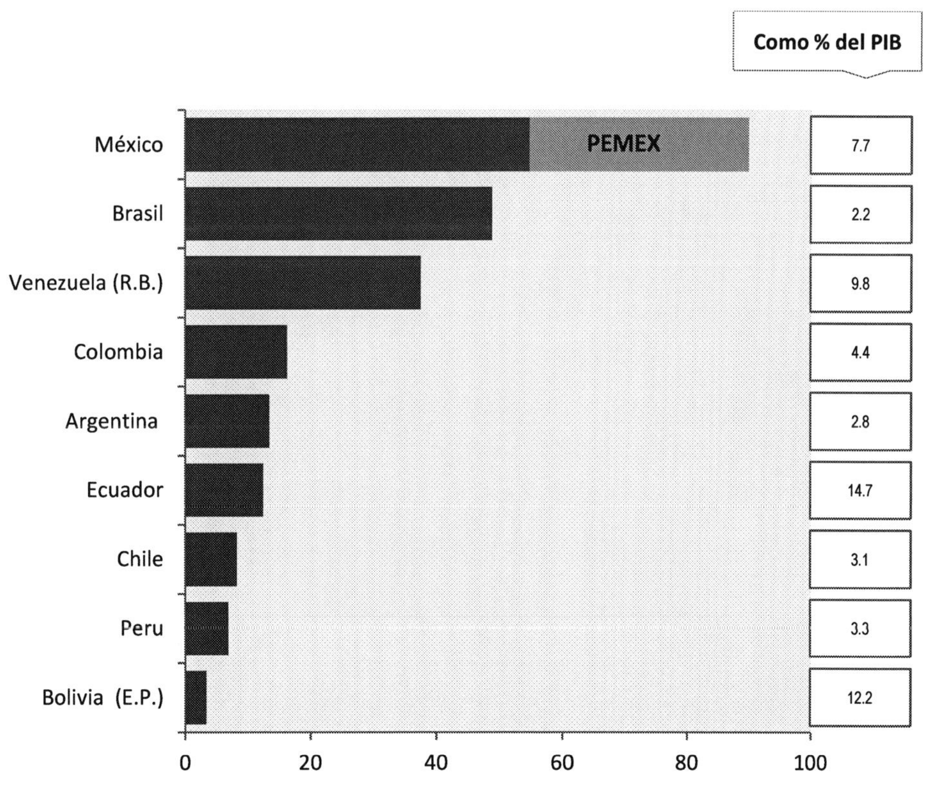

Fuente: CEPAL.

StatLink http://dx.doi.org/10.1787/888932970684

Factores causantes del aumento en los ingresos provenientes de recursos naturales no renovables

Gran parte del rápido aumento en los ingresos fiscales asociados con los recursos naturales no renovables se explica por el crecimiento de sus precios, más que por cambios en el volumen producido. Entre 2000 y 2012, los precios internacionales de las materias primas aumentaron considerablemente como consecuencia del incremento de la demanda frente a una oferta relativamente inelástica. Los precios del petróleo crudo y el cobre, dos de las principales materias primas de la región, se han más que triplicado. En particular, el precio del cobre casi se quintuplicó en 2011 con respecto al 2000 (Gráfico S.2). Los precios del hierro se dispararon, con un aumento del 1 297% entre 2000 y 2011, aunque experimentaron un ligero retroceso en 2012. Si bien la crisis económica mundial atenuó el aumento en 2009, los precios de muchos productos primarios se han mantenido en un nivel elevado luego de la crisis.

La producción ha respondido lentamente a los cambios en los precios, en gran parte debido a los lapsos de tiempo, relativamente largos, que tienen lugar entre los cambios en los precios y la demanda de mercado y la realización de nuevas inversiones (Gráfico S.2). La producción de cobre entre 2000 y 2011 aumentó un 31,9% en términos de volumen (toneladas métricas), explicado principalmente por un incremento del 130% en Perú. La producción de hierro en Brasil, el principal exportador, casi se duplicó en volumen. Sin embargo, la producción de petróleo crudo registró un aumento modesto en el período (4.9%). Entre los principales productores de crudo de la región, la República Bolivariana de Venezuela y México registraron una disminución en sus niveles de producción, mientras que los de Brasil aumentaron considerablemente (57%). En cuanto a los productores más pequeños, Colombia (38%) y Ecuador (25%) también registraron aumentos, mientras que la producción en la Argentina se redujo (-19%).

Gráfico S.2. **Producción y precios del cobre y petróleo crudo, 2000-12**

(índice 2000=100)

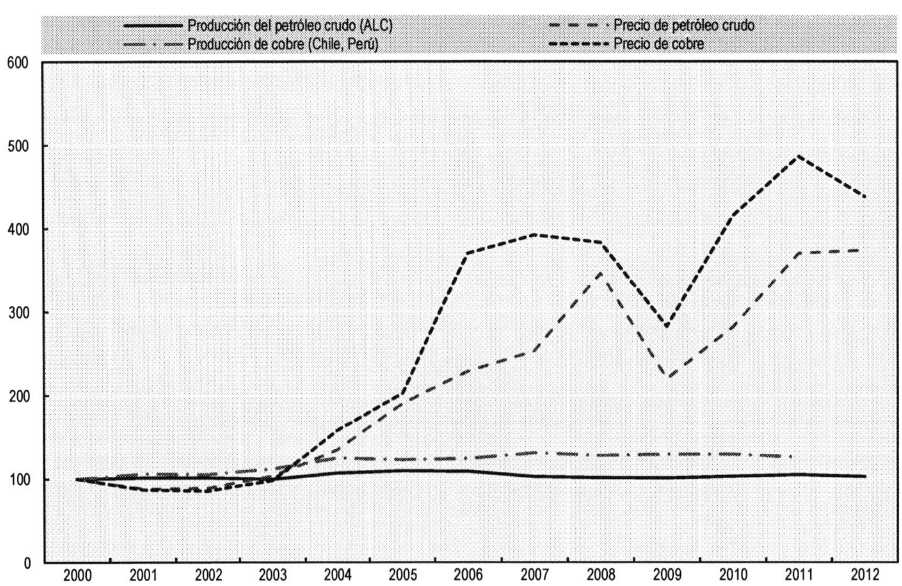

Fuente: CEPAL, sobre le base de datos de USGS (producción de cobre), IEA (producción de petróleo crudo), y CEPAL Stat (precios).

StatLink http://dx.doi.org/10.1787/888932970703

Si bien los factores de mercado pueden haber jugado un papel predominante, en varios países las reformas fiscales también han aumentado la apropiación de las rentas procedentes de recursos naturales por parte del Estado. La evidencia sugiere que la participación del Estado en las rentas económicas y el aporte fiscal procedente de los sectores exportadores de recursos naturales no renovables (minerales e hidrocarburos) aumentó en el último período de auge 2003-08, en contraste con el desempeño del período precedente 1990-2003, lo que puede interpretarse como una mejora en la efectividad de los marcos institucionales (Aquatella, 2012).

Como se destaca en CEPAL (2013), entre 2005 y 2012 las reformas legales más importantes dirigidas a asegurar el control público de los recursos naturales no renovables se enfocaron en el sector de hidrocarburos. Estas medidas incluyeron la nacionalización de dicho sector a través de empresas mixtas en la República Bolivariana de Venezuela (entre 2005 y 2007), la nacionalización de hidrocarburos y la reestatización de la mina de estaño Huanani en el Estado Plurinacional de Bolivia (2006), la renegociación de contratos petroleros en el Ecuador con la estipulación de que el gobierno capturaría el 100% de los eventuales incrementos del precio del petróleo (2010), la expropiación del 51% de las acciones de YPF en la Argentina (2012) y la nacionalización de la mina de Colquirí, en Oruro, en el Estado Plurinacional de Bolivia (2012).

Además, los gobiernos han establecido otros mecanismos de apropiación estatal, como el uso de regalías, habitualmente basadas en la producción, e impuestos específicos (Cuadro S.1). Esto ha sido especialmente importante en el sector de la minería, donde la captación de recursos por la vía de la participación estatal en empresas ha sido de menor importancia relativa. Las regalías y los impuestos han permitido asegurar un pago mínimo por los recursos a los gobiernos, tanto nacionales como subnacionales, como ocurre en un número creciente de países donde se han introducido reformas en los sistemas de regalías, incluidos el Estado Plurinacional de Bolivia (2005), el Ecuador (2010), Colombia (2011) y el Perú (2011). A su vez, en la mayoría de los casos se ha aplicado el tradicional impuesto a la renta con tasas diferenciales junto con otros gravámenes especiales, a menudo con tasas progresivas, sobre las empresas públicas o privadas dedicadas a la explotación de recursos no renovables. Esto se ha reforzado mediante reformas llevadas a cabo en Chile (2005), el Perú (2011) y la República Bolivariana de Venezuela (2006, 2008 y 2011).

Las nuevas medidas - anunciadas o promulgadas- en 2013 sugieren que mientras los legisladores buscan aumentar la contribución fiscal de los recursos naturales no renovables, también están preocupados por la necesidad de fortalecer la inversión privada. La reforma energética anunciada por el gobierno de México incluye, por primera vez desde la nacionalización del sector petrolero, un rol para la inversión del sector privado a través de la utilización de los contratos de reparto de utilidades. En Brasil se encuentra en debate un nuevo marco de regulación de la minería que fijaría el límite superior de las regalías en 4%, o al doble de su nivel actual para hierro y carbón. Ecuador promulgó recientemente una reforma minera que intenta aumentar tanto la inversión en el país, especialmente en los proyectos de pequeñas y medianas empresas, como la contribución fiscal del sector a través de regalías mínimas y un impuesto sobre las ganancias extraordinarias (que se ha retrasado).

Cuadro S.1. **Características de los regímenes fiscales aplicados a la explotación de los recursos naturales no renovables en América Latina**

País y producto	Regalías (alícuotas)	Impuesto sobre la renta (alícuota general)	Otros impuestos sobre los ingresos (alícuotas)	Otros gravámenes	Participación pública
Argentina (petróleo y minería)	12-15%; ó 5% para yacimientos marginales (petróleo) 0-3% (minería)	Impuesto a las ganancias: 35%		Derechos de exportación (25%- 45%- 100% para hidrocarburos y 5-10%, minería); Impuestos sobre los combustibles líquidos, gas natural, gas oil, gas licuado, naftas y gas natural comprimido; Canon minero	YPF (hidrocarburos)
Bolivia (E.P.) (hidrocarburos)	Regalías departamentales: 11% Regalías nacionales compensatorias: 1% Regalías nacionales (Tesoro Nacional): 6%	Impuesto sobre las Utilidades de las Empresas (IUE): 25%	Impuesto a las utilidades - beneficiarios del exterior: 12.5%	Impuesto Directo a los Hidrocarburos (IDH): 32% Impuesto Especial a los Hidrocarburos y Derivados (IEHD)	YPFB (hidrocarburos)
Brasil (hidrocarburos)	10% del valor de producción (puede reducirse hasta 5%, dependiendo del riesgo geológico y otros factores) (petróleo); 0.2-3% (minería, CFEM)	EL ISR es del 15%, más un recargo del 10% si beneficios son superiores a R$ 240,000 por año	Participaciones especiales: 10-40% Impuesto a las utilidades - beneficiarios del exterior: 15% (o 25% para pagos a parios fiscales)	Contribución social sobre el beneficio neto: 9%; CIDE: 10%; impuesto estatal sobre la venta de petróleo e hidrocarburos (ICMS combustibles)	Petrobras (hidrocarburos)
Chile (minería)		Impuesto sobre los ingresos de primera categoría: 20%	Impuesto sobre remesas de utilidades 35% y 4% sobre remesas de intereses; Para empresas públicas: impuesto especial del 40% sobre las utilidades	Impuesto específico sobre la renta operacional de la actividad minera: tasas progresivas entre 0,5% y 14% impuesto a las Fuerzas Armadas (Ley Reservada): 10% sobre el retorno en moneda extranjera por la venta al exterior de la producción de cobre de CODELCO	CODELCO (cobre)
Colombia (petróleo y minería)	8-25% (petróleo) 1-12% (minería)	Impuesto a las sociedades: 25% Impuesto sobre la Renta para la Equidad (CREE): 9% para 2013-2015 y luego 8%		Impuesto de transporte sobre oleoductos; Impuesto nacional a la gasolina y al ACPM; Derechos económicos de la ANH	Ecopetrol (hidrocarburos)
Ecuador (petróleo)	12.5-18.5% (de la producción bruta de petróleo crudo)	Impuesto sobre la renta: 23%	El Estado se reserva el 25% de los ingresos brutos del área del contrato	Participación laboral: el Estado recibe 12% de las utilidades (destinado a los gobiernos autónomos descentralizados).	Petroecuador (hidrocarburos)
México (petróleo)		Impuesto a los rendimientos petroleros (PEMEX): 30% Impuesto sobre la renta (ciertas compañías subsidiarias): 30%	Impuesto empresarial de tasa única (IETU) (ciertas compañías subsidiarias): 17.5%	Derechos sobre hidrocarburos Impuesto especial sobre producción y servicios (IEPS gasolina) Impuesto a la Importación de Mercancías	Pemex (hidrocarburos)

Cuadro S.1. **Características de los regímenes fiscales aplicados a la explotación de los recursos naturales no renovables en América Latina (*cont*)**

País y producto	Regalías (alícuotas)	Impuesto sobre la renta (alícuota general)	Otros impuestos sobre los ingresos (alícuotas)	Otros gravámenes	Participación pública
Perú (hidrocarburos y minería)	1-12% sobre utilidad operativo (minería); 5-35%, dependiendo del método usado en el contrato (hidrocarburos)	Impuesto sobre la renta: 30%	Dividendos y distribución de utilidades: 4.1%	Impuesto especial minero (IEM): 2-8.4% y Gravamen especial a la minería (GEM): 4-13,12% (sobre utilidad operativa); Impuesto Selectivo al Consumo de Combustible	
Venezuela (R.B) (petróleo)	30% del valor extraído	Impuesto sobre la Renta Petrolera (ISLR): 50%		Impuesto sobre precios extraordinarios; Impuesto a la Extracción (33% del valor); Impuesto de Registro de Exportación (0.1% del valor exportado)	PDVSA (hidrocarburos)

Fuente: CEPAL, sobre la base de CEPAL (2013).

Como se señala en Aquatella (2012), históricamente los países de la región han tenido dificultades para lograr traducir los períodos de bonanza exportadora de sus recursos naturales en procesos de desarrollo económico de largo plazo. Sin embargo, en los últimos años, América Latina demostró los beneficios de contar con la capacidad de desplegar políticas anticíclicas que amortiguaron el impacto de la crisis internacional a partir del manejo de los ahorros fiscales captados durante el auge de precios registrado entre 2003 y 2008. Entre los instrumentos para lograrlo están los fondos de estabilización, financiados con los ingresos excedentes de la exportación de cobre, como el de Chile, o a partir de las rentas petroleras, como en el caso de Colombia, el Ecuador, México y la República Bolivariana de Venezuela.

Tendencias en los ingresos provenientes de recursos naturales no renovables

La contribución fiscal de los recursos naturales no renovables creció significativamente durante la última década (Gráfico S.3). Los ingresos aumentaron de un promedio de 4.3% del PIB en la primera mitad de la década a 7.2% del PIB en 2008; un incremento de 3 puntos porcentuales en 3 años. Aunque la mayoría de los países siguieron esta tendencia, en ciertos casos el aumento fue más pronunciado, como en Ecuador (8.2), Chile (6.8 en 2007) y el Estado Plurinacional de Bolivia (6.2).

Gráfico S.3. **Ingresos fiscales totales e ingresos provenientes de recursos naturales no renovables**

(en porcentajes del PIB)

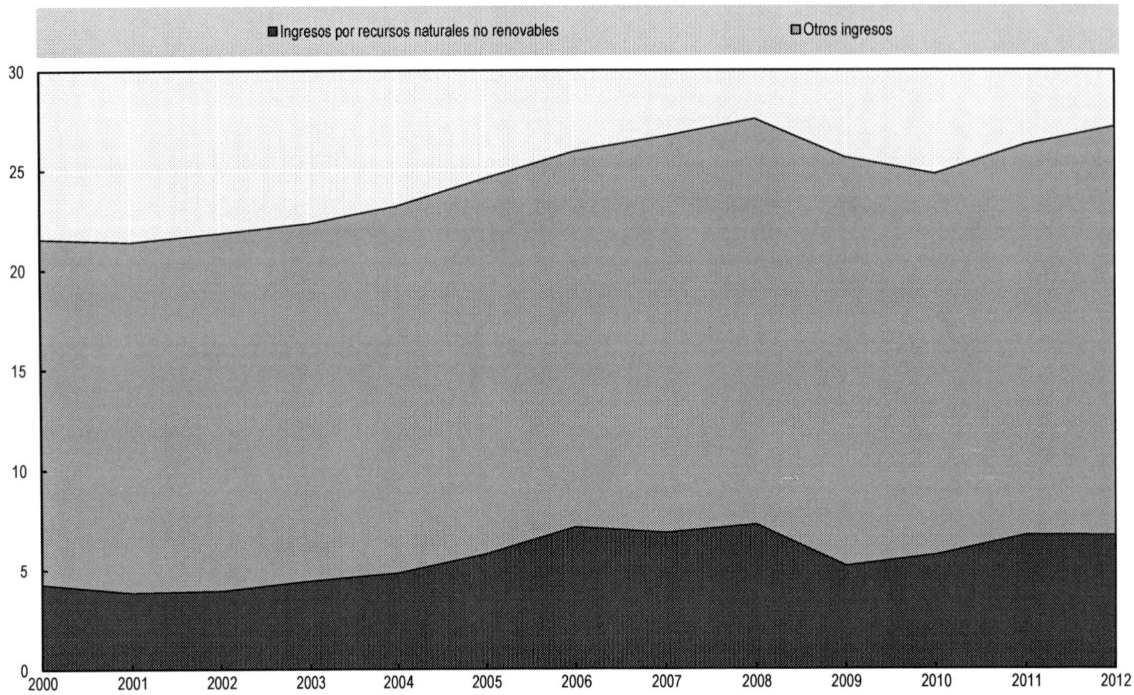

Nota: Incluye Argentina (SPNNF), Bolivia (E.P.) (GG), Brasil (GG), Chile (GC), Colombia (GC), Ecuador (SPNF), México (SP), Perú (GG) y Venezuela (R.B.) (GC).

Fuente: CEPAL.

StatLink http://dx.doi.org/10.1787/888932970722

Sin embargo, con la misma rapidez con que estos ingresos aumentaron, luego cayeron en 2009 con el inicio de la crisis económica y financiera mundial, disminuyendo 2,1 puntos porcentuales del PIB entre 2008 y 2009. No obstante, en ciertos casos el descenso fue más pronunciado: Ecuador (5.7 puntos porcentuales), Chile (5.7 entre 2007 y 2009) y la República Bolivariana de Venezuela (4.6). Aunque antes de la crisis estos ingresos crecieron más rápidamente que los demás recursos públicos, su posterior desempeño estuvo marcado por la volatilidad: un crecimiento relativamente fuerte en 2010 y 2011 para luego estancarse en 2012.

Estas tendencias generales contrastan con una dinámica más diferenciada cuando se observa el desempeño de grupos determinados de materias primas, como los hidrocarburos y los minerales. Si bien los ingresos de ambos grupos experimentaron un declive importante como porcentaje del PIB en 2009 – el descenso en ingresos de los minerales ya había empezado en 2008 – luego de la crisis, mostraron un desempeño fuertemente diferenciado (Gráfico S.4). Los ingresos por hidrocarburos registraron una recuperación sostenida como porcentaje del PIB, con un retorno a los niveles de 2006-08 a finales de 2011. En cambio, los ingresos por minerales se estancaron en niveles menores a los de los años de auge, a pesar que los precios se han mantenido relativamente elevados y la producción ha permanecido estable. Este resultado se explica, en gran medida, por los reducidos márgenes de beneficios como consecuencia del aumento en los costos de producción de los principales países exportadores de minerales y, en menor medida, por la apreciación de los tipos de cambio que a su vez resultó en la generación de menores ingresos en moneda nacional. El caso de CODELCO, la cuprífera estatal chilena, es ilustrativo de estas tendencias; los informes anuales de la empresa muestran un fuerte aumento en los costos de producción entre 2010 y 2012 en comparación con los niveles de 2006-07 (Gráfico S.5).

Gráfico S.4. **Ingresos provenientes de recursos naturales no renovables, por grupos seleccionados de materias primas, 2000-12**

(para 8 países LAC, en porcentajes del PIB)

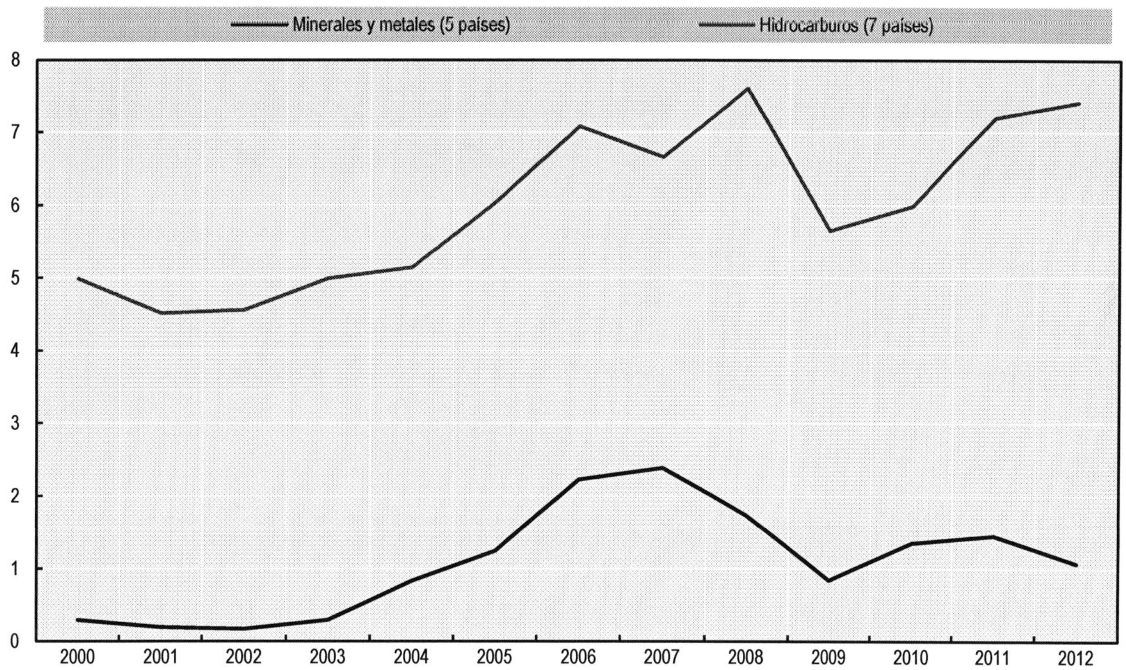

Nota: Los datos desagregados para Argentina no estaban disponibles por lo que el país no se incluye en este gráfico. Para Bolivia (E.P.), Brasil, Colombia y Perú los datos fueron separados por grupo de materias primas, entonces la suma de los dos grupos es mayor que los países cubiertos.

Fuente: CEPAL.

StatLink http://dx.doi.org/10.1787/888932970741

Gráfico S.5. **Ingresos y costos de venta de CODELCO, 2000-12**

(miles de millones de dólares)

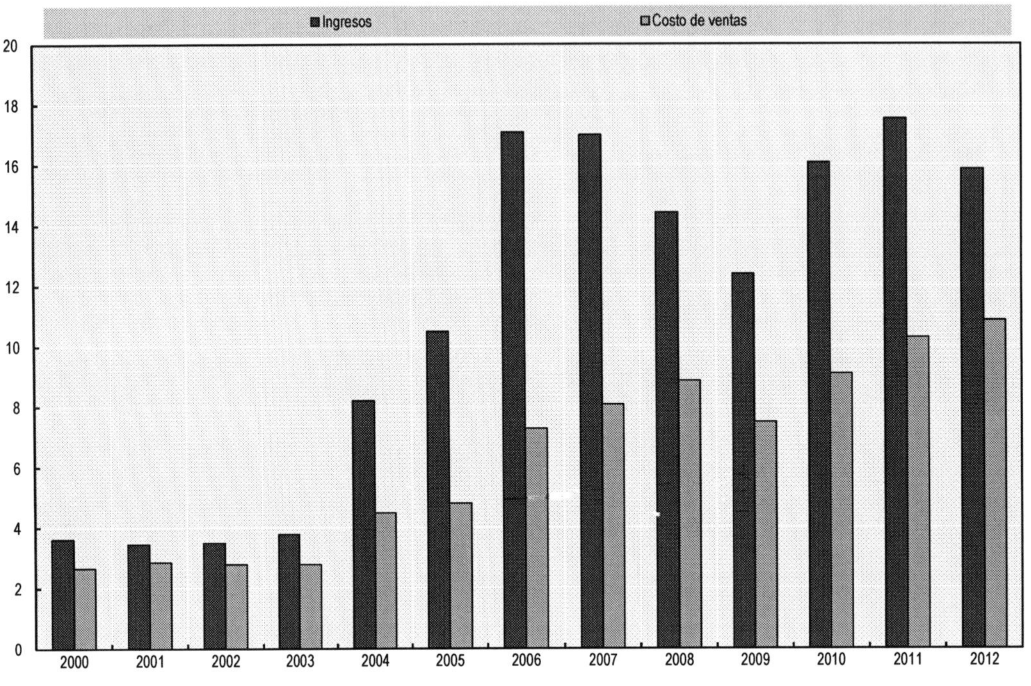

Nota: CODELCO se refiere a la Corporación Nacional del Cobre de Chile.

Fuente: CEPAL, sobre la base de datos de Bloomberg.

StatLink http://dx.doi.org/10.1787/888932970760

Más allá de estas tendencias, los ingresos fiscales provenientes de recursos naturales no renovables siguen siendo muy importantes como porcentaje de los ingresos fiscales totales en muchos países. En particular, el Estado Plurinacional de Bolivia, el Ecuador, México y la República Bolivariana de Venezuela muestran un alto nivel de dependencia, dado que los ingresos públicos basados en recursos naturales representan más del 30% del total (Gráfico S.6). Para estos países, el alto nivel de los ingresos por recursos naturales no renovables implica una mayor participación en las rentas que generan pero también un mayor riesgo debido a la dinámica del mercado mundial. En los países que no forman parte de este grupo, la crisis no necesariamente sirvió para frenar la importancia de estos ingresos. Colombia y Ecuador, por ejemplo, muestran una mayor participación de los ingresos por recursos naturales en sus ingresos totales después de la crisis en comparación con los ingresos anteriores a la crisis.

Gráfico S.6. **Participación relativa de los ingresos por recursos naturales no renovables en los ingresos totales**

(en porcentajes)

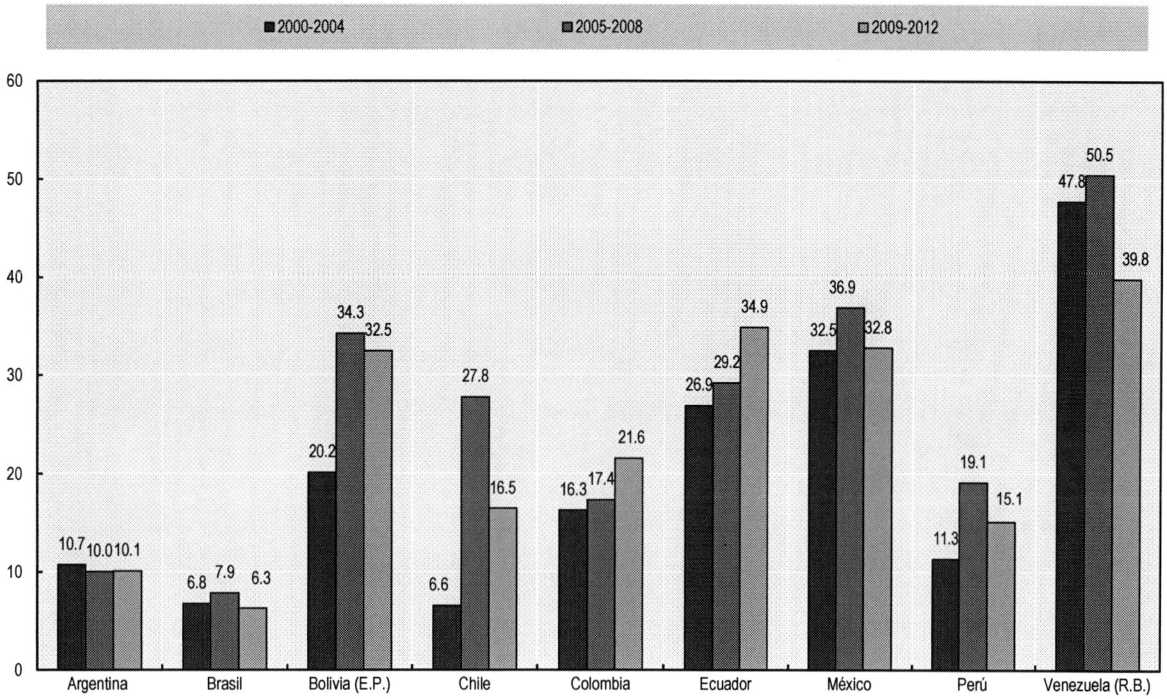

Nota: Véase el Gráfico S.3 para una descripción de la cobertura de los datos por país.

Fuente: CEPAL.

StatLink http://dx.doi.org/10.1787/888932970779

Referencias

Aquatella, J. (2012); "Rentas de recursos naturales no-renovables en América Latina y el Caribe: Evolución 1990 -2010 y participación estatal", Seminario "Gobernanza de los Recursos Naturales en ALC", División de Recursos Naturales e Infraestructura, CEPAL, abril.

CEPAL (Comisión Económica para América Latina y el Caribe) (2013), "Panorama fiscal de América Latina y el Caribe: reformas tributarias y renovación del pacto fiscal", Santiago de Chile, Chile.

PART II

Tax Levels and Tax Structures, 1990-2012

PARTE II

Niveles impositivos y estructuras tributarias, 1990-2012

Part II / Parte II

A. Comparative Tables, 1990-2012

In all of the following tables a dash (-) indicates zero and a blank space not available or not applicable. The main series in this volume cover the years 1990 to 2012.

Figures referring to 1991-94, 1996-99 and 2001-06 have been omitted because of lack of space. Complete series are, however, available on line at www.latameconomy.org.

A. Cuadros comparativos, 1990-2012

En todos los cuadros siguientes, un guión (-) indica cero, y un espacio en blanco, la indisponibilidad o inaplicabilidad. Las principales series de datos de esta sección cubren el periodo que va de 1990 a 2012.

Las cifras relativas a 1991-94, 1996-99 y 2001-06 se han omitido por falta de espacio. Sin embargo, las series completas están disponibles en línea en www.latameconomy.org.

Table 1 - Cuadro 1

Total tax revenue as percentage of GDP[1] / Total de ingresos tributarios en porcentaje del PIB[1]

	1990	1994	1995	1996	1997	1998	1999	2000	2001	2002	
Argentina	16.1	21.5	20.3	19.7	20.6	21.0	21.2	21.5	20.9	19.9	Argentina
Bolivia[2,3]	7.2	11.1	11.8	11.8	11.9	12.8	11.8	14.7	13.1	14.5	Bolivia[2,3]
Brazil	28.2	29.2	27.0	26.4	26.6	27.4	28.7	30.1	31.0	31.7	Brasil
Chile	17.0	18.5	18.4	19.6	19.1	18.8	18.1	18.8	19.0	19.0	Chile
Colombia	9.0	13.2	13.8	14.7	15.6	15.0	15.0	14.6	16.3	16.2	Colombia
Costa Rica	16.1	17.6	16.3	17.8	17.9	18.3	17.7	18.2	19.3	19.5	Costa Rica
Dominican Republic	8.3	10.1	10.6	10.4	11.7	11.7	12.0	12.4	13.8	13.7	República Dominicana
Ecuador	7.1	7.8	7.9	7.4	8.3	8.8	8.7	10.1	11.5	12.3	Ecuador
El Salvador	10.5	12.2	13.0	12.3	12.2	12.3	12.2	12.2	12.3	12.9	El Salvador
Guatemala	9.0	9.2	10.4	11.3	11.4	11.5	12.3	12.4	12.7	13.7	Guatemala
Honduras	16.2	16.5	18.1	16.6	16.0	18.7	19.4	15.3	15.4	15.6	Honduras
Mexico[4,5]	15.8	15.7	15.2	15.3	15.9	15.1	15.8	16.9	17.1	16.5	México[4,5]
Nicaragua	n.a.	14.1	14.1	14.5	16.0	16.9	16.7	16.9	16.4	17.3	Nicaragua
Panama	14.7	16.2	17.1	17.4	17.1	16.5	17.2	16.7	15.6	15.1	Panamá
Paraguay[2]	5.4	12.1	13.6	12.7	12.7	12.6	14.2	14.5	14.2	13.4	Paraguay[2]
Peru	11.8	15.0	15.4	15.8	16.0	15.7	14.3	13.9	14.1	13.7	Perú
Uruguay	19.6	20.7	21.0	21.2	21.9	22.0	21.6	21.6	22.0	21.1	Uruguay
Venezuela[2]	18.7	14.8	13.3	14.2	17.6	12.9	13.8	13.6	12.2	11.2	Venezuela[2]
Unweighted average:											*Promedio no ponderado:*
LAC (18)[6]	13.6	15.3	15.4	15.5	16.0	16.0	16.2	16.4	16.5	16.5	AL (18)[6]
OECD (34)[7]	32.9	34.0	34.4	34.8	34.8	34.8	35.1	35.2	34.7	34.4	OCDE (34)[7]

Table 1 - Cuadro 1 (cont'd)

Total tax revenue as percentage of GDP[1] / Total de ingresos tributarios en porcentaje del PIB[1]

	2003	2004	2005	2006	2007	2008	2009	2010	2011	2012	
Argentina	23.4	26.4	26.9	27.4	29.1	30.8	31.5	33.5	34.7	37.3	Argentina
Bolivia[2,3]	13.3	15.5	19.1	21.8	22.6	20.5	22.7	20.7	24.2	26.0	Bolivia[2,3]
Brazil	31.2	32.1	33.1	33.1	33.8	34.0	32.6	33.2	34.9	36.3	Brasil
Chile	18.7	19.1	20.7	22.0	22.8	21.4	17.2	19.5	21.2	20.8	Chile
Colombia	16.7	17.5	18.1	19.1	19.1	18.8	18.6	18.0	18.8	19.6	Colombia
Costa Rica	19.4	19.3	19.8	20.3	21.7	22.4	20.8	20.5	21.0	21.0	Costa Rica
Dominican Republic	12.0	12.9	14.7	15.0	16.0	15.0	13.1	12.8	12.9	13.5	República Dominicana
Ecuador	11.4	11.4	11.7	12.4	12.8	14.0	14.9	16.8	17.9	20.2	Ecuador
El Salvador	13.3	13.2	14.1	15.1	15.2	15.1	14.4	14.8	14.8	15.7	El Salvador
Guatemala	13.5	13.4	13.1	13.8	13.9	12.9	12.2	12.3	12.6	12.3	Guatemala
Honduras	16.2	17.0	16.9	17.6	19.0	18.9	17.1	17.3	16.9	17.5	Honduras
Mexico[4,5]	17.4	17.1	18.1	18.2	17.7	20.9	17.4	18.9	19.7	19.6	México[4,5]
Nicaragua	19.1	19.8	20.9	17.1	17.4	17.3	17.4	18.3	19.1	19.5	Nicaragua
Panama	15.0	14.7	14.6	16.0	16.7	16.9	17.4	18.1	18.1	18.5	Panamá
Paraguay[2]	11.6	13.1	13.8	14.2	13.9	14.6	16.1	16.5	17.0	17.6	Paraguay[2]
Peru	14.5	14.7	15.8	17.2	17.8	18.2	16.3	17.4	17.8	18.1	Perú
Uruguay	21.5	22.7	23.8	25.4	25.0	26.1	27.1	27.0	27.3	26.3	Uruguay
Venezuela[2]	11.9	13.3	15.9	16.3	16.8	14.1	14.3	11.4	12.9	13.7	Venezuela[2]
Unweighted average:											*Promedio no ponderado:*
LAC (18)[6]	16.7	17.4	18.4	19.0	19.5	19.5	18.9	19.3	20.1	20.7	AL (18)[6]
OECD (34)[7]	34.3	34.3	34.8	35.0	35.0	34.5	33.6	33.8	34.1	n.a	OCDE (34)[7]

n.a. : indicates not available

1. The figures exclude local government revenues for Argentina (but include provincial revenues), Bolivia, Costa Rica (up to 1997), Dominican Republic, Ecuador, El Salvador, Honduras, Nicaragua, Panama (up to 1998), Paraguay (up to 2004, 2011 and 2012), Peru (up to 2004), Uruguay (2012) and Venezuela as the data are not available.

1. Las cifras excluyen los ingresos de gobiernos locales en Argentina (pero incluye ingresos de las provincias), Bolivia, Costa Rica (hasta 1997), República Dominicana, Ecuador, El Salvador, Honduras, Nicaragua, Panamá (hasta 1998), Paraguay (hasta 2004, 2011 y 2012), Perú (hasta 2004), Uruguay (2012) y Venezuela dado que los datos no están disponibles.

2. Estimated figures for 2011 and 2012. / 2. Datos estimados para el 2011 y el 2012.

3. In ECLAC data the excise tax on hydrocarbons is treated as non tax revenues.

3. En los datos de CEPAL, el Impuesto Directo sobre Hidrocarburos (IDH) es considerado como regalía en los ingresos no tributarios

4. In ECLAC and CIAT data, fees levied on hydrocarbon production are treated as non tax revenues.

4. En los datos de CEPAL y CIAT, los derechos sobre la producción de hidrocarburos son tratados como ingresos no tributarios.

5. Estimated figure for 2012 including expected revenues for state and local governments. / 5. La data estimada incluye ingresos esperados a nivel estatal y local para el 2012.

6. Represents a group of 18 Latin American countries. Chile and Mexico are also part of the OECD (34) group.

6. Representa un grupo de 18 países de América Latina. Chile y México son también parte del grupo OCDE (34).

7. Represents the unweighted average for OECD member countries. / 7. Representa el promedio no ponderado para los países miembros de la OCDE.

StatLink http://dx.doi.org/10.1787/888932971007

Table 2 - Cuadro 2

Tax revenue of main headings/Ingresos tributarios en las principales partidas

A. As percentage of GDP[1/]En porcentaje del PIB[1]

2012

	1000 Income & Profits Renta & utilidades	2000 Social Security Seguridad social	3000 Payroll Nómina	4000 Property Patrimonio	5000 Goods & Services Bienes & servicios	6000 Other Otros	
Argentina	6.5	8.3	-	3.3	18.8	0.4	Argentina
Bolivia[2]	4.0	1.5	-	1.9	17.0	1.5	Bolivia[2]
Brazil[3]	7.6	8.8	0.8	2.1	15.4	0.2	Brasil[3]
Chile	8.3	1.1	-	0.9	10.6	0.0	Chile
Colombia	6.6	2.4	-	2.0	7.6	1.0	Colombia
Costa Rica	3.9	6.2	0.9	0.4	9.4	0.2	Costa Rica
Dominican Republic	3.3	0.1	0.7	0.8	8.6	0.0	República Dominicana
Ecuador	3.9	5.7	-	-	10.5	0.1	Ecuador
El Salvador	5.0	1.7	-	0.1	8.9	-	El Salvador
Guatemala	3.4	1.5	-	0.1	7.0	0.2	Guatemala
Honduras	4.8	3.0	-	0.1	9.6	0.0	Honduras
Mexico[3]	5.4	2.9	0.3	0.3	10.7	0.2	México[3]
Nicaragua	5.4	4.4	-	-	9.6	0.0	Nicaragua
Panama	5.5	6.0	0.2	0.7	5.7	0.4	Panamá
Paraguay[2]	2.7	4.1 [3]	-	n.a.	9.9	0.1	Paraguay[2]
Peru	7.7	1.8	0.0	0.4	7.7	0.5	Perú
Uruguay	5.7	7.2	-	1.3	12.1	0.0	Uruguay
Venezuela[2]	4.3	0.4 [3]	-	0.0	8.7	0.2	Venezuela[2]
Unweighted average:							*Promedio no ponderado:*
LAC (18)[4]	5.2	3.9	0.2	0.8	10.4	0.3	AL (18)[4]
OECD (34)[3,5]	11.4	9.1	0.4	1.8	11.0	0.4	OCDE (34)[3,5]

B. As percentage of total taxation[1/]En porcentaje del total de ingresos tributarios[1]

2012

	1000 Income & Profits Renta & utilidades	2000 Social Security Seguridad social	3000 Payroll Nómina	4000 Property Patrimonio	5000 Goods & Services Bienes & servicios	6000 Other Otros	
Argentina	17.3	22.2	-	9.0	50.4	1.0	Argentina
Bolivia[2]	15.6	5.9	-	7.4	65.5	5.6	Bolivia[2]
Brazil[3]	21.7	25.2	2.4	6.0	44.1	0.7	Brasil[3]
Chile	39.7	5.2	-	4.2	50.7	0.2	Chile
Colombia	33.5	12.4	-	10.4	38.6	5.1	Colombia
Costa Rica	18.7	29.7	4.3	1.7	44.6	0.9	Costa Rica
Dominican Republic	24.5	0.4	5.1	6.0	64.0	0.0	República Dominicana
Ecuador	19.5	27.9	-	-	51.9	0.7	Ecuador
El Salvador	31.8	10.8	-	0.5	56.9	-	El Salvador
Guatemala	27.8	12.5	-	1.2	56.8	1.8	Guatemala
Honduras	27.6	17.2	-	0.5	54.6	0.0	Honduras
Mexico[3]	27.3	14.5	1.5	1.5	54.1	1.1	México[3]
Nicaragua	27.7	22.9	-	-	49.4	0.0	Nicaragua
Panama	29.6	32.4	1.1	3.9	30.9	2.2	Panamá
Paraguay[2]	15.8	24.5	-	-	59.0	0.6	Paraguay[2]
Peru	42.6	10.2	0.0	2.0	42.4	2.8	Perú
Uruguay	21.9	27.3		4.9	46.0	0.0	Uruguay
Venezuela[2]	31.6	3.1	-	0.2	63.3	1.8	Venezuela[2]
Unweighted average:							*Promedio no ponderado:*
LAC (18)[4]	26.4	16.9	0.8	3.3	51.3	1.4	AL (18)[4]
OECD (34)[3,5]	33.5	26.2	1.1	5.4	32.9	1.0	OCDE (34)[3,5]

1. The figures exclude local government revenues for Argentina (but include provincial revenues), Bolivia, Costa Rica (up to 1997), Dominican Republic, Ecuador, El Salvador, Honduras, Nicaragua, Panama (up to 1998), Paraguay (up to 2004, 2011 and 2012), Peru (up to 2004), Uruguay (2012) and Venezuela as the data are not available.

1. Las cifras excluyen los ingresos de gobiernos locales en Argentina (pero incluye ingresos de las provincias), Bolivia, Costa Rica (hasta 1997), República Dominicana, Ecuador, El Salvador, Honduras, Nicaragua, Panamá (hasta 1998), Paraguay (hasta 2004, 2011 y 2012), Perú (hasta 2004), Uruguay (2012) y Venezuela dado que los datos no están disponibles.

2. Estimated data. / 2. Datos estimados.

3. Data for 2011 is used. / 3. Se utilizan datos del 2011.

4. Represents a group of 18 Latin American countries. Chile and Mexico are also part of the OECD (34) group.

4. Representa un grupo de 18 países de América Latina. Chile y México son también parte del grupo OCDE (34).

5. Represents the unweighted average for OECD member countries. / 5. Representa el promedio no ponderado para los países miembros de la OCDE.

StatLink http://dx.doi.org/10.1787/888932971026

Table 3 - Cuadro 3

Taxes on income and profits (1000)/Impuestos sobre la renta y las utilidades (1000)

A. As percentage of GDP[1]/En porcentaje del PIB[1]

	1990	2000	2007	2008	2009	2010	2011	2012	
Argentina	0.6	4.0	5.4	5.3	5.0	5.4	6.0	6.5	Argentina
Bolivia	0.8	1.9	3.0	3.8	3.9	3.9	3.8	4.0	Bolivia
Brazil	5.1	5.8	7.2	7.7	7.2	6.9	7.6	7.3	Brasil
Chile	3.9	4.4	10.4	8.0	5.4	7.5	8.5	8.3	Chile
Colombia	2.7	3.4	5.6	5.1	5.6	4.8	5.4	6.6	Colombia
Costa Rica	1.8	2.6	3.9	4.4	4.1	3.9	4.0	3.9	Costa Rica
Dominican Republic	2.2	1.8	3.4	3.0	2.5	2.1	2.3	3.3	República Dominicana
Ecuador	0.9	1.6	2.5	3.8	4.0	3.5	3.9	3.9	Ecuador
El Salvador	2.0	3.3	4.6	4.7	4.6	4.4	4.4	5.0	El Salvador
Guatemala	1.6	2.5	3.3	3.3	3.2	3.1	3.4	3.4	Guatemala
Honduras	3.4	2.8	5.1	5.1	4.6	4.7	5.1	4.8	Honduras
Mexico	4.3	4.6	4.9	5.2	5.0	5.2	5.4	5.2	México
Nicaragua	n.a.	2.3	4.2	4.4	4.7	4.6	5.2	5.4	Nicaragua
Panama	3.6	4.2	4.7	4.8	5.3	5.0	4.3	5.5	Panamá
Paraguay	1.1	1.9	1.8	1.9	2.8	2.2	2.5	2.7	Paraguay
Peru	0.7	2.8	7.3	7.1	5.9	6.5	7.5	7.7	Perú
Uruguay	0.9	2.0	3.4	5.4	5.6	5.7	5.7	5.7	Uruguay
Venezuela	15.6	5.9	7.6	5.8	5.5	3.6	3.9	4.3	Venezuela
Unweighted average:									*Promedio no ponderado:*
LAC (18)[2]	3.0	3.2	4.9	4.9	4.7	4.6	4.9	5.2	AL (18)[2]
OECD (34)[3]	12.5	12.5	12.7	12.3	11.3	11.2	11.4	n.a.	OCDE (34)[3]

B. As percentage of total taxation1/En porcentaje del total de ingresos tributarios[1]

	1990	2000	2007	2008	2009	2010	2011	2012	
Argentina	3.7	18.5	18.7	17.2	15.8	16.2	17.3	17.3	Argentina
Bolivia	11.1	12.6	13.4	18.3	17.0	18.7	15.7	15.6	Bolivia[4]
Brazil	18.1	19.3	21.4	22.8	22.1	20.7	21.7	20.1	Brasil
Chile	23.2	23.3	45.7	37.5	31.1	38.4	40.1	39.7	Chile
Colombia	29.9	23.3	29.2	27.1	29.9	26.7	28.6	33.5	Colombia
Costa Rica	11.1	14.4	18.0	19.6	19.6	19.2	19.0	18.7	Costa Rica
Dominican Republic	26.0	14.6	21.0	20.3	19.2	16.6	18.1	24.5	República Dominicana
Ecuador	12.8	15.9	19.4	27.0	27.0	20.7	22.1	19.5	Ecuador
El Salvador	18.9	26.7	30.5	31.0	32.0	29.6	29.9	31.8	El Salvador
Guatemala	18.1	19.9	23.8	25.4	25.8	25.1	27.1	27.8	Guatemala
Honduras	21.2	18.3	27.0	27.1	26.8	27.0	30.1	27.6	Honduras
Mexico	27.1	27.3	27.7	24.8	28.6	27.8	27.3	n.a.	México
Nicaragua	n.a.	13.6	24.1	25.3	27.2	25.2	27.5	27.7	Nicaragua
Panama	24.3	25.0	28.0	28.2	30.7	27.4	23.8	29.6	Panamá
Paraguay[4]	21.1	13.1	12.7	13.4	17.2	13.4	15.2	15.8	Paraguay[4]
Peru	5.7	19.8	40.7	39.2	36.4	37.5	42.3	42.6	Perú
Uruguay	4.8	9.4	13.6	20.7	20.8	21.2	20.8	21.9	Uruguay
Venezuela[4]	83.7	43.2	45.2	41.4	38.6	31.7	30.3	31.6	Venezuela[4]
Unweighted average:									*Promedio no ponderado:*
LAC (18)[2]	21.2	19.9	25.6	25.9	25.9	24.6	25.4	26.2	AL (18)[2]
OECD (34)[3]	37.1	35.0	35.9	35.3	33.5	33.1	33.5	n.a.	OCDE (34)[3]

n.a.: indicates not available

1. The figures exclude local government revenues for Argentina (but include provincial revenues), Bolivia, Costa Rica (up to 1997), Dominican Republic, Ecuador, El Salvador, Honduras, Nicaragua, Panama (up to 1998), Paraguay (up to 2004, 2011 and 2012), Peru (up to 2004), Uruguay (2012) and Venezuela as the data are not available.

1. Las cifras excluyen los ingresos de gobiernos locales en Argentina (pero incluye ingresos de las provincias), Bolivia, Costa Rica (hasta 1997), República Dominicana, Ecuador, El Salvador, Honduras, Nicaragua, Panamá (hasta 1998), Paraguay (hasta 2004, 2011 y 2012), Perú (hasta 2004), Uruguay (2012) y Venezuela dado que los datos no están disponibles.

2. Represents a group of 18 Latin American countries. Chile and Mexico are also part of the OECD (34) group.

2. Representa un grupo de 18 países de América Latina. Chile y México son también parte del grupo OCDE (34).

3. Represents the unweighted average for OECD member countries. / 3. Representa el promedio no ponderado para los países miembros de la OCDE.

4. Estimated figures for 2011 and 2012. / 4. Datos estimados para 2011 y 2012.

StatLink http://dx.doi.org/10.1787/888932971045

Table 4 - Cuadro 4

Social security contributions (2000)/Contribuciones a la seguridad social (2000)

A. As percentage of GDP[1]/En porcentaje del PIB[1]

	1990	2000	2007	2008	2009	2010	2011	2012	
Argentina	4.1	3.4	4.5	5.1	6.7	7.1	7.4	8.3	Argentina
Bolivia	n.a.	1.3	1.1	1.1	1.2	1.2	1.6	1.5	Bolivia
Brazil	6.8	7.1	8.1	8.1	8.5	8.4	8.8	9.7	Brasil
Chile	1.5	1.4	1.3	1.4	1.4	1.3	1.3	1.1	Chile
Colombia	0.7	3.0	2.9	2.7	2.8	2.8	2.4	2.4	Colombia
Costa Rica	4.4	5.1	5.5	5.7	5.9	6.0	6.2	6.2	Costa Rica
Dominican Republic	0.1	0.1	0.1	0.1	0.1	0.1	0.1	0.1	República Dominicana
Ecuador	1.6	1.2	3.5	3.4	3.3	3.8	5.2	5.7	Ecuador
El Salvador	1.4	2.0	1.6	1.7	1.7	1.7	1.7	1.7	El Salvador
Guatemala	1.4	1.9	1.9	1.8	1.9	1.9	1.9	1.5	Guatemala
Honduras	1.4	1.6	2.6	2.8	2.9	2.9	2.1	3.0	Honduras
Mexico	2.1	2.8	2.7	2.6	2.9	2.9	2.9	2.9	México
Nicaragua	n.a.	3.4	3.6	3.8	4.1	4.4	4.4	4.4	Nicaragua
Panama	4.5	6.4	5.6	5.8	5.7	6.2	6.5	6.0	Panamá
Paraguay[2]	0.4	3.7	3.3	3.4	3.9	3.7	3.8	4.1	Paraguay[2]
Peru	0.9	1.7	1.6	1.7	1.7	1.7	1.7	1.8	Perú
Uruguay	6.0	6.4	5.2	5.5	6.3	6.4	6.7	7.2	Uruguay
Venezuela[2]	0.9	0.7	0.9	0.8	1.0	0.5	0.4	0.4	Venezuela[2]
Unweighted average:									*Promedio no ponderado:*
LAC (18)[3]	2.4	3.0	3.1	3.2	3.4	3.5	3.6	3.8	AL (18)[3]
OECD (34)[4]	7.6	8.9	8.8	8.9	9.2	9.1	9.1	n.a.	OCDE (34)[4]

B. As percentage of total taxation[1]/En porcentaje del total de ingresos tributarios[1]

	1990	2000	2007	2008	2009	2010	2011	2012	
Argentina	25.3	15.8	15.5	16.6	21.4	21.2	21.5	22.2	Argentina
Bolivia[2]	n.a.	8.7	4.8	5.4	5.5	5.8	6.6	5.9	Bolivia[2]
Brazil	24.0	23.5	23.9	23.9	25.9	25.2	25.2	26.8	Brasil
Chile	9.0	7.3	5.6	6.4	8.3	6.9	6.3	5.2	Chile
Colombia	7.9	20.6	15.2	14.2	14.8	15.8	12.6	12.4	Colombia
Costa Rica	27.2	28.0	25.2	25.3	28.5	29.4	29.6	29.7	Costa Rica
Dominican Republic	0.8	1.0	0.4	0.4	0.5	0.8	0.5	0.4	República Dominicana
Ecuador	22.5	12.3	27.4	24.2	22.1	22.5	28.9	27.9	Ecuador
El Salvador	13.3	16.4	10.8	11.0	12.1	11.6	11.2	10.8	El Salvador
Guatemala	15.6	15.5	14.0	14.2	15.2	15.3	15.0	12.5	Guatemala
Honduras	8.8	10.6	13.6	14.7	17.2	16.7	12.3	17.2	Honduras
Mexico	13.4	16.5	15.3	12.7	16.7	15.4	14.5	n.a.	México
Nicaragua	n.a.	19.9	20.6	21.7	23.6	24.1	22.9	22.9	Nicaragua
Panama	30.4	38.2	33.5	34.2	33.0	34.0	36.0	32.4	Panamá
Paraguay[2]	8.3	25.6	23.4	23.7	24.5	22.7	23.3	24.5	Paraguay[2]
Peru	7.7	12.3	8.7	9.2	10.7	9.5	9.6	10.2	Perú
Uruguay	30.5	29.6	20.7	20.9	23.3	23.7	24.5	27.3	Uruguay
Venezuela[2]	4.9	5.4	5.1	5.3	6.7	4.8	3.4	3.1	Venezuela[2]
Unweighted average:									*Promedio no ponderado:*
LAC (18)[3]	15.6	17.1	15.8	15.8	17.2	17.0	16.9	17.2	AL (18)[3]
OECD (34)[4]	22.0	24.6	24.6	25.4	26.6	26.5	26.2	n.a.	OCDE (34)[4]

n.a.: indicates not available

1. The figures exclude local government revenues for Argentina (but include provincial revenues), Bolivia, Costa Rica (up to 1997), Dominican Republic, Ecuador, El Salvador, Honduras, Nicaragua, Panama (up to 1998), Paraguay (up to 2004, 2011 and 2012), Peru (up to 2004), Uruguay (2012) and Venezuela as the data are not available.

1. Las cifras excluyen los ingresos de gobiernos locales en Argentina (pero incluye ingresos de las provincias), Bolivia, Costa Rica (hasta 1997), República Dominicana, Ecuador, El Salvador, Honduras, Nicaragua, Panamá (hasta 1998), Paraguay (hasta 2004, 2011 y 2012), Perú (hasta 2004), Uruguay (2012) y Venezuela dado que los datos no están disponibles.

2. Estimated figures for 2011 and 2012. / 2. Datos estimados para 2011 y 2012.

3. Represents a group of 18 Latin American countries. Chile and Mexico are also part of the OECD (34) group.

3. Representa un grupo de 18 países de América Latina. Chile y México son también parte del grupo OCDE (34).

4. Represents the unweighted average for OECD member countries. / 4. Representa el promedio no ponderado para los países miembros de la OCDE.

StatLink http://dx.doi.org/10.1787/888932971064

Table 5 - Cuadro 5

Taxes on property (4000)/Impuestos sobre la propiedad (4000)

A. As percentage of GDP[1]/En porcentaje del PIB[1]

	1990	2000	2007	2008	2009	2010	2011	2012	
Argentina	2.1	1.4	3.0	3.0	2.9	3.0	3.1	3.3	Argentina
Bolivia	1.3	1.8	2.2	2.2	1.9	1.8	1.9	1.9	Bolivia
Brazil	1.8	2.4	2.9	1.9	1.9	2.0	2.1	n.a.	Brasil
Chile	1.0	1.3	1.1	1.2	0.8	0.7	0.8	0.9	Chile
Colombia	0.2	1.0	1.5	1.9	1.6	1.5	2.1	2.0	Colombia
Costa Rica	0.1	0.3	0.3	0.3	0.3	0.3	0.3	0.4	Costa Rica
Dominican Republic	0.1	0.1	0.7	0.7	0.7	0.7	0.7	0.8	República Dominicana
Ecuador	-	-	-	-	-	-	-	-	Ecuador
El Salvador	0.5	0.1	0.1	0.1	0.1	0.1	0.1	0.1	El Salvador
Guatemala	0.1	0.1	0.2	0.2	0.2	0.2	0.2	0.1	Guatemala
Honduras	0.1	0.2	0.1	0.1	0.1	0.1	0.1	0.1	Honduras
Mexico	0.2	0.2	0.3	0.3	0.3	0.3	0.3	n.a.	México
Nicaragua	n.a.	-	0.0	-	-	-	-	-	Nicaragua
Panama	0.7	0.5	0.8	0.7	0.7	0.8	0.7	0.7	Panamá
Paraguay	0.3	-	0.3	0.3	0.3	0.3	n.a.	n.a.	Paraguay
Peru	1.8	0.0	0.6	0.6	0.5	0.5	0.4	0.4	Perú
Uruguay	1.6	2.2	2.5	2.4	2.4	2.2	2.1	1.3	Uruguay
Venezuela	0.1	0.5	0.5	0.9	0.0	0.0	0.0	0.0	Venezuela
Unweighted average:									*Promedio no ponderado:*
LAC (18)[2]	0.8	0.7	1.0	1.0	0.9	0.9	0.9	0.9	AL (18)[2]
OECD (34)[3]	1.8	1.9	1.9	1.8	1.8	1.8	1.8	n.a.	OCDE (34)[3]

B. As percentage of total taxation[1]/En porcentaje del total de ingresos tributarios[1]

	1990	2000	2007	2008	2009	2010	2011	2012	
Argentina	12.7	6.4	10.1	9.7	9.2	9.0	9.0	9.0	Argentina
Bolivia[4]	18.7	12.4	9.6	10.5	8.5	8.9	7.9	7.4	Bolivia[4]
Brazil	6.5	8.1	8.5	5.6	5.8	5.9	6.0	n.a.	Brasil
Chile	6.2	7.0	4.9	5.4	4.8	3.6	4.0	4.2	Chile
Colombia	2.2	6.6	7.8	9.9	8.8	8.5	11.1	10.4	Colombia
Costa Rica	0.3	1.4	1.4	1.3	1.4	1.6	1.6	1.7	Costa Rica
Dominican Republic	0.7	1.0	4.5	4.8	5.0	5.2	5.6	6.0	República Dominicana
Ecuador	-	-	-	-	-	-	-	-	Ecuador
El Salvador	5.1	0.7	0.7	0.5	0.5	0.5	0.5	0.5	El Salvador
Guatemala	1.6	1.0	1.2	1.3	1.5	1.5	1.4	1.2	Guatemala
Honduras	0.8	1.2	0.7	0.5	0.5	0.5	0.5	0.5	Honduras
Mexico	1.5	1.4	1.7	1.4	1.7	1.6	1.5	n.a.	México
Nicaragua	n.a.	-	0.0	-	-	-	-	-	Nicaragua
Panama	4.9	3.2	4.7	4.1	4.2	4.4	4.0	3.9	Panamá
Paraguay	4.9	-	2.1	2.2	2.0	1.7	n.a.	n.a.	Paraguay
Peru	15.3	0.0	3.2	3.2	3.3	3.0	2.2	2.0	Perú
Uruguay	8.4	10.2	10.2	9.1	9.0	8.1	7.8	4.9	Uruguay
Venezuela[4]	0.3	3.7	3.3	6.5	0.2	0.2	0.2	0.2	Venezuela4
Unweighted average:									*Promedio no ponderado:*
LAC (18)[2]	5.6	3.8	4.4	4.5	3.9	3.8	3.9	3.7	AL (18)[2]
OECD (34)[3]	5.7	5.5	5.6	5.4	5.5	5.5	5.4	n.a.	OCDE (34)[3]

n.a. : indicates not available

1. The figures exclude local government revenues for Argentina (but include provincial revenues), Bolivia, Costa Rica (up to 1997), Dominican Republic, Ecuador, El Salvador, Honduras, Nicaragua, Panama (up to 1998), Paraguay (up to 2004, 2011 and 2012), Peru (up to 2004), Uruguay (2012) and Venezuela as the data are not available.

1. Las cifras excluyen los ingresos de gobiernos locales en Argentina (pero incluye ingresos de las provincias), Bolivia, Costa Rica (hasta 1997), República Dominicana, Ecuador, El Salvador, Honduras, Nicaragua, Panamá (hasta 1998), Paraguay (hasta 2004, 2011 y 2012), Perú (hasta 2004), Uruguay (2012) y Venezuela dado que los datos no están disponibles.

2. Represents a group of 18 Latin American countries. Chile and Mexico are also part of the OECD (34) group.

2. Representa un grupo de 18 países de América Latina. Chile y México son también parte del grupo OCDE (34).

3. Represents the unweighted average for OECD member countries. / 3. Representa el promedio no ponderado para los países miembros de la OCDE.

4. Estimated figures for 2011 and 2012. / 4. Datos estimados para 2011 y 2012.

StatLink http://dx.doi.org/10.1787/888932971083

Table 6 - Cuadro 6

Taxes on goods and services (5000)/Impuestos sobre bienes y servicios (5000)

A. As percentage of GDP[1]/En porcentaje del PIB[1]

	1990	2000	2007	2008	2009	2010	2011	2012	
Argentina	9.0	12.1	15.8	17.0	16.4	17.5	17.8	18.8	Argentina
Bolivia	5.1	10.0	16.5	16.4	14.1	14.5	16.5	17.0	Bolivia
Brazil[2]	13.5	13.9	14.7	15.2	14.1	14.8	15.4	15.6	Brasil[2]
Chile	10.7	12.0	10.0	10.8	9.6	10.0	10.5	10.6	Chile
Colombia	4.8	6.4	8.1	8.2	7.5	7.7	7.8	7.6	Colombia
Costa Rica	7.9	9.3	11.1	11.1	9.5	9.2	9.5	9.4	Costa Rica
Dominican Republic	5.8	9.3	11.0	10.5	9.2	9.2	9.0	8.6	República Dominicana
Ecuador	4.4	7.3	6.8	6.8	7.2	9.1	8.7	10.5	Ecuador
El Salvador	5.4	6.9	8.8	8.7	8.0	8.7	8.6	8.9	El Salvador
Guatemala	5.5	7.7	8.3	7.5	6.8	7.0	7.0	7.0	Guatemala
Honduras	11.2	10.7	11.1	10.9	9.5	9.7	9.6	9.6	Honduras
Mexico[2]	8.7	8.9	9.4	12.4	8.7	9.9	10.7	11.0	México[2]
Nicaragua	n.a.	11.2	9.6	9.2	8.5	9.3	9.4	9.6	Nicaragua
Panama	5.5	4.9	5.2	5.3	5.2	5.7	6.0	5.7	Panamá
Paraguay	2.8	8.4	8.4	8.7	8.9	10.0	10.0	9.9	Paraguay
Peru	7.8	8.5	7.8	8.2	7.4	8.0	7.8	7.7	Perú
Uruguay	11.1	11.2	13.9	12.9	12.7	12.7	12.8	12.1	Uruguay
Venezuela	2.1	6.5	7.8	6.6	7.8	7.2	8.0	8.7	Venezuela
Unweighted average:									*Promedio no ponderado:*
LAC (18)[3]	7.1	9.2	10.2	10.3	9.5	10.0	10.3	10.5	AL (18)[3]
OECD (34)[4]	10.4	11.3	11.0	10.8	10.7	11.0	11.0	n.a.	OCDE (34)[4]

B. As percentage of total taxation[1]/En porcentaje del total de ingresos tributarios[1]

	1990	2000	2007	2008	2009	2010	2011	2012	
Argentina	55.7	56.5	54.3	55.2	52.2	52.4	51.2	50.4	Argentina
Bolivia[5]	70.9	68.0	72.9	80.1	61.9	70.2	68.3	65.5	Bolivia[5]
Brazil	47.7	46.3	43.4	44.8	43.2	44.6	44.1	n.a.	Brasil
Chile	62.9	63.8	43.8	50.6	55.9	51.3	49.3	50.7	Chile
Colombia	53.8	43.8	42.2	43.4	40.6	42.9	41.7	38.6	Colombia
Costa Rica	49.0	51.1	51.1	49.4	45.9	45.1	45.1	44.6	Costa Rica
Dominican Republic	69.9	74.6	69.1	70.0	69.9	72.0	70.0	64.0	República Dominicana
Ecuador	62.1	71.8	53.2	48.3	48.4	54.2	48.8	51.9	Ecuador
El Salvador	51.3	56.2	57.9	57.5	55.5	58.3	58.4	56.9	El Salvador
Guatemala	61.0	62.4	59.9	58.0	55.8	56.7	55.2	56.8	Guatemala
Honduras	69.1	70.0	58.6	57.6	55.4	55.8	57.1	54.6	Honduras
Mexico	55.3	53.0	53.1	59.2	50.2	52.6	54.1	n.a.	México
Nicaragua	n.a.	66.3	55.2	52.9	49.1	50.7	49.5	49.4	Nicaragua
Panama	37.6	29.5	31.0	31.2	30.1	31.4	33.4	30.9	Panamá
Paraguay[5]	51.4	58.0	60.1	59.9	55.5	60.5	61.0	59.0	Paraguay[5]
Peru	65.6	60.9	43.9	45.1	45.3	46.1	43.6	42.4	Perú
Uruguay	56.7	51.8	55.5	49.3	46.9	47.1	46.9	46.0	Uruguay
Venezuela[5]	11.1	47.7	46.5	46.8	54.6	63.4	61.7	63.3	Venezuela[5]
Unweighted average:									*Promedio no ponderado:*
LAC (18)[3]	54.8	57.3	52.9	53.3	50.9	53.1	52.2	51.6	AL (18)[3]
OECD (34)[4]	32.9	33.0	32.0	32.1	32.5	33.1	32.9	n.a.	OCDE (34)[4]

n.a.: indicates not available

1. The figures exclude local government revenues for Argentina (but include provincial revenues), Bolivia, Costa Rica (up to 1997), Dominican Republic, Ecuador, El Salvador, Honduras, Nicaragua, Panama (up to 1998), Paraguay (up to 2004, 2011 and 2012), Peru (up to 2004), Uruguay (2012) and Venezuela as the data are not available.

1. Las cifras excluyen los ingresos de gobiernos locales en Argentina (pero incluye ingresos de las provincias), Bolivia, Costa Rica (hasta 1997), República Dominicana, Ecuador, El Salvador, Honduras, Nicaragua, Panamá (hasta 1998), Paraguay (hasta 2004, 2011 y 2012), Perú (hasta 2004), Uruguay (2012) y Venezuela dado que los datos no están disponibles.

2. Estimated figures for 2012. / 2. Datos estimados para el 2012.

3. Represents a group of 18 Latin American countries. Chile and Mexico are also part of the OECD (34) group.

3. Representa un grupo de 18 países de América Latina. Chile y México son también parte del grupo OCDE (34).

4. Represents the unweighted average for OECD member countries. / 4. Representa el promedio no ponderado para los países miembros de la OCDE.

5. Estimated figures for 2011 and 2012. / 5. Datos estimadoes para 2011 y 2012.

StatLink http://dx.doi.org/10.1787/888932971102

Table 7 - Cuadro 7

Taxes on general consumption (5110)/Impuestos generales sobre el consumo (5110)

A. As percentage of GDP[1]/En porcentaje del PIB[1]

	1990	2000	2007	2008	2009	2010	2011	2012	
Argentina	3.9	8.6	10.4	10.7	10.9	11.4	11.9	13.0	Argentina
Bolivia	3.2	5.1	6.5	7.0	6.3	6.7	7.3	7.6	Bolivia
Brazil	13.4	13.1	13.2	13.7	12.9	13.2	13.6	n.a.	Brasil
Chile	6.3	7.9	7.5	8.4	7.3	7.6	7.8	8.0	Chile
Colombia	2.3	4.6	6.2	6.5	6.0	6.1	6.4	6.3	Colombia
Costa Rica	3.2	4.5	5.9	6.0	4.9	4.8	5.0	5.0	Costa Rica
Dominican Republic	1.3	2.6	4.9	4.7	4.2	4.3	4.2	4.0	República Dominicana
Ecuador	2.0	4.6	4.9	4.6	4.8	5.8	5.5	6.4	Ecuador
El Salvador	2.8	5.4	6.9	6.8	6.1	6.7	6.8	7.0	El Salvador
Guatemala	2.4	4.7	5.9	5.5	4.9	5.1	5.2	5.3	Guatemala
Honduras	2.7	4.8	6.1	6.3	5.2	5.4	5.7	5.6	Honduras
Mexico	3.3	3.1	3.6	3.8	3.4	3.9	3.7	3.8	México
Nicaragua	n.a.	5.9	5.8	5.6	5.3	5.6	6.0	6.1	Nicaragua
Panama	1.3	0.6	1.0	2.3	2.3	2.9	3.3	3.3	Panamá
Paraguay	-	4.7	5.0	5.5	5.6	6.3	6.5	6.5	Paraguay
Peru	1.4	5.1	5.9	6.8	6.0	6.6	6.5	6.4	Perú
Uruguay	5.5	6.5	9.3	9.2	9.0	8.9	8.9	8.7	Uruguay
Venezuela	-	4.1	5.6	4.6	5.9	5.5	6.2	6.8	Venezuela
Unweighted average:									*Promedio no ponderado:*
LAC (18)[2]	3.2	5.3	6.4	6.5	6.2	6.5	6.7	6.6	AL (18)[2]
OECD (34)[3]	5.8	6.8	6.9	6.8	6.7	6.9	6.9	n.a.	OCDE (34)[3]

B. As percentage of total taxation[1]/En porcentaje del total de ingresos tributarios[1]

	1990	2000	2007	2008	2009	2010	2011	2012	
Argentina	23.9	40.2	35.9	34.7	34.5	34.1	34.5	34.7	Argentina
Bolivia[4]	44.8	34.6	28.9	33.9	27.8	32.6	30.1	29.3	Bolivia[4]
Brazil	47.4	43.4	38.9	40.3	39.5	39.8	39.1	n.a.	Brasil
Chile	37.4	41.8	32.9	39.4	42.5	38.7	37.0	38.4	Chile
Colombia	26.1	31.4	32.7	34.4	32.2	33.8	34.1	32.0	Colombia
Costa Rica	20.0	24.9	27.1	26.6	23.7	23.6	23.6	23.6	Costa Rica
Dominican Republic	15.2	21.1	30.7	31.5	31.7	33.6	32.8	29.7	República Dominicana
Ecuador	28.1	45.2	38.3	32.6	32.4	34.3	30.6	31.8	Ecuador
El Salvador	26.2	44.4	45.5	45.1	42.2	45.1	46.2	45.0	El Salvador
Guatemala	27.2	37.9	42.4	42.4	40.0	41.4	41.5	43.2	Guatemala
Honduras	16.9	31.5	32.0	33.2	30.5	31.0	33.6	31.8	Honduras
Mexico	20.8	18.7	20.4	18.0	19.7	20.5	19.0	n.a.	México
Nicaragua	n.a.	34.8	33.7	32.5	30.8	30.8	31.3	31.5	Nicaragua
Panama	9.0	3.6	6.2	13.6	13.3	15.9	18.4	17.7	Panamá
Paraguay[4]	-	32.1	36.2	37.5	34.6	38.3	40.1	38.9	Paraguay[4]
Peru	12.1	36.8	33.2	37.2	36.8	37.9	36.4	35.4	Perú
Uruguay	28.1	30.2	37.0	35.0	33.3	33.0	32.6	33.2	Uruguay
Venezuela[4]	-	30.2	33.5	32.8	41.2	48.2	48.0	49.7	Venezuela[4]
Unweighted average:									*Promedio no ponderado:*
LAC (18)[2]	22.5	32.4	32.5	33.4	32.6	34.0	33.8	34.1	AL (18)[2]
OECD (34)[3]	18.1	19.7	19.8	19.8	20.0	20.5	20.3	n.a.	OCDE (34)[3]

n.a.: indicates not available

1. The figures exclude local government revenues for Argentina (but include provincial revenues), Bolivia, Costa Rica (up to 1997), Dominican Republic, Ecuador, El Salvador, Honduras, Nicaragua, Panama (up to 1998), Paraguay (up to 2004, 2011 and 2012), Peru (up to 2004), Uruguay (2012) and Venezuela as the data are not available.

1. Las cifras excluyen los ingresos de gobiernos locales en Argentina (pero incluye ingresos de las provincias), Bolivia, Costa Rica (hasta 1997), República Dominicana, Ecuador, El Salvador, Honduras, Nicaragua, Panamá (hasta 1998), Paraguay (hasta 2004, 2011 y 2012), Perú (hasta 2004), Uruguay (2012) y Venezuela dado que los datos no están disponibles.

2. Represents a group of 18 Latin American countries. Chile and Mexico are also part of the OECD (34) group.

2. Representa un grupo de 18 países de América Latina. Chile y México son también parte del grupo OCDE (34).

3. Represents the unweighted average for OECD member countries. / 3. Representa el promedio no ponderado para los países miembros de la OCDE.

4. Estimated figures for 2011 and 2012. / 4. Datos estimados para 2011 y 2012.

StatLink http://dx.doi.org/10.1787/888932971121

Table 8 - Cuadro 8

Taxes on specific goods and services (5120)/Impuestos específicos sobre bienes y servicios (5120)

A. As percentage of GDP[1]/En porcentaje del PIB[1]

	1990	2000	2007	2008	2009	2010	2011	2012	
Argentina	4.9	3.2	5.1	6.1	5.3	5.9	5.5	5.6	Argentina
Bolivia	1.9	4.9	9.9	9.5	7.8	7.8	9.2	9.4	Bolivia
Brazil	-	0.7	1.2	1.3	1.0	1.2	1.3	n.a.	Brasil
Chile	3.9	3.5	2.0	1.9	1.7	1.9	2.0	2.0	Chile
Colombia	2.5	1.8	1.8	1.7	1.6	1.6	1.4	1.3	Colombia
Costa Rica	4.3	4.3	4.8	4.6	4.1	3.9	4.0	3.6	Costa Rica
Dominican Republic	4.4	6.5	6.0	5.6	4.9	4.8	4.7	4.5	República Dominicana
Ecuador	2.4	2.6	1.8	2.0	2.2	3.1	3.0	3.8	Ecuador
El Salvador	2.6	1.4	1.9	1.9	1.9	2.0	1.8	1.9	El Salvador
Guatemala	2.9	2.9	2.3	1.9	1.8	1.7	1.6	1.4	Guatemala
Honduras	8.5	5.9	5.1	4.6	4.3	4.3	4.0	4.0	Honduras
Mexico	5.4	5.6	5.6	8.4	5.1	5.9	6.8	n.a.	México
Nicaragua	n.a.	5.3	3.7	3.5	3.2	3.6	3.5	3.5	Nicaragua
Panama	2.3	4.0	3.8	2.7	2.6	2.7	2.6	2.4	Panamá
Paraguay	2.8	3.8	3.2	3.1	3.2	3.4	3.4	3.4	Paraguay
Peru	6.3	3.3	1.9	1.4	1.4	1.4	1.3	1.3	Perú
Uruguay	5.1	3.7	3.9	3.1	3.1	3.3	3.4	3.4	Uruguay
Venezuela	2.1	2.4	2.2	2.0	1.9	1.7	1.8	1.9	Venezuela
Unweighted average:									*Promedio no ponderado:*
LAC (18)[2]	3.7	3.7	3.7	3.6	3.2	3.3	3.4	3.3	AL (18)[2]
OECD (34)[3]	4.0	3.8	3.4	3.4	3.4	3.5	3.5	n.a.	OCDE (34)[3]

B. As percentage of total taxation[1]/En porcentaje del total de ingresos tributarios[1]

	1990	2000	2007	2008	2009	2010	2011	2012	
Argentina	30.6	15.0	17.6	19.7	16.8	17.6	16.0	15.0	Argentina
Bolivia[4]	26.1	33.4	44.0	46.1	34.1	37.6	38.2	36.1	Bolivia[4]
Brazil	-	2.4	3.7	3.7	2.9	3.5	3.7	n.a.	Brasil
Chile	25.6	22.0	10.9	11.2	13.4	12.6	12.3	12.2	Chile
Colombia	27.8	12.4	9.5	9.0	8.4	9.1	7.6	6.6	Colombia
Costa Rica	26.8	23.9	22.0	20.6	19.7	18.9	19.2	17.1	Costa Rica
Dominican Republic	53.6	51.9	37.3	37.7	37.2	37.5	36.2	33.2	República Dominicana
Ecuador	33.8	26.1	13.7	14.6	14.7	18.6	17.0	18.9	Ecuador
El Salvador	25.0	11.8	12.5	12.4	13.3	13.3	12.3	11.8	El Salvador
Guatemala	32.8	23.4	16.6	14.6	14.6	14.1	12.5	11.7	Guatemala
Honduras	52.2	38.5	26.7	24.5	24.9	24.9	23.5	22.8	Honduras
Mexico	34.0	33.4	31.6	40.3	29.4	31.2	34.3	n.a.	México
Nicaragua	n.a.	31.5	21.5	20.4	18.4	19.9	18.3	17.9	Nicaragua
Panama	15.5	23.8	22.9	15.9	15.1	14.7	14.2	13.2	Panamá
Paraguay[4]	51.4	25.9	22.7	21.1	19.9	20.8	20.9	20.2	Paraguay[4]
Peru	53.5	24.1	10.7	7.9	8.4	8.1	7.2	7.0	Perú
Uruguay	25.9	17.3	15.8	11.7	11.5	12.2	12.6	12.8	Uruguay
Venezuela[4]	11.1	17.5	13.0	14.0	13.4	15.1	13.6	13.6	Venezuela[4]
Unweighted average:									*Promedio no ponderado:*
LAC (18)[2]	30.9	24.1	19.6	19.2	17.6	18.3	17.7	16.9	AL (18)[2]
OECD (34)[3]	13.2	11.5	10.4	10.5	10.6	10.8	10.7	n.a.	OCDE (34)[3]

n.a.: indicates not available

1. The figures exclude local government revenues for Argentina (but include provincial revenues), Bolivia, Costa Rica (up to 1997), Dominican Republic, Ecuador, El Salvador, Honduras, Nicaragua, Panama (up to 1998), Paraguay (up to 2004, 2011 and 2012), Peru (up to 2004), Uruguay (2012) and Venezuela as the data are not available.

1. Las cifras excluyen los ingresos de gobiernos locales en Argentina (pero incluye ingresos de las provincias), Bolivia, Costa Rica (hasta 1997), República Dominicana, Ecuador, El Salvador, Honduras, Nicaragua, Panamá (hasta 1998), Paraguay (hasta 2004, 2011 y 2012), Perú (hasta 2004), Uruguay (2012) y Venezuela dado que los datos no están disponibles.

2. Represents a group of 18 Latin American countries. Chile and Mexico are also part of the OECD (34) group.

2. Representa un grupo de 18 países de América Latina. Chile y México son también parte del grupo OCDE (34).

3. Represents the unweighted average for OECD member countries. / 3. Representa el promedio no ponderado para los países miembros de la OCDE.

4. Estimated figures for 2011 and 2012. / 4. Datos estimados para 2011 y 2012.

StatLink http://dx.doi.org/10.1787/888932971140

Table 9 - Cuadro 9

Gross domestic product for tax reporting years at market prices, in billions of national currency units

Producto interno bruto para los años fiscales a precios de mercado, en millardos de moneda local

	1990	2000	2007	2008	2009	2010	2011	2012	
Argentina	63	284	812	1 033	1 145	1 443	1 842	2 164	Argentina
Bolivia	15	52	103	121	122	138	166	187	Bolivia
Brazil	0	1 179	2 661	3 032	3 239	3 770	4 143	4 403	Brasil
Chile	10 482	42 095	90 429	93 848	96 444	111 008	121 493	130 527	Chile
Colombia	28 651	208 531	431 072	480 087	504 647	544 924	621 615	664 473	Colombia
Costa Rica	664	4 915	13 598	15 702	16 845	19 087	20 748	22 685	Costa Rica
Dominican Republic	77	388	1 364	1 576	1 679	1 902	2 119	2 317	República Dominicana
Ecuador	15	18	51	62	63	68	77	84	Ecuador
El Salvador	5	13	20	21	21	21	23	24	El Salvador
Guatemala	31	133	262	296	308	333	371	391	Guatemala
Honduras	13	107	234	262	276	299	335	362	Honduras
Mexico	810	6 021	11 291	12 153	11 893	13 029	14 351	15 456	México
Nicaragua	n.a.	50	137	160	166	183	216	247	Nicaragua
Panama	6 077	11 621	19 794	23 002	24 163	26 590	31 316	36 253	Panamá
Paraguay	6 474	24 737	69 426	80 735	79 117	94 934	105 203	108 832	Paraguay
Peru	5	186	336	371	382	435	486	526	Perú
Uruguay	12	276	549	636	682	779	897	1 014	Uruguay
Venezuela	2	80	495	678	707	1 017	1 357	1 635	Venezuela

n.a.: indicates not available

Source: OECD National Accounts data for Chile and Mexico and official National Accounts data for the other countries.

Fuente: Datos de Cuentas Nacionales de la OCDE para Chile y México y estadísticas oficiales de Cuentas Nacionales para el resto de países.

StatLink http://dx.doi.org/10.1787/888932971159

B. Comparative charts / B. Gráficos comparativos

Chart 1. **Tax revenue of main headings as percentage of total tax revenue, 2012**
Gráfico 1. **Ingresos tributarios de categorías principales como porcentaje del ingreso tributario total, 2012**

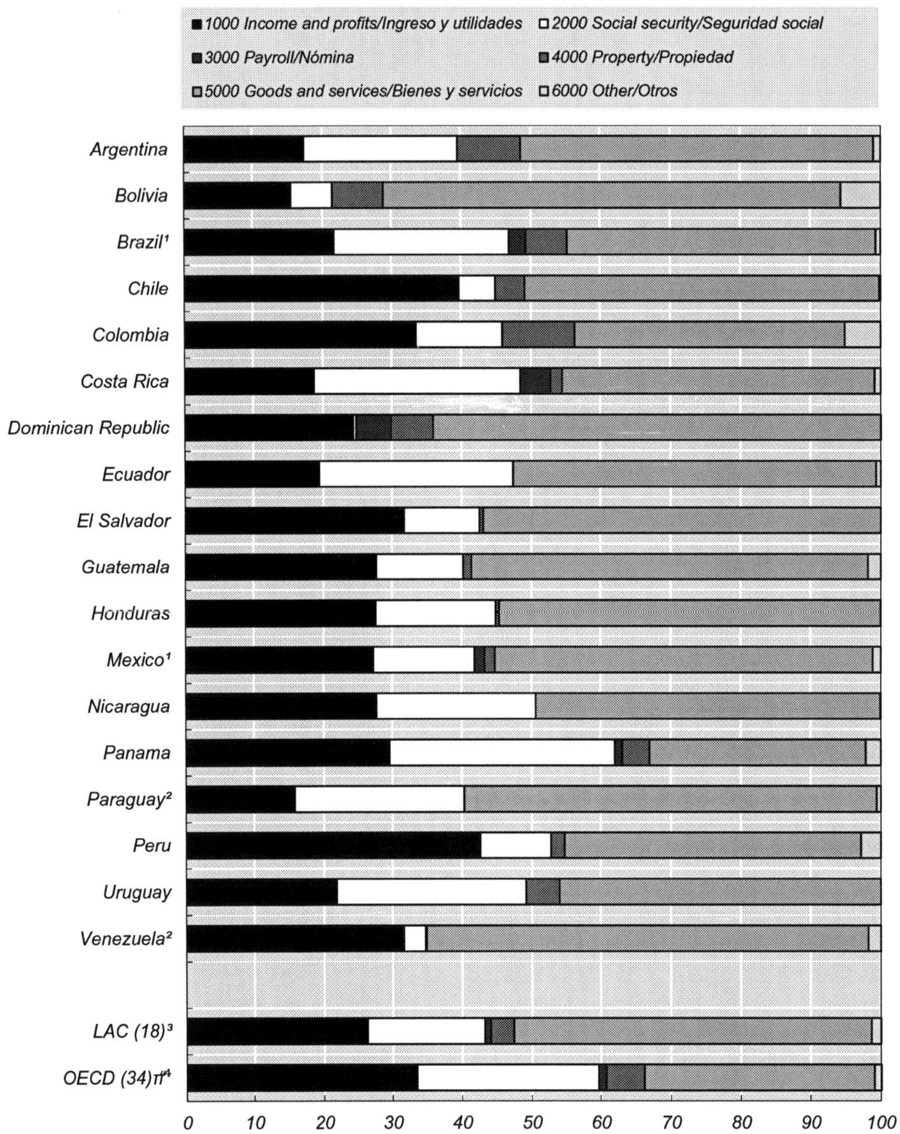

1. Data for 2011 is used.
1. Se utilizan datos del 2011.
2. Estimated data.
2. Datos estimados.
3. Represents the unweighted average for a group of 18 Latin American countries. Chile and Mexico are also part of the OECD (34) group.
3. Representa el promedio no ponderado para un grupo de 18 países de América Latina. Chile y México son también parte del grupo OCDE (34).
4. Represents the unweighted average for OECD member countries.
4. Representa el promedio no ponderado para los países miembros de la OCDE.

Source: Table 2B in Part II.A/Cuadro 2B en Parte II.A.

StatLink http://dx.doi.org/10.1787/888932970798

Chart 2. **Tax structures in selected Latin American countries, 1990-2012**

Receipts as percentage of total tax revenues

Gráfico 2. **Estructuras impositivas en países seleccionados de América Latina, 1990-2012**

Ingresos como porcentaje de los ingresos tributarios totales

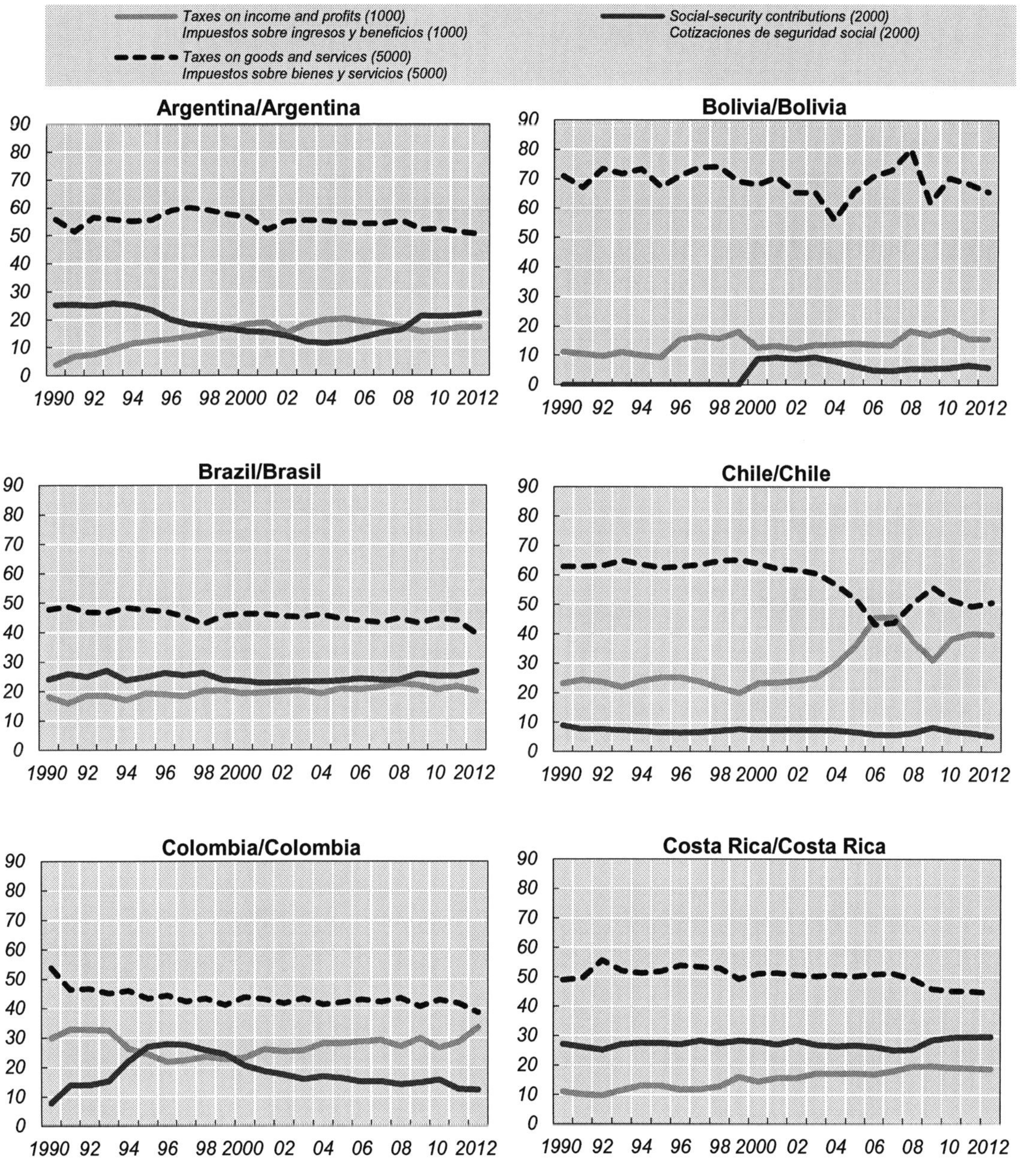

Chart 2. **Tax structures in selected Latin American countries, 1990-2012** ***(cont)***

Receipts as percentage of total tax revenues

Gráfico 2. **Estructuras impositivas en países seleccionados de América Latina, 1990-2012** ***(cont)***

Ingresos como porcentaje de los ingresos tributarios totales

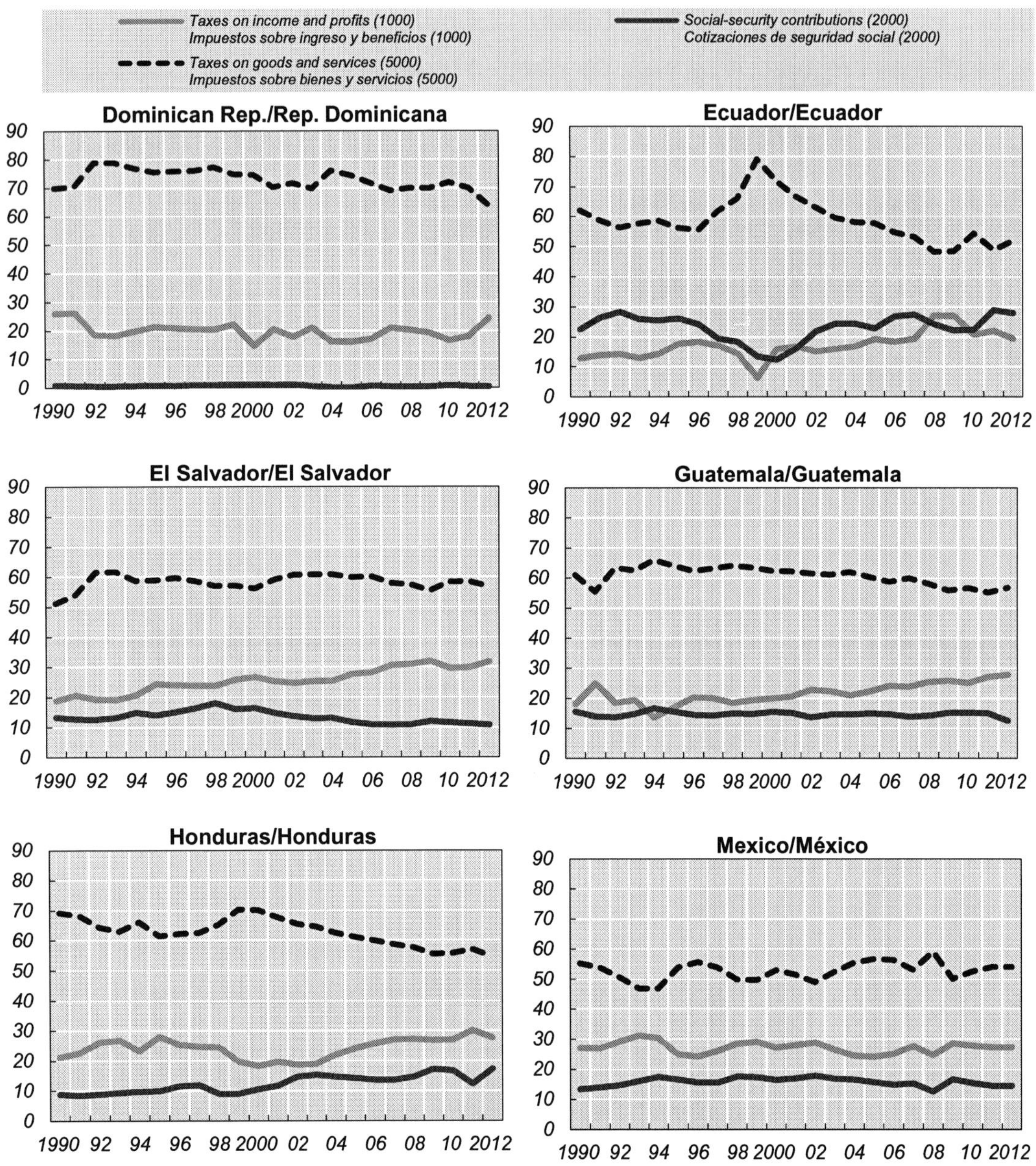

Chart 2. **Tax structures in selected Latin American countries, 1990-2012** ***(cont)***

Receipts as percentage of total tax revenues

Gráfico 2. **Estructuras impositivas en países seleccionados de América Latina, 1990-2012** ***(cont)***

Ingresos como porcentaje de los ingresos tributarios totales

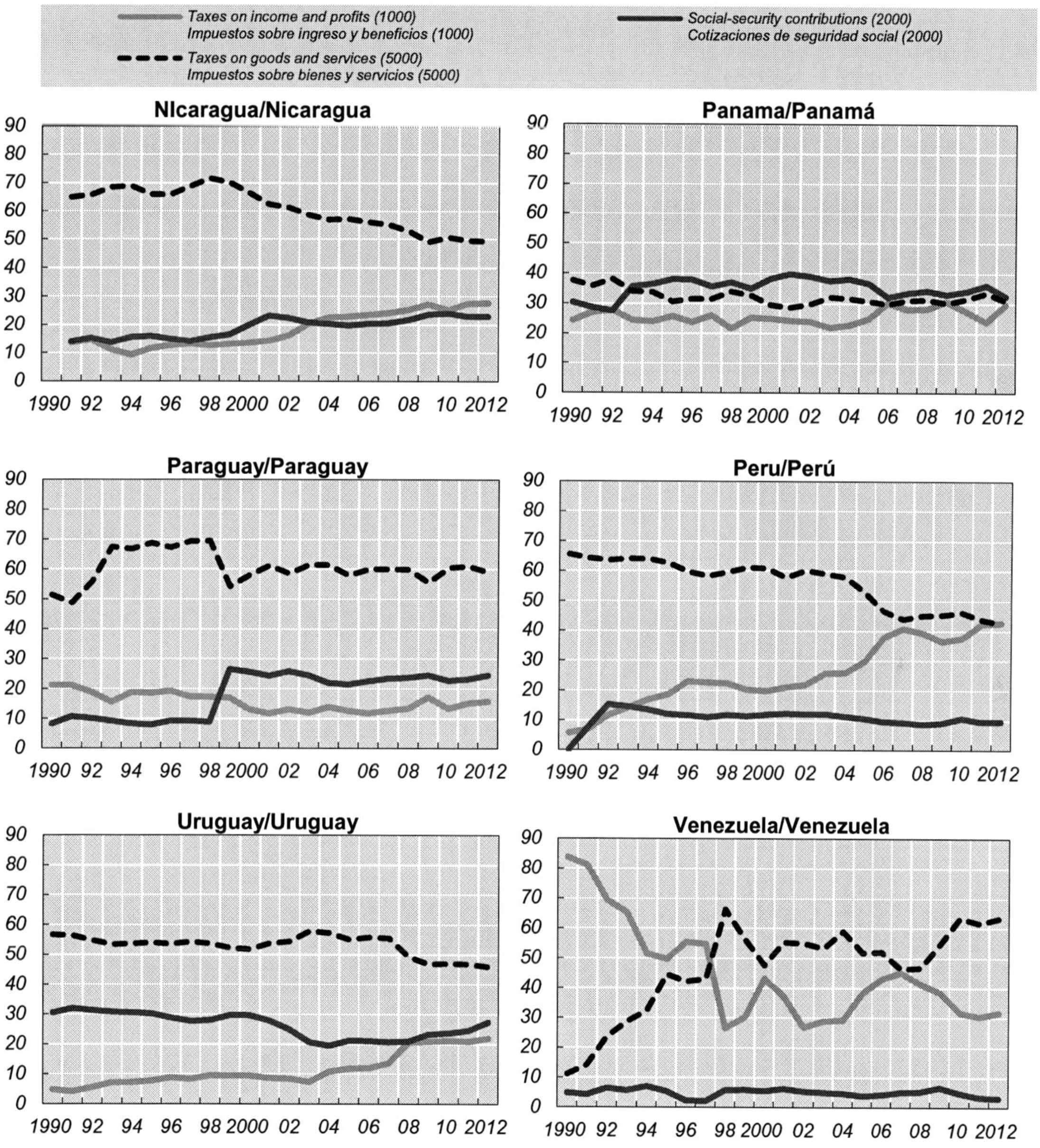

StatLink http://dx.doi.org/10.1787/888932970817

PART III / Parte III

Country Tables, 1990-2012 – Tax revenues

Cuadros país, 1990-2012 – Ingresos tributarios

Table 10 - Cuadro 10

ARGENTINA - ARGENTINA

Details of tax revenue, in millions of argentinean pesos

	1990	2000	2007	2008	2009	2010	2011	2012
Total tax revenue	10 217	61 078	236 513	317 584	360 951	483 012	638 355	808 053
1000 Taxes on income, profits and capital gains	382	11 303	44 226	54 722	56 887	78 427	110 118	140 108
1100 Of individuals	11	3 937	12 777	17 615	19 573	23 980	35 436	54 498
1110 On income and profits	-	3 854	12 715	17 534	19 460	23 858	35 279	54 283
1120 On capital gains	11	82	62	80	114	122	157	215
1200 Corporate	-	6 575	29 145	34 026	33 921	50 664	70 717	81 934
1210 On profits	-	6 575	29 145	34 026	33 921	50 664	70 717	81 934
Corporate income taxes		5 956	27 837	33 031	32 702	49 012	69 356	80 486
Tax on assets		19	9	7	6	4	4	5
Tax on assumed minimum income		600	1 299	988	1 213	1 648	1 357	1 443
1220 On capital gains	-	-	-	-		-	-	-
1300 Unallocable between 1100 and 1200	371	792	2 304	3 082	3 392	3 783	3 965	3 676
Non resident taxpayers	-	792	2 304	3 082	3 392	3 783	3 965	3 676
Other	371	-	-	-	-	-	-	-
2000 Social security contributions	2 583	9 670	36 606	52 565	77 231	102 460	137 186	179 776
2100 Employees	-	2 486	7 052	12 917	28 871	37 990	51 715	70 087
2110 On a payroll basis		2 486	7 052	12 917	28 871	37 990	51 715	70 087
2120 On an income tax basis		-	-	-	-	-	-	-
2200 Employers	-	6 069	23 939	32 459	40 473	54 713	75 550	100 029
2210 On a payroll basis		6 069	23 939	32 459	40 473	54 713	75 550	100 029
2220 On an income tax basis		-	-	-	-	-	-	-
2300 Self-employed or non-employed	98	1 115	5 615	7 189	7 886	9 757	9 922	9 661
2310 On a payroll basis	98	1 115	5 615	7 189	7 886	9 757	9 922	9 661
2320 On an income tax basis	-	-	-	-	-	-	-	-
2400 Unallocable between 2100, 2200 and 2300	2 485	-	-	-	-	-	-	-
2410 On a payroll basis	2 485							
2420 On an income tax basis	-							
3000 Taxes on payroll and workforce	-	-	-	-	-	-	-	-
4000 Taxes on property	1 302	3 896	23 978	30 858	33 167	43 538	57 521	72 431
4100 Recurrent taxes on immovable property	412	1 809	3 025	3 929	4 170	5 035	6 092	9 814
4110 Households	-	-	-	-	-	-	-	-
4120 Others	412	1 809	3 025	3 929	4 170	5 035	6 092	9 814
4200 Recurrent taxes on net wealth	3	1 084	2 557	3 446	4 123	5 248	6 018	7 408
4210 Individual	-	1 024	2 492	3 375	4 041	5 147	5 892	7 263
Personal assets		1 024	2 492	3 375	4 041	5 147	5 892	7 263
Recurrent taxes on net wealth		-	-	-	-	-	-	-
4220 Corporate	3	60	65	71	82	101	126	145
4300 Estate, inheritance and gift taxes	-	-	-	-	-	-	-	-
4310 Estate and inheritance taxes								
4320 Gift taxes								
4400 Taxes on financial and capital transactions	656	933	18 390	23 480	24 871	33 252	45 411	55 208
Immovable property transfers	-	54	382	439	372	539	775	721
Movable property transfers	-	-	-	-	-	-	-	-
Bank accounts' credits and debits	415	-	15 065	19 495	20 561	26 885	36 179	43 931
Provincial taxes on financial and capital transactions	160	833	2 942	3 546	3 937	5 829	8 457	10 556
Stamp taxes	81	46	-	-	-	-	-	-
4500 Non-recurrent taxes	-	70	6	4	4	3	0	1
4510 On net wealth		-	-	-	-	-	-	-
4520 Other non-recurrent taxes		70	6	4	4	3	0	1
4600 Other recurrent taxes on property	231	-	-	-	-	-	-	-

Table 10 - Cuadro 10 *(cont)*

ARGENTINA - ARGENTINA

Details of tax revenue, in millions of argentinean pesos

	1990	2000	2007	2008	2009	2010	2011	2012
5000 Taxes on goods and services	5 692	34 510	128 332	175 234	188 344	253 092	327 004	407 662
5100 Taxes on production, sale, transfer, etc	5 559	33 706	126 411	172 726	185 117	249 494	322 083	401 206
5110 General taxes	2 437	24 540	84 891	110 212	124 407	164 478	220 074	280 298
5111 Value added taxes	1 591	18 426	60 757	77 335	84 935	113 330	149 547	188 509
5112 Sales tax	-	-	-	-	-	-	-	-
5113 Other	846	6 114	24 134	32 877	39 472	51 148	70 527	91 789
5120 Taxes on specific goods and services	3 122	9 166	41 520	62 514	60 709	85 016	102 009	120 908
5121 Excises	2 082	5 850	13 167	16 439	19 523	26 208	30 849	40 800
Alcoholic beverages	-	36	95	116	169	238	318	422
Non alcoholic beverages	-	90	312	411	441	501	634	912
Beers	-	50	149	228	226	212	242	332
Tobacco products	-	1 875	3 881	4 686	5 751	6 884	8 620	10 310
Liquid fuels and gas	1 068	3 478	7 469	9 701	11 593	15 269	18 131	25 785
Electricity	72	205	538	556	559	591	616	610
Motor vehicles	-	20	0	15	36	27	24	153
Other	942	96	724	726	747	2 485	2 263	2 275
5122 Profits of fiscal monopolies	-	-	-	-	-	-	-	-
5123 Customs and import duties	219	1 976	7 015	8 988	7 700	11 428	14 678	16 640
Import duties	166	1 938	6 859	8 803	7 526	11 183	14 373	16 313
Import fees	53	38	156	185	174	246	305	327
5124 Taxes on exports	724	32	20 450	36 055	32 042	45 547	54 163	61 316
5125 Taxes on investment goods	-	-	-	-	-	-	-	-
5126 Taxes on specific services	-	1 233	674	769	1 190	1 428	1 822	1 430
Insurance services		194	11	13	17	21	27	35
Financial services		855	1	1	0	-	-	-
Telephone services		33	417	480	779	936	1 166	1 391
Other specific services		151	246	275	395	472	629	5
5127 Other taxes on internat trade and transactions	97	74	214	263	255	404	497	721
5128 Other taxes	-	-	-	-	-	-	-	-
5130 Unallocable between 5110 and 5120	-	-	-	-	-	-	-	-
5200 Taxes on use of goods and perform activities	133	804	1 921	2 508	3 228	3 598	4 921	6 456
5210 Recurrent taxes	133	804	1 921	2 508	3 228	3 598	4 921	6 456
5211 Paid by households: motor vehicles	-	-	-	-	-	-	-	-
5212 Paid by others: motor vehicles	133	804	1 921	2 508	3 228	3 598	4 921	6 456
5213 Paid in respect of other goods	-	-	-	-	-	-	-	-
5220 Non-recurrent taxes	-	-	-	-	-	-	-	-
5300 Unallocable between 5100 and 5200	-	-	-	-	-	-	-	-
6000 Other taxes	258	1 698	3 371	4 205	5 321	5 496	6 526	8 075
6100 Paid solely by business	-	354	1 063	1 355	1 550	2 093	2 983	3 825
Simplified system for small taxpayers		354	1 063	1 355	1 550	2 093	2 983	3 825
6200 Other	258	1 345	2 307	2 850	3 771	3 403	3 543	4 250
Tax debt payments	135	24	38	237	1 629	293	710	934
Special payments	80	-	-	-	-	-	-	-
Other national level	-	12	-	-	-	-	-	-
Other provincial level	43	1 309	2 269	2 613	2 143	3 110	2 833	3 316
Total tax revenue on cash basis	10 217	61 078	236 513	317 584	360 951	483 012	638 355	808 053

Year ending 31st December.
The data are on cash basis.
The figures exclude local government revenues as the data are not available.
Heading 5212: In ECLAC data, property tax on motor vehicles is classified in category 4000.
Source: Subsecretaría de Ingresos Públicos, Dirección Nacional de Coordinación Fiscal con las Provincias, Ministry of Economy and Production.

StatLink http://dx.doi.org/10.1787/888932971178

Table 11 - Cuadro 11

BOLIVIA - BOLIVIA

Details of tax revenue, in millions of bolivianos

	1990	2000	2007	2008	2009	2010	2011	2012
Total tax revenue	1 108	7 651	23 295	24 753	27 682	28 495	44 214	52 550
1000 Taxes on income, profits and capital gains	123	967	3 118	4 540	4 700	5 326	6 331	7 556
1100 Of individuals	-	-	-	-	-	-	-	-
1110 On income and profits	-	-	-	-	-	-	-	-
1120 On capital gains	-	-	-	-	-	-	-	-
1200 Corporate	61	806	2 923	4 308	4 445	5 089	6 072	7 296
1210 On profits	61	806	2 923	4 308	4 445	5 089	6 072	7 296
Presumed profit of enterprises	60	2	-	-	-	-	-	-
Mining profits	-	0	153	80	61	473	616	322
Tax regularization	0	0	-	-	-	-	-	-
Corporate tax	-	546	2 251	3 657	3 761	3 874	4 724	6 256
Corporate tax remittances	-	258	519	571	623	742	732	718
1220 On capital gains	-	-	-	-	-	-	-	-
1300 Unallocable between 1100 and 1200	62	161	195	232	255	237	260	260
2000 Social security contributions	-	666	1 109	1 347	1 515	1 645	2 665	2 878
2100 Employees	-	-	-	-	-	-	-	-
2110 On a payroll basis								
2120 On an income tax basis								
2200 Employers	-	-	-	-	-	-	-	-
2210 On a payroll basis								
2220 On an income tax basis								
2300 Self-employed or non-employed	-	-	-	-	-	-	-	-
2310 On a payroll basis								
2320 On an income tax basis								
2400 Unallocable between 2100, 2200 and 2300	-	666	1 109	1 347	1 515	1 645	2 665	2 878
2410 On a payroll basis	-	666	1 109	1 347	1 515	1 645	2 665	2 878
2420 On an income tax basis	-	-	-	-	-	-	-	-
3000 Taxes on payroll and workforce	-	-	-	-	-	-	-	-
4000 Taxes on property	208	946	2 240	2 607	2 360	2 541	3 174	3 603
4100 Recurrent taxes on immovable property	-	-	-	-	-	-	-	-
4110 Households	-	-	-	-	-	-	-	-
4120 Others	-	-	-	-	-	-	-	-
4200 Recurrent taxes on net wealth	-	-	-	-	-	-	-	-
4210 Individual			-	-	-	-	-	-
4220 Corporate			-	-	-	-	-	-
4300 Estate, inheritance and gift taxes	1	3	11	14	18	20	22	23
4310 Estate and inheritance taxes								
4320 Gift taxes								
4400 Taxes on financial and capital transactions	136	943	2 229	2 593	2 342	2 521	3 152	3 580
4500 Non-recurrent taxes	-	-	-	-	-	-	-	-
4510 On net wealth								
4520 Other non-recurrent taxes								
4600 Other recurrent taxes on property	71	-	-	-	-	-	-	-

Table 11 - Cuadro 11 *(cont)*

BOLIVIA - BOLIVIA

Details of tax revenue, in millions of bolivianos

	1990	2000	2007	2008	2009	2010	2011	2012
5000 Taxes on goods and services	786	5 206	16 981	19 816	17 142	20 011	27 469	31 782
5100 Taxes on production, sale, transfer, etc	786	5 206	16 981	19 816	17 142	20 011	27 469	31 782
5110 General taxes	497	2 649	6 734	8 393	7 705	9 293	12 109	14 245
5111 Value added taxes	497	2 649	6 734	8 393	7 705	9 293	12 109	14 245
5112 Sales tax	-	-	-	-	-	-	-	-
5113 Other	-	-	-	-	-	-	-	-
5120 Taxes on specific goods and services	289	2 557	10 247	11 423	9 437	10 718	15 360	17 537
5121 Excises	83	1 930	9 111	9 986	8 220	9 126	13 077	14 992
Excises (Internal)	61	244	598	717	739	933	1 204	1 157
Excises (Imports)	22	298	485	594	367	379	642	580
Special tax on hydrocarbons and derivatives	-	1 387	2 073	2 031	650	1 070	2 236	1 144
Excise tax on hydrocarbons	-	-	5 954	6 644	6 465	6 744	8 996	12 111
5122 Profits of fiscal monopolies	-	-	-	-	-	-	-	-
5123 Customs and import duties	204	612	1 103	1 406	1 179	1 545	2 218	2 485
5124 Taxes on exports	-	-	-	-	-	-	-	-
5125 Taxes on investment goods	-	-	-	-	-	-	-	-
5126 Taxes on specific services	2	15	33	31	38	47	65	60
Air departure tax	2	15	33	31	38	47	52	51
Tax on gambling	-	-	-	-	-	-	13	9
5127 Other taxes on internat trade and transactions	-	-	-	-	-	-	-	-
5128 Other taxes	-	-	-	-	-	-	-	-
5130 Unallocable between 5110 and 5120	-	-	-	-	-	-	-	-
5200 Taxes on use of goods and perform activities	-	-	-	-	-	-	-	-
5210 Recurrent taxes								
5211 Paid by households: motor vehicles								
5212 Paid by others: motor vehicles								
5213 Paid in respect of other goods								
5220 Non-recurrent taxes								
5300 Unallocable between 5100 and 5200	-	-	-	-	-	-	-	-
6000 Other taxes	-9	-135	-152	-3 557	1 964	-1 029	4 574	6 732
6100 Paid solely by business	4	6	8	11	12	12	13	14
Simplified tax regime	3	6	8	11	11	12	13	14
Integrated tax system	1	0	0	0	0	0	0	0
6200 Other	-13	-141	-160	-3 568	1 953	-1 041	4 562	6 718
Rural property tax	2	1	7	9	12	14	17	22
Fiscal notes	135	701	1 665	2 166	5 834	2 552	3 989	5 836
Rebates	-169	-878	-2 111	-6 231	-4 403	-4 029	-	-
Total tax revenue on cash basis	1 108	7 651	23 295	24 753	27 682	28 495	44 214	52 550

Year ending 31st December.

The data are on cash basis.

Heading 2000: The data for social security contributions are available from the year 2000 only.

Heading 5121: In ECLAC data the excise tax on hydrocarbons (IDH) is treated as non tax revenues.

Source: Ministry of Economy and Public Finance.

StatLink http://dx.doi.org/10.1787/888932971197

Table 12 - Cuadro 12

BRAZIL - BRASIL

Details of tax revenue, in millions of reais

	1990	2000	2007	2008	2009	2010	2011	2012
Total tax revenue	3	354 883	900 043	1 029 744	1 056 603	1 251 674	1 444 569	1 597 020
1000 Taxes on income, profits and capital gains	1	68 667	192 629	234 380	233 564	258 505	313 928	321 670
1100 Of individuals	0	3 406	12 586	13 792	13 469	16 174	20 438	-
1110 On income and profits	0	3 406	12 586	13 792	13 469	16 174	20 438	-
1120 On capital gains	-	-	-	-	-	-	-	-
1200 Corporate	0	25 430	98 788	120 184	120 215	128 123	153 392	57 520
1210 On profits	0	25 430	98 788	120 184	120 215	128 123	153 392	57 520
Corporate income tax	0	16 680	65 605	78 521	77 024	82 391	94 798	-
Social contribution on net profits (CSLL)	0	8 750	33 183	41 664	43 190	45 733	58 594	57 520
1220 On capital gains	-	-	-	-				
1300 Unallocable between 1100 and 1200	0	39 831	81 255	100 403	99 880	114 207	140 098	264 150
Withholding taxes	0	39 831	81 255	100 403	99 880	114 207	140 098	-
2000 Social security contributions	1	83 469	215 190	246 502	274 017	315 476	363 969	427 680
2100 Employees	-	-	-	-	-	-	-	-
2110 On a payroll basis								
2120 On an income tax basis								
2200 Employers	0	18 709	43 602	50 518	57 183	64 271	74 979	79 970
2210 On a payroll basis	0	18 709	43 602	50 518	57 183	64 271	74 979	79 970
2220 On an income tax basis	-	-	-	-	-	-	-	-
2300 Self-employed or non-employed	-	-	-	-	-	-	-	-
2310 On a payroll basis								
2320 On an income tax basis								
2400 Unallocable between 2100, 2200 and 2300	1	64 760	171 588	195 984	216 833	251 205	288 990	347 710
2410 On a payroll basis	1	64 760	171 588	195 984	216 833	251 205	288 990	347 710
Social security contributions (Federal)	1	59 334	154 324	179 424	200 552	232 838	268 641	325 300
Social security contributions (State)	0	4 423	13 481	12 678	11 948	13 273	14 325	15 370
Social security contributions (Municipal)	0	1 003	3 783	3 882	4 333	5 095	6 023	7 040
2420 On an income tax basis	-	-	-	-	-	-	-	-
3000 Taxes on payroll and workforce	0	6 749	19 310	23 309	25 224	33 038	34 182	-
PASEP contributions	-	1 312	4 039	4 894	5 115	9 865	6 936	-
Payroll-based contribution to education	0	2 791	7 089	8 776	9 589	11 049	13 115	-
"S" system contributions	0	2 646	6 592	7 826	8 524	9 887	11 663	-
Other	-	-	1 592	1 812	1 996	2 236	2 467	-
4000 Taxes on property	0	28 818	76 378	57 925	60 808	73 987	86 221	31 450
4100 Recurrent taxes on immovable property	0	4 753	12 941	13 941	15 295	17 637	19 902	680
4110 Households	-	-	-	-	-	-	-	-
4120 Others	0	4 753	12 941	13 941	15 295	17 637	19 902	680
Tax on rural land property (ITR)	0	234	313	395	414	483	568	680
Tax on urban land property (IPTU)	0	4 519	12 628	13 546	14 882	17 154	19 334	-
4200 Recurrent taxes on net wealth	-	-	-	-	-	-	-	-
4210 Individual								
4220 Corporate								
4300 Estate, inheritance and gift taxes	0	329	1 208	1 489	1 677	2 517	2 766	-
4310 Estate and inheritance taxes	0	329	1 208	1 489	1 677	2 517	2 766	-
4320 Gift taxes	-	-	-	-	-	-	-	-
4400 Taxes on financial and capital transactions	0	18 442	47 603	25 464	23 732	32 472	39 446	30 770
Tax on financial operations (IOF)	0	3 096	7 817	20 168	19 223	26 571	31 998	30 770
Real estate property transfers (ITBI)	0	950	3 467	4 324	4 546	5 919	7 369	-
Other	-	14 396	36 320	971	-36	-18	79	-
4500 Non-recurrent taxes	-	-	-	-	-	-	-	-
4510 On net wealth								
4520 Other non-recurrent taxes								
4600 Other recurrent taxes on property	0	5 294	14 626	17 031	20 103	21 361	24 107	-

Table 12 - Cuadro 12 *(cont)*

BRAZIL - BRASIL

Details of tax revenue, in millions of reais

	1990	2000	2007	2008	2009	2010	2011	2012
5000 Taxes on goods and services	2	164 144	390 391	461 228	455 971	558 674	636 421	630 250
5100 Taxes on production, sale, transfer, etc	2	162 575	383 345	453 039	448 033	542 045	617 411	630 250
5110 General taxes	2	154 130	350 384	415 059	416 975	497 791	564 210	596 400
5111 Value added taxes	1	100 978	207 303	246 178	247 557	293 449	324 976	375 710
Tax on the circulation of goods and services (ICMS)	1	82 279	186 681	221 213	227 564	267 977	297 299	329 780
Tax on industrialized products (IPI)	0	18 699	20 622	24 965	19 993	25 472	27 677	45 930
5112 Sales tax	0	47 046	122 296	143 864	142 000	171 503	200 718	220 690
Contribution for financing social security (COFINS)	0	38 707	100 556	118 431	116 281	140 809	164 815	174 470
PIS contribution	0	8 339	21 741	25 433	25 719	30 694	35 903	46 220
5113 Other	0	6 106	20 784	25 017	27 419	32 839	38 516	-
5120 Taxes on specific goods and services	-	8 445	32 962	37 980	31 057	44 254	53 202	33 850
5121 Excises	-	-	18 560	17 657	12 568	19 576	22 481	2 740
5122 Profits of fiscal monopolies	-	-	-	-	-	-	-	-
5123 Customs and import duties	-	8 445	12 216	17 101	15 834	21 118	26 759	31 110
5124 Taxes on exports	-	-	-	-	-	-	-	-
5125 Taxes on investment goods	-	-	-	-	-	-	-	-
5126 Taxes on specific services	-	-	1 381	2 305	1 511	2 348	2 455	-
5127 Other taxes on international trade and transactions	-	-	-	-	-	-	-	-
5128 Other taxes	-	-	805	917	1 145	1 211	1 507	-
5130 Unallocable between 5110 and 5120	-	-	-	-	-	-	-	-
5200 Taxes on use of goods and perform activities	0	1 569	7 046	8 189	7 938	16 629	19 010	-
5210 Recurrent taxes	0	1 569	7 046	8 189	7 938	16 629	19 010	-
5211 Paid by households: motor vehicles	0	1 569	7 046	8 189	7 938	16 629	19 010	-
5212 Paid by others: motor vehicles								
5213 Paid in respect of other goods								
5220 Non-recurrent taxes								
5300 Unallocable between 5100 and 5200	-	-	-	-	-	-	-	-
6000 Other taxes	0	3 036	6 145	6 401	7 021	11 995	9 848	185 970
6100 Paid solely by business	-	-	307	186	180	212	356	560
Revenue service development fund (FUNDAF)	-	-	307	186	180	212	356	560
6200 Other	0	3 036	5 839	6 215	6 841	11 784	9 492	185 410
Other federal taxes	0	941	39	45	44	22	-	57 800
Other social contributions	0	1 273	1 935	2 076	2 513	3 120	-	-
Other state taxes	0	322	1 498	1 716	1 795	-	-	49 520
Other municipal taxes	0	377	2 367	2 379	2 488	8 642	9 492	78 090
Total tax revenue on cash basis	3	354 883	900 043	1 029 744	1 056 603	1 251 674	1 444 569	1 597 020

Year ending 31st December.

The data are on cash basis.

Headings 3000, 5112 and 6200: For years prior to 2000, as well as for 2012, the PASEP contributions under heading 3000 are included in the total for PIS contributions under heading 5112. For 2012, revenue from the other taxes under heading 3000 is included in category 6200.

Headings 5111 and 5121: From 2007 to 2011, a portion of the IPI is levied separately as an excise tax on automobiles, beverages, and tobacco products.

Heading 6200: The figure for 2012 includes IPTU (heading 4120), ITCD (heading 4300), ITBI (4400), IPVA (4600), ISS (5113) and Taxas Estaduais (5211).

Source: Figures published by Secretaria da Receita Federal (Ministry of Finance) in Carga Tributária no Brasil.

StatLink http://dx.doi.org/10.1787/888932971216

Table 13 - Cuadro 13

CHILE - CHILE

Details of tax revenue, in millions of chilean pesos

	1990	2000	2007	2008	2009	2010	2011	2012
Total tax revenue	1 777 218	7 901 998	20 599 131	20 081 681	16 595 349	21 678 481	25 762 449	27 196 360
1000 Taxes on income, profits and capital gains	412 974	1 841 630	9 412 056	7 536 172	5 162 043	8 329 060	10 322 824	10 803 031
1100 Of individuals	99 154	604 100	989 348	1 146 546	1 252 672	1 492 837	1 690 230	1 893 620
Second category tax	65 552	490 980	993 129	1 110 643	1 239 815	1 449 099	1 663 293	1 917 675
Global complementary tax	33 603	113 120	-3 781	35 903	12 857	43 738	26 936	-24 055
1110 On income and profits								
1120 On capital gains								
1200 Corporate	219 586	882 896	6 054 487	4 805 522	4 110 485	4 448 745	6 021 408	7 560 906
First category tax	200 891	815 747	5 084 996	4 252 551	3 729 488	3 913 870	5 254 907	6 770 329
Surtax on state owned enterprises	16 074	47 634	113 334	92 949	44 974	194 203	116 725	80 084
Mining tax	-	-	835 452	417 214	312 473	298 558	598 790	619 150
Other	2 621	19 516	20 705	42 808	23 550	42 114	50 987	91 343
1210 On profits								
1220 On capital gains								
1300 Unallocable between 1100 and 1200	94 233	354 634	2 368 221	1 584 104	-201 114	2 387 478	2 611 186	1 348 506
Additional tax	59 082	350 301	1 462 715	1 363 357	1 023 497	1 414 057	1 187 866	1 178 917
Other	35 151	4 332	905 507	220 747	-1 224 610	973 421	1 423 320	169 589
2000 Social security contributions	159 559	576 758	1 148 647	1 289 225	1 371 750	1 493 987	1 623 818	1 422 554
2100 Employees	154 021	553 937	1 098 620	1 229 912	1 312 793	1 433 159	1 565 828	1 422 554
2110 On a payroll basis	154 021	553 937	1 098 620	1 229 912	1 312 793	1 433 159	1 565 828	1 742 526
2120 On an income tax basis	-	-	-	-	-	-	-	-
2200 Employers	5 538	22 821	50 027	59 313	58 957	60 828	57 990	59 942
2210 On a payroll basis	5 538	22 821	50 027	59 313	58 957	60 828	57 990	59 942
2220 On an income tax basis	-	-	-	-	-	-	-	-
2300 Self-employed or non-employed	-	-	-	-	-	-	-	-
2310 On a payroll basis								
2320 On an income tax basis								
2400 Unallocable between 2100, 2200 and 2300	-	-	-	-	-	-	-	-
2410 On a payroll basis								
2420 On an income tax basis								
3000 Taxes on payroll and workforce	-	-	-	-	-	-	-	-
4000 Taxes on property	109 319	554 037	1 013 571	1 080 090	795 084	785 364	1 027 627	1 138 062
4100 Recurrent taxes on immovable property	59 968	302 244	496 311	541 268	532 279	549 125	731 191	746 674
4110 Households								
4120 Others								
4200 Recurrent taxes on net wealth	-	-	-	-	-	-	-	-
4210 Individual								
4220 Corporate								
4300 Estate, inheritance and gift taxes	3 444	10 906	28 501	35 554	200 203	39 338	30 876	66 719
4310 Estate and inheritance taxes								
4320 Gift taxes								
4400 Taxes on financial and capital transactions	45 907	240 886	488 759	503 269	62 602	196 901	265 560	324 669
4500 Non-recurrent taxes	-	-	-	-	-	-	-	-
4510 On net wealth								
4520 Other non-recurrent taxes								
4600 Other recurrent taxes on property	-	-	-	-	-	-	-	-

Table 13 - Cuadro 13 *(cont)*

CHILE - CHILE

Details of tax revenue, in millions of chilean pesos

	1990	2000	2007	2008	2009	2010	2011	2012
5000 Taxes on goods and services	1 118 722	5 041 769	9 023 834	10 166 189	9 271 910	11 131 188	12 700 180	13 777 358
5100 Taxes on production, sale, transfer, etc	1 074 009	4 789 827	8 578 804	9 650 260	8 724 696	10 514 822	11 963 914	13 036 137
5110 General taxes	664 421	3 306 350	6 781 501	7 912 009	7 051 079	8 399 926	9 536 786	10 447 374
5111 Value added taxes	664 421	3 306 350	6 781 501	7 912 009	7 051 079	8 399 926	9 536 786	10 447 374
5112 Sales tax	-	-	-	-	-	-	-	-
5113 Other	-	-	-	-	-	-	-	-
5120 Taxes on specific goods and services	409 588	1 483 477	1 797 303	1 738 251	1 673 617	2 114 896	2 427 128	2 588 763
5121 Excises	166 050	816 160	1 300 012	1 190 726	1 248 243	1 561 205	1 750 916	1 892 713
Cigarettes and tobacco	60 604	283 275	455 595	504 480	556 651	647 637	744 302	783 995
Gasoline and diesel	105 445	532 885	844 249	661 380	684 698	913 568	1 006 614	1 108 718
Oil stabilisation fund	-	-	168	24 866	6 894	-	-	-
5122 Profits of fiscal monopolies	-	-	-	-	-	-	-	-
5123 Customs and import duties	222 486	548 571	300 416	307 265	162 987	267 331	301 828	314 441
5124 Taxes on exports	-	-	-	-	-	-	-	-
5125 Taxes on investment goods	-	-	-	-	-	-	-	-
5126 Taxes on specific services	21 052	118 746	196 875	240 260	262 387	286 360	374 384	381 609
5127 Other taxes on internat trade and transactions	-	-	-	-	-	-	-	-
5128 Other taxes	-	-	-	-	-	-	-	-
5130 Unallocable between 5110 and 5120	-	-	-	-	-	-	-	-
5200 Taxes on use of goods and perform activities	44 714	251 942	445 030	515 929	547 214	616 366	736 266	741 221
5210 Recurrent taxes	44 714	251 942	445 030	515 929	547 214	616 366	736 266	741 221
Motor vehicles	24 469	93 880	155 158	177 167	171 141	197 145	267 116	267 116
5211 Paid by households: motor vehicles	-	-	-	-	-	-	-	-
5212 Paid by others: motor vehicles	-	-	-	-	-	-	-	-
5213 Paid in respect of other goods	20 245	158 062	289 872	338 762	376 073	419 221	469 150	474 105
Municipal permits	18 401	136 138	263 996	307 349	342 861	382 245	425 138	425 138
Mining patents	3 374	34 730	25 184	30 391	32 690	36 213	42 944	47 899
Other	-1 530	-12 806	692	1 022	522	763	1 068	1 068
5220 Non-recurrent taxes	-	-	-	-	-	-	-	-
5300 Unallocable between 5100 and 5200	-	-	-	-	-	-	-	-
6000 Other taxes	-23 356	-112 195	1 023	10 005	-5 438	-61 117	88 000	55 355
6100 Paid solely by business	-	-	-	-	-	-	-	-
6200 Other	-23 356	-112 195	1 023	10 005	-5 438	-61 117	88 000	55 355
Total tax revenue on cash basis	1 777 218	7 901 998	20 599 131	20 081 681	16 595 349	21 678 481	25 762 449	27 196 360

Year ending 31st December.

The data are on cash basis.

Heading 5121: In ECLAC data, figures from the Oil Prices Stabilisation Fund (FEPP) are considered as non tax revenues.

Source: Servicio de Impuestos Internos (Chile's Tax Service).

StatLink http://dx.doi.org/10.1787/888932971235

Table 14 - Cuadro 14

COLOMBIA - COLOMBIA

Details of tax revenue, in millions of colombian pesos

	1990	2000	2007	2008	2009	2010	2011	2012
Total tax revenue	2 579 426	30 512 910	82 309 367	90 247 961	93 871 843	98 006 164	117 024 569	130 201 595
1000 Taxes on income, profits and capital gains	771 694	7 103 525	24 010 404	24 448 371	28 090 176	26 190 739	33 495 576	43 649 796
1100 Of individuals	47 210	127 908	813 650	583 411	571 952	741 826	795 276	868 206
1110 On income and profits	47 210	127 908	813 650	583 411	571 952	741 826	795 276	868 206
1120 On capital gains	-	-	-	-	-	-	-	-
1200 Corporate	359 758	1 180 627	10 534 870	8 910 177	11 107 651	7 771 373	11 340 109	20 307 550
1210 On profits	359 758	1 180 627	10 534 870	8 910 177	11 107 651	7 771 373	11 340 109	20 307 550
Ecopetrol	-	246 231	1 500 000	1 807 944	3 878 357	2 990 687	6 951 384	7 913 516
Other	359 758	934 396	9 034 870	7 102 233	7 229 294	4 780 686	4 388 725	12 394 034
1220 On capital gains	-	-	-	-	-	-	-	-
1300 Unallocable between 1100 and 1200	364 726	5 794 990	12 661 884	14 954 783	16 410 573	17 677 540	21 360 191	22 474 040
2000 Social security contributions	203 596	6 275 803	12 492 906	12 809 259	13 922 895	15 500 589	14 783 716	16 145 691
2100 Employees	-	-	-	-	-	-	-	-
2110 On a payroll basis								
2120 On an income tax basis								
2200 Employers	-	1 286 803	2 798 906	3 178 259	3 587 147	4 022 503	4 479 886	4 728 094
2210 On a payroll basis		1 286 803	2 798 906	3 178 259	3 587 147	4 022 503	4 479 886	4 728 094
2220 On an income tax basis								
2300 Self-employed or non-employed	-	-	-	-	-	-	-	-
2310 On a payroll basis								
2320 On an income tax basis								
2400 Unallocable between 2100, 2200 and 2300	203 596	4 989 000	9 694 000	9 631 000	10 335 748	11 478 085	10 303 830	11 417 597
2410 On a payroll basis	203 596	4 989 000	9 694 000	9 631 000	10 335 748	11 478 085	10 303 830	11 417 597
2420 On an income tax basis	-	-	-	-	-	-	-	-
3000 Taxes on payroll and workforce	-	-	-	-	-	-	-	-
4000 Taxes on property	56 160	2 027 654	6 459 259	8 932 264	8 220 499	8 359 387	13 017 232	13 569 222
4100 Recurrent taxes on immovable property	56 160	991 070	2 298 829	2 532 996	3 076 434	3 163 084	3 707 079	3 917 577
4110 Households	-	-	-	-	-	-	-	-
4120 Others	56 160	991 070	2 298 829	2 532 996	3 076 434	3 163 084	3 707 079	3 917 577
4200 Recurrent taxes on net wealth	-	-	1 170 908	3 199 668	2 022 787	1 970 530	4 240 547	4 183 293
4210 Individual	-	-	1 170 908	3 199 668	2 022 787	1 970 530	4 240 547	4 183 293
4220 Corporate			-	-	-	-	-	-
4300 Estate, inheritance and gift taxes	-	-	-	-	-	-	-	-
4310 Estate and inheritance taxes								
4320 Gift taxes								
4400 Taxes on financial and capital transactions	-	1 036 584	2 989 522	3 199 600	3 121 278	3 225 773	5 069 606	5 468 352
4500 Non-recurrent taxes	-	-	-	-	-	-	-	-
4510 On net wealth								
4520 Other non-recurrent taxes								
4600 Other recurrent taxes on property	-	-	-	-	-	-	-	-

Table 14 - Cuadro 14 *(cont)*

COLOMBIA - COLOMBIA

Details of tax revenue, in millions of colombian pesos

	1990	2000	2007	2008	2009	2010	2011	2012
5000 Taxes on goods and services	1 388 653	13 367 908	34 750 053	39 194 218	38 090 163	42 063 441	48 790 355	50 246 323
5100 Taxes on production, sale, transfer, etc	1 388 653	13 367 908	34 750 053	39 194 218	38 090 163	42 063 441	48 790 355	50 246 323
5110 General taxes	672 368	9 585 866	26 910 512	31 074 221	30 185 624	33 118 301	39 941 309	41 698 551
5111 Value added taxes	583 078	8 445 776	23 377 821	27 064 094	25 910 469	28 811 682	35 093 071	36 291 054
5112 Sales tax	89 290	1 140 090	3 532 691	4 010 127	4 275 155	4 306 620	4 848 238	5 407 497
Industry and commerce tax (State)	89 290	1 140 090	3 532 691	4 010 127	4 275 155	4 306 620	4 848 238	5 407 497
5113 Other	-	-	-	-	-	-	-	-
5120 Taxes on specific goods and services	716 285	3 782 042	7 839 541	8 119 997	7 904 539	8 945 140	8 849 045	8 547 773
5121 Excises	404 699	2 037 944	3 579 755	3 828 119	3 903 697	4 293 141	4 768 330	5 026 180
Petrol	141 270	833 004	1 211 511	1 287 969	1 291 493	1 418 766	1 603 227	1 755 000
Tobacco (State)	52 898	213 410	330 016	333 170	317 317	391 852	471 441	447 731
Beer (State)	85 722	471 137	1 203 838	1 268 054	1 381 248	1 434 560	1 444 067	1 565 738
Liquors (State)	124 808	520 393	834 390	938 925	913 640	1 047 963	1 249 595	1 257 711
5122 Profits of fiscal monopolies	-	-	-	-	-	-	-	-
5123 Customs and import duties	311 586	1 744 097	4 259 786	4 291 878	4 000 842	4 651 999	4 080 716	3 521 593
Custom duties	180 989	1 744 097	4 259 786	4 291 878	4 000 842	4 651 999	4 080 716	3 521 593
Imports surcharge	130 597	-	-	-	-	-	-	-
5124 Taxes on exports	-	-	-	-	-	-	-	-
5125 Taxes on investment goods	-	-	-	-	-	-	-	-
5126 Taxes on specific services	-	-	-	-	-	-	-	-
5127 Other taxes on internat trade and transactions	-	-	-	-	-	-	-	-
5128 Other taxes	-	-	-	-	-	-	-	-
5130 Unallocable between 5110 and 5120	-	-	-	-	-	-	-	-
5200 Taxes on use of goods and perform activities	-	-	-	-	-	-	-	-
5210 Recurrent taxes								
5211 Paid by households: motor vehicles								
5212 Paid by others: motor vehicles								
5213 Paid in respect of other goods								
5220 Non-recurrent taxes								
5300 Unallocable between 5100 and 5200	-	-	-	-	-	-	-	-
6000 Other taxes	159 323	1 738 020	4 596 744	4 863 849	5 548 110	5 892 008	6 937 690	6 590 563
6100 Paid solely by business	-	-	-	-	-	-	-	-
6200 Other	159 323	1 738 020	4 596 744	4 863 849	5 548 110	5 892 008	6 937 690	6 590 563
Stamp tax	-	401 497	759 787	768 580	611 832	357 160	123 923	55 240
Other	78 306	79 287	86 297	88 790	120 721	125 688	142 267	154 000
Other (sub-national)	81 017	1 257 236	3 750 660	4 006 478	4 815 557	5 409 160	6 671 500	6 381 323
Total tax revenue on cash basis	2 579 426	30 512 910	82 309 367	90 247 961	93 871 843	98 006 164	117 024 569	130 201 595

Year ending 31st December.

The data are on cash basis.

Includes the reported consolidated revenues of the territorial entities (departments and municipalities).

Source: Ministry of Finance and Central Bank of Colombia.

StatLink http://dx.doi.org/10.1787/888932971254

Table 15 - Cuadro 15

COSTA RICA - COSTA RICA

Details of tax revenue, in millions of colones

	1990	2000	2007	2008	2009	2010	2011	2012
Total tax revenue	106 778	893 812	2 948 447	3 515 365	3 501 310	3 905 683	4 356 629	4 757 915
1000 Taxes on income, profits and capital gains	11 820	128 805	531 552	689 225	687 420	748 093	828 691	891 669
1100 Of individuals	-	-	123 194	104 536	156 936	202 849	233 486	307 489
1110 On income and profits			123 194	104 536	156 936	202 849	233 486	307 489
1120 On capital gains			-	-	-	-	-	-
1200 Corporate	-	-	348 826	481 736	444 242	450 312	486 001	461 481
1210 On profits			348 826	481 736	444 242	450 312	486 001	461 481
1220 On capital gains			-	-	-	-	-	-
1300 Unallocable between 1100 and 1200	11 820	128 805	59 531	102 953	86 241	94 932	109 204	122 699
2000 Social security contributions	29 065	249 886	742 115	889 807	996 692	1 148 663	1 291 105	1 414 755
2100 Employees	-	3 405	6 964	7 465	8 777	9 649	11 014	12 936
2110 On a payroll basis		3 405	6 964	7 465	8 777	9 649	11 014	12 936
2120 On an income tax basis		-	-	-	-	-	-	-
2200 Employers	-	-	-	-	-	-	-	-
2210 On a payroll basis								
2220 On an income tax basis								
2300 Self-employed or non-employed	-	5 858	20 987	24 555	30 656	33 778	36 733	39 462
2310 On a payroll basis		5 858	20 987	24 555	30 656	33 778	36 733	39 462
2320 On an income tax basis		-	-	-	-	-	-	-
2400 Unallocable between 2100, 2200 and 2300	29 065	240 623	714 164	857 787	957 260	1 105 236	1 243 358	1 362 357
2410 On a payroll basis								
2420 On an income tax basis								
3000 Taxes on payroll and workforce	7 054	41 918	110 609	135 865	148 902	165 443	182 538	205 971
4000 Taxes on property	366	12 681	42 658	46 610	48 040	63 663	70 927	81 868
4100 Recurrent taxes on immovable property	-	5 310	21 568	27 700	34 233	47 607	50 279	2 638
Land tax		-	-	-	-	-	-	-
Additional land tax		-	-	-	-	-	-	-
Tax on sumptuary constructions		-	-	-	-	-	-	-
Immovable property tax		-	-	-	55	3 527	2 475	2 638
Municipal immovable property tax		5 310	21 568	27 700	34 178	44 080	47 804	58 280
4110 Households								
4120 Others								
4200 Recurrent taxes on net wealth	-	4 284	-	-	-	-	-	-
4210 Individual		-						
4220 Corporate		4 284						
Tax on corporate assets		4 284						
4300 Estate, inheritance and gift taxes	-	-	-	-	-	-	-	-
4310 Estate and inheritance taxes								
4320 Gift taxes								
4400 Taxes on financial and capital transactions	366	3 007	19 366	17 204	12 734	14 743	19 053	20 950
4500 Non-recurrent taxes	-	-	-	-	-	-	-	-
4510 On net wealth								
4520 Other non-recurrent taxes								
4600 Other recurrent taxes on property	-	80	1 724	1 706	1 072	1 313	1 595	-

Table 15 - Cuadro 15 *(cont)*

COSTA RICA - COSTA RICA

Details of tax revenue, in millions of colones

	1990	2000	2007	2008	2009	2010	2011	2012
5000 Taxes on goods and services	52 360	456 707	1 505 545	1 737 642	1 606 222	1 762 591	1 963 833	2 122 589
5100 Taxes on production, sale, transfer, etc	49 980	437 334	1 449 974	1 665 700	1 524 363	1 664 652	1 872 449	2 015 909
5110 General taxes	21 326	222 775	797 850	936 721	830 538	920 298	1 029 811	1 122 978
5111 Value added taxes	21 326	222 775	797 850	936 721	830 538	920 298	1 029 811	1 122 978
5112 Sales tax	-	-	-	-	-	-	-	-
5113 Other	-	-	-	-	-	-	-	-
5120 Taxes on specific goods and services	28 654	213 499	648 428	722 432	688 697	739 494	837 573	813 013
5121 Excises	11 096	157 204	447 168	485 696	481 147	523 617	596 268	629 423
Fuels and energy	-	-	250 577	268 070	308 274	320 638	359 425	354 149
Alcoholic beverages	-	8 229	23 802	29 413	29 639	28 035	32 936	35 620
Non alcoholic beverages	-	-	18 263	22 716	24 426	26 566	27 804	30 205
Soaps	-	-	883	1 009	1 110	1 317	1 425	1 487
Cement	-	-	-	220	253	227	250	247
Tobacco	-	-	-	-	-	-	-	19 852
Abolished specific taxes on production and consumption	-	31 756	-	-	-	-	-	-
Other specific taxes on consumption	11 096	117 219	153 643	164 268	117 444	146 834	174 428	187 863
Transfers of exempted vehicles	-	-	-	-	-	-	-	-
5122 Profits of fiscal monopolies	-	-	-	-	-	-	-	-
5123 Customs and import duties	15 053	40 485	134 576	156 816	117 256	126 135	146 511	152 275
Import duties	13 977	32 336	107 565	124 550	97 001	103 851	122 355	128 358
Custom duties	1 076	8 149	27 011	32 266	20 255	22 284	24 156	23 917
Import duties on animals	-	-	-	-	-	-	-	-
Temporary import surcharges	-	-	-	-	-	-	-	-
5124 Taxes on exports	2 226	2 238	2 432	4 667	4 677	3 973	3 990	3 823
Export duties	2 226	1 835	2 260	4 508	4 534	3 816	3 827	3 663
Export duties Law 133	-	-	-	-	-	-	-	-
Export duties Law 5519	-	253	-	-	-	-	-	-
Tax on banana exports	-	150	172	160	143	157	163	160
Export duties on flora and fauna	-	-	-	-	-	-	-	-
5125 Taxes on investment goods	-	-	-	-	-	-	-	-
5126 Taxes on specific services	280	13 488	63 419	74 376	84 619	84 270	88 744	25 579
Casinos and gambling	-	225	442	458	411	445	288	213
Electronic betting business	-	-	-	-	-	-	-	-
Port cargo movements	-	6	0	-	12	-	-	-
Overseas departure tax	-	-	22 799	24 939	24 794	24 322	23 902	25 366
10% on public shows	-	26	-	-	-	-	-	-
Pro-national airport's stamp tax	-	6	-	-	-	-	-	-
Stamp tax on the use of borders and ports	280	2 697	-	-	-	-	-	-
Municipal licences and permits	-	8 692	31 888	39 841	52 492	52 637	55 606	-
Municipal tax on constructions	-	1 836	8 290	9 137	6 910	6 866	8 948	-
5127 Other taxes on internat trade and transactions	-	83	832	877	998	1 499	2 060	1 913
5128 Other taxes	-	-	-	-	-	-	-	-
5130 Unallocable between 5110 and 5120	-	1 061	3 696	6 547	5 128	4 860	5 065	79 918
5200 Taxes on use of goods and perform activities	2 380	19 357	55 536	71 871	81 705	97 803	91 266	106 557
5210 Recurrent taxes	2 380	19 357	55 536	71 871	81 705	97 803	91 266	106 557
5211 Paid by households: motor vehicles	-	-	-	-	-	-	-	-

Table 15 - Cuadro 15 *(cont)*

COSTA RICA - COSTA RICA

Details of tax revenue, in millions of colones

	1990	2000	2007	2008	2009	2010	2011	2012
5212 Paid by others: motor vehicles	1 425	15 487	52 511	68 299	77 924	94 101	85 152	101 903
Property tax on vehicles, aircraft and boats	1 425	15 374	52 511	68 299	77 924	94 101	85 152	101 903
Special tax on the use of public roads	-	113	-	-	-	-	-	-
5213 Paid in respect of other goods	955	3 870	3 025	3 572	3 781	3 702	6 114	4 654
Hunting and fishing licences	-	0	-	-	-	-	0	-
Hunting and fishing licences (Ministry of Natural Resources, Energy and Mines)	-	4	0	-	-	-	-	-
Spirits license	-	-	-	-	-	-	-	-
Revenue stamps	955	3 866	3 025	3 572	3 781	3 702	6 114	4 654
Sport stamp tax	-	0	-	-	-	-	-	-
5220 Non-recurrent taxes	-	-	-	-	-	-	-	-
5300 Unallocable between 5100 and 5200	-	15	35	71	153	136	118	123
6000 Other taxes	6 113	3 816	15 968	16 216	14 034	17 230	19 535	41 063
6100 Paid solely by business	-	15	1 629	1 068	521	459	526	22 724
6200 Other	6 113	3 801	14 339	15 148	13 513	16 771	19 009	18 339
Transfers of vehicles, aircraft and boats	497	2 530	9 937	10 554	9 612	12 311	13 672	12 947
Total tax revenue on cash basis	106 778	893 812	2 948 447	3 515 365	3 501 310	3 905 683	4 356 629	4 757 915

Year ending 31st December.

The data are on cash basis.

The figures for years up to and including 1997 exclude local government revenues as the data are not available.

Heading 2000: In ECLAC data, social security contributions include INA, IMAS, and FODESAF.

Heading 3000: In ECLAC data, social security contributions from decentralized institutions are considered in category 2000.

Heading 5121: In ECLAC data, the tax on transfers of vehicles is classified as a property tax 4000.

Heading 5212: In ECLAC data, Property tax on vehicles, aircraft and boats is classified in category 4000.

Heading 6000: In ECALC data, the tax on the transfer of used vehicles Law No. 7088 of 30/11/87 is classified as a property tax (4000).

Source: Secretaría Técnica de la Autoridad Presupuestaria, Ministry of Finance and Contraloría General de la República.

StatLink http://dx.doi.org/10.1787/888932971273

Table 16 - Cuadro 16

DOMINICAN REPUBLIC - REPÚBLICA DOMINICANA

Details of tax revenue, in millions of dominican pesos

	1990	2000	2007	2008	2009	2010	2011	2012
Total tax revenue	6 416	48 310	217 965	236 166	220 373	243 943	273 132	312 064
1000 Taxes on income, profits and capital gains	1 670	7 060	45 805	47 866	42 367	40 496	49 426	76 315
1100 Of individuals	-	366	5 237	5 913	3 676	3 941	4 894	5 772
1110 On income and profits	-	348	5 098	5 700	3 438	3 754	4 441	5 473
1120 On capital gains	-	18	139	213	238	187	453	299
1200 Corporate	-	4 679	29 203	26 999	22 546	21 475	25 083	46 624
1210 On profits	-	4 605	29 063	26 853	22 414	21 325	24 900	46 411
1220 On capital gains	-	74	140	146	132	151	182	213
Casinos	-	59	140	146	132	151	182	213
Racetracks	-	15	-	-	-	-	-	-
1300 Unallocable between 1100 and 1200	1 670	2 015	11 365	14 954	16 145	15 080	19 450	23 919
2000 Social security contributions	53	490	860	860	1 009	1 845	1 328	1 250
2100 Employees	-	-	-	-	-	-	-	-
2110 On a payroll basis								
2120 On an income tax basis								
2200 Employers	-	-	-	-	-	-	-	-
2210 On a payroll basis								
2220 On an income tax basis								
2300 Self-employed or non-employed	-	-	-	-	-	-	-	-
2310 On a payroll basis								
2320 On an income tax basis								
2400 Unallocable between 2100, 2200 and 2300	53	490	860	860	1 009	1 845	1 328	1 250
2410 On a payroll basis	-	-	-	-	-	-	-	-
2420 On an income tax basis	-	-	-	-	-	-	-	-
3000 Taxes on payroll and workforce	-	3 722	9 428	10 668	11 761	13 147	15 779	15 959
4000 Taxes on property	46	505	9 713	11 441	11 127	12 738	15 306	18 867
4100 Recurrent taxes on immovable property	9	115	1 875	2 567	2 702	3 004	5 235	8 351
4110 Households	9	115	594	552	473	555	629	686
4120 Others	-	-	1 281	2 016	2 230	2 449	4 605	7 665
Tax on assets	-	-	1 281	2 016	2 230	2 449	2 790	3 044
Tax on financial assets (Law 139-11)	-	-	-	-	-	-	1 816	4 620
4200 Recurrent taxes on net wealth	-	-	-	-	-	-	-	-
4210 Individual								
4220 Corporate								
4300 Estate, inheritance and gift taxes	11	96	143	221	199	231	237	227
4310 Estate and inheritance taxes								
4320 Gift taxes								
4400 Taxes on financial and capital transactions	22	217	7 123	7 876	7 181	8 125	8 255	8 723
Tax on checks	-	-	3 833	4 472	3 919	4 262	4 492	4 852
Real estate operations	22	217	3 291	3 404	3 262	3 864	3 763	3 872
4500 Non-recurrent taxes	3	32	270	324	282	488	578	609
4510 On net wealth	3	32	270	324	282	488	578	609
4520 Other non-recurrent taxes	-	-	-	-	-	-	-	-
4600 Other recurrent taxes on property	1	46	302	462	763	891	1 002	957
5000 Taxes on goods and services	4 488	36 038	150 604	165 306	154 105	175 716	191 294	199 673
5100 Taxes on production, sale, transfer, etc	4 410	35 281	148 276	163 286	151 840	173 403	188 560	196 473
5110 General taxes	973	10 195	66 982	74 319	69 877	81 871	89 610	92 819
5111 Value added taxes	973	10 195	66 982	74 319	69 877	81 871	89 610	92 819
5112 Sales tax	-	-	-	-	-	-	-	-
5113 Other	-	-	-	-	-	-	-	-

Table 16 - Cuadro 16 *(cont)*

DOMINICAN REPUBLIC - REPÚBLICA DOMINICANA

Details of tax revenue, in millions of dominican pesos

	1990	2000	2007	2008	2009	2010	2011	2012
5120 Taxes on specific goods and services	3 437	25 086	81 294	88 966	81 964	91 531	98 950	103 654
5121 Excises	500	6 474	51 906	57 192	52 445	60 144	67 174	71 033
Vehicle registration	-	-	4 140	4 798	3 163	4 234	4 268	4 505
Transfer tax	18	160	251	386	507	533	572	682
Alcoholic beverages	251	2 451	13 101	13 030	13 343	15 054	16 240	17 089
Tobacco products	102	469	3 283	4 180	4 131	4 529	4 241	4 470
Petroleum products	89	3 143	29 985	33 905	30 373	34 598	40 303	42 460
Other	39	251	1 145	894	927	1 197	1 549	1 827
5122 Profits of fiscal monopolies	-	-	-	-	-	-	-	-
5123 Customs and import duties	1 548	13 469	19 425	21 182	18 293	19 492	18 850	18 920
Customs duties	615	13 456	19 336	21 141	18 264	19 455	18 801	18 776
Other	933	13	89	41	29	37	49	144
5124 Taxes on exports	6	4	83	128	132	146	181	264
5125 Taxes on investment goods	-	-	-	-	-	-	-	-
5126 Taxes on specific services	347	1 593	9 215	10 017	10 799	11 407	12 404	13 128
Telecommunications	85	-	3 867	4 100	4 592	4 886	4 947	5 124
Insurance premiums	33	584	2 211	2 796	2 978	3 088	3 238	3 437
Travel tickets	204	809	3 131	3 073	3 222	3 428	3 632	3 951
Hotels	22	191	-	-	-	-	-	-
Others	4	9	7	48	6	5	588	616
5127 Other taxes on international trade and transactions	1 037	3 546	665	447	295	342	340	309
Exchange commission	857	3 412	233	187	45	70	-	-
Consular fees	77	32	342	143	138	132	138	130
Other	103	102	90	117	112	140	202	179
5128 Other taxes	-	-	-	-	-	-	-	-
5130 Unallocable between 5110 and 5120	-	-	-	-	-	-	-	-
5200 Taxes on use of goods and perform activities	77	757	2 329	2 020	2 265	2 313	2 733	3 199
5210 Recurrent taxes	77	757	2 329	2 020	2 265	2 313	2 733	3 199
5211 Paid by households: motor vehicles	45	268	1 391	1 183	1 225	1 277	1 300	1 271
5212 Paid by others: motor vehicles	-	-	-	-	-	-	-	-
5213 Paid in respect of other goods	33	489	938	837	1 040	1 036	1 433	1 929
Licenses to carry firearms	17	237	316	214	346	296	253	194
Licenses to operate gambling houses	-	114	217	187	199	211	571	1 076
Licenses to operate slot machines	4	60	371	385	409	457	528	567
Other	12	78	34	51	86	72	82	92
5220 Non-recurrent taxes	-	-	-	-	-	-	-	-
5300 Unallocable between 5100 and 5200	-	-	-	-	-	-	-	-
6000 Other taxes	159	495	1 555	25	5	-	-	0
6100 Paid solely by business	-	-	-	-	-	-	-	-
6200 Other	159	495	1 555	25	5	-	-	0
Total tax revenue on cash basis	6 416	48 310	217 965	236 166	220 373	243 943	273 132	312 064

Year ending 31st December.

The data are on a cash basis.

The data exclude local government revenues as the data are not available.

Heading 2000: The data exclude social security contributions to general government managed by the private sector.

Heading 5121: In ECLAC data, the tax on transfer of movable goods is classified as a propety tax (4000).

Heading 6000: In ECLAC data, the Vehicle transfer tax is classified as a property tax (4000).

Source: Ministerio de Hacienda - Ministry of Finance

StatLink http://dx.doi.org/10.1787/888932971292

Table 17 - Cuadro 17

ECUADOR - ECUADOR

Details of tax revenue, in millions of US dollars

	1990	2000	2007	2008	2009	2010	2011	2012
Total tax revenue	1 076	1 851	6 545	8 667	9 318	11 343	13 736	17 007
1000 Taxes on income, profits and capital gains	138	293	1 268	2 339	2 518	2 353	3 030	3 313
1100 Of individuals	-	-	-	-	-	-	-	-
1110 On income and profits								
1120 On capital gains								
1200 Corporate	-	-	-	-	-	-	-	-
1210 On profits	-	-	-	-	-	-	-	-
1220 On capital gains	-	-	-	-	-	-	-	-
1300 Unallocable between 1100 and 1200	138	293	1 268	2 339	2 518	2 353	3 030	3 313
2000 Social security contributions	243	228	1 795	2 097	2 061	2 549	3 971	4 752
2100 Employees	-	-	-	-	-	-	-	-
2110 On a payroll basis		-	-	-	-	-	-	-
2120 On an income tax basis								
2200 Employers	-	-	-	-	-	-	-	-
2210 On a payroll basis		-	-	-	-	-	-	-
2220 On an income tax basis		-	-	-	-	-	-	-
2300 Self-employed or non-employed	-	-	-	-	-	-	-	-
2310 On a payroll basis		-	-	-	-	-	-	-
2320 On an income tax basis		-	-	-	-	-	-	-
2400 Unallocable between 2100, 2200 and 2300	243	228	1 795	2 097	2 061	2 549	3 971	4 752
2410 On a payroll basis	-	-	-	-	-	-	-	-
2420 On an income tax basis	-	-	-	-	-	-	-	-
3000 Taxes on payroll and workforce	-	-	-	-	-	-	-	-
4000 Taxes on property	-	-	-	-	-	-	-	-
4100 Recurrent taxes on immovable property	-	-	-	-	-	-	-	-
4110 Households								
4120 Others								
4200 Recurrent taxes on net wealth	-	-	-	-	-	-	-	-
4210 Individual	-	-	-	-	-	-	-	-
4220 Corporate	-	-	-	-	-	-	-	-
4300 Estate, inheritance and gift taxes	-	-	-	-	-	-	-	-
4310 Estate and inheritance taxes								
4320 Gift taxes								
4400 Taxes on financial and capital transactions	-	-	-	-	-	-	-	-
4500 Non-recurrent taxes	-	-	-	-	-	-	-	-
4510 On net wealth								
4520 Other non-recurrent taxes								
4600 Other recurrent taxes on property	-	-	-	-	-	-	-	-
5000 Taxes on goods and services	668	1 330	3 479	4 183	4 508	6 152	6 707	8 830
5100 Taxes on production, sale, transfer, etc	665	1 319	3 407	4 088	4 390	5 997	6 533	8 636
5110 General taxes	302	836	2 509	2 825	3 019	3 886	4 200	5 415
5111 Value added taxes	302	836	2 509	2 825	3 019	3 886	4 200	5 415
5112 Sales tax	-	-	-	-	-	-	-	-
5113 Other	-	-	-	-	-	-	-	-

Table 17 - Cuadro 17 *(cont)*

ECUADOR - ECUADOR

Details of tax revenue, in millions of US dollars

	1990	2000	2007	2008	2009	2010	2011	2012
5120 Taxes on specific goods and services	363	483	898	1 263	1 372	2 110	2 332	3 221
5121 Excises	90	75	220	474	448	530	618	685
Alcohol products	-	30	70	-	-	-	-	-
Soft drinks and mineral water	-	9	15	-	-	-	-	-
Cigarettes	-	24	74	-	-	-	-	-
Luxury goods and vehicles	-	11	61	-	-	-	-	-
5122 Profits of fiscal monopolies	-	-	-	-	-	-	-	-
5123 Customs and import duties	227	217	679	789	923	1 152	1 156	1 261
5124 Taxes on exports	-	-	-	-	-	-	-	-
5125 Taxes on investment goods	-	-	-	-	-	-	-	-
5126 Taxes on specific services	7	17	-	-	-	428	558	1 275
Exit taxes	7	17	-	-	-	428	558	1 275
5127 Other taxes on internat trade and transactions	40	175	-	-	-	-	-	-
On capital movements	-	169	-	-	-	-	-	-
On purchase of foreign exchange	22	4	-	-	-	-	-	-
On credit operations in national currency	18	2	-	-	-	-	-	-
5128 Other taxes	-	-	-	-	-	-	-	-
5130 Unallocable between 5110 and 5120	-	-	-	-	-	-	-	-
5200 Taxes on use of goods and perform activities	3	11	72	95	118	156	174	194
5210 Recurrent taxes								
5211 Paid by households: motor vehicles								
5212 Paid by others: motor vehicles	3	11	72	95	118	156	174	194
Annual tax on motor vehicles	3	11	72	95	118	156	174	194
5213 Paid in respect of other goods								
5220 Non-recurrent taxes								
5300 Unallocable between 5100 and 5200	-	-	-	-	-	-	-	-
6000 Other taxes	27	-	3	48	231	289	28	111
6100 Paid solely by business	-	-	-	-	-	-	-	-
6200 Other	27	-	3	48	231	289	28	111
Total tax revenue on accrual basis	1 076	1 851	6 545	8 667	9 318	11 343	13 736	17 007

Year ending 31st December.

The data are on an accrual basis.

Social security data is recorded at the nonfinancial public sector level.

The figures exclude local government revenues as the data are not available.

Heading 5212: In ECLAC data, the annual tax on motor vehicles is classified as a property tax (4000).

Source: Banco Central del Ecuador

StatLink http://dx.doi.org/10.1787/888932971311

Table 18 - Cuadro 18

EL SALVADOR - EL SALVADOR

Details of tax revenue, in millions of US dollars

	1990	2000	2007	2008	2009	2010	2011	2012
Total tax revenue	506	1 607	3 056	3 240	2 966	3 180	3 410	3 726
1000 Taxes on income, profits and capital gains	95	429	933	1 004	948	940	1 020	1 184
1100 Of individuals	-	-	395	536	444	571	456	697
1110 On income and profits			395	536	444	571	456	697
1120 On capital gains			-	-	-	-	-	-
1200 Corporate	-	-	573	518	559	423	631	555
1210 On profits			573	518	559	423	631	555
1220 On capital gains			-	-	-	-	-	-
1300 Unallocable between 1100 and 1200	95	429	-35	-49	-55	-55	-66	-68
Income tax	95	429	-	-	-	-	-	-
Income tax refunds	-	-	-35	-49	-55	-55	-66	-68
2000 Social security contributions	67	263	331	356	358	369	382	404
2100 Employees	-	75	88	96	96	99	100	106
2110 On a payroll basis		75	88	96	96	99	100	106
2120 On an income tax basis		-	-	-	-	-	-	-
2200 Employers	-	176	214	230	230	238	245	260
2210 On a payroll basis		176	214	230	230	238	245	260
2220 On an income tax basis		-	-	-	-	-	-	-
2300 Self-employed or non-employed	-	13	29	29	31	33	36	38
2310 On a payroll basis		13	29	29	31	33	36	38
2320 On an income tax basis		-	-	-	-	-	-	-
2400 Unallocable between 2100, 2200 and 2300	67	-	-	-	-	-	-	-
2410 On a payroll basis	67							
2420 On an income tax basis	-							
3000 Taxes on payroll and workforce	-	-	-	-	-	-	-	-
4000 Taxes on property	26	12	21	18	13	16	16	20
4100 Recurrent taxes on immovable property	-	-	-	-	-	-	-	-
4110 Households								
4120 Others								
4200 Recurrent taxes on net wealth	16	-	-	-	-	-	-	-
4210 Individual	16							
4220 Corporate	-							
4300 Estate, inheritance and gift taxes	-	-	-	-	-	-	-	-
4310 Estate and inheritance taxes								
4320 Gift taxes								
4400 Taxes on financial and capital transactions	10	12	21	18	13	16	16	20
4500 Non-recurrent taxes	-	-	-	-	-	-	-	-
4510 On net wealth								
4520 Other non-recurrent taxes								
4600 Other recurrent taxes on property	-	-	-	-	-	-	-	-

Table 18 - Cuadro 18 *(cont)*

EL SALVADOR - EL SALVADOR

Details of tax revenue, in millions of US dollars

	1990	2000	2007	2008	2009	2010	2011	2012
5000 Taxes on goods and services	259	903	1 770	1 863	1 646	1 855	1 992	2 118
5100 Taxes on production, sale, transfer, etc	259	903	1 770	1 863	1 646	1 855	1 992	2 118
5110 General taxes	133	714	1 389	1 461	1 251	1 433	1 574	1 677
5111 Value added taxes	-	714	1 389	1 461	1 251	1 433	1 574	1 677
5112 Sales tax	-	-	-	-	-	-	-	-
5113 Other	133	-	-	-	-	-	-	-
5120 Taxes on specific goods and services	127	189	381	402	395	422	418	441
5121 Excises	65	49	169	194	202	218	203	226
Consumption of products	65	49	-	-	-	0	0	0
Alcoholic beverages	-	-	40	43	44	44	52	64
Cigarettes	-	-	30	27	31	31	38	40
Soft drinks	-	-	27	24	24	31	35	40
Beer	-	-	1	-	1	1	1	1
Weapons, ammunition and explosives	-	-	1	1	1	1	-	-
Special Contribution- Sugar	-	-	-	33	34	35	-	-
Special Contribution- Public transportation	-	-	70	65	68	69	69	71
Special Contribution- FOVIAL	-	-	-	-	-	7	8	9
5122 Profits of fiscal monopolies	-	-	-	-	-	-	-	-
5123 Customs and import duties	61	141	204	179	138	148	167	180
5124 Taxes on exports	-	-	-	-	-	-	-	-
5125 Taxes on investment goods	-	-	-	-	-	-	-	-
5126 Taxes on specific services	-	-	8	30	55	56	48	36
5127 Other taxes on internat trade and transactions	-	-	-	-	-	-	-	-
5128 Other taxes	-	-	-	-	-	-	-	-
5130 Unallocable between 5110 and 5120	-	-	-	-	-	-	-	-
5200 Taxes on use of goods and perform activities	-	-	-	-	-	-	-	-
5210 Recurrent taxes								
5211 Paid by households: motor vehicles								
5212 Paid by others: motor vehicles								
5213 Paid in respect of other goods								
5220 Non-recurrent taxes								
5300 Unallocable between 5100 and 5200	-	-	-	-	-	-	-	-
6000 Other taxes	58	0	-	-	-	-	-	-
6100 Paid solely by business	-	-						
6200 Other	58	0						
Total tax revenue on cash basis	506	1 607	3 056	3 240	2 966	3 180	3 410	3 726

Year ending 31st December.

The data are on cash basis.

The figures exclude local government revenues as the data are not available.

Heading 1000: For 2002 and from 2006 onwards sub-headings 1100 and 1200 are presented on a gross basis.

Heading 2000: Corresponds to social security contributions paid to the Salvadoran Institute of Social Security.

Heading 2000: Data on public pension contributions are not available for 2011 and 2012.

Source: Dirección General de Tesorería, Ministry of Finance (for national taxes). Central Reserve Bank of El Salvador from 1990 to 1996 and Salvadoran Institute of Social Security for subsequent years (for social security contribution figures).

StatLink http://dx.doi.org/10.1787/888932971330

Table 19 - Cuadro 19

GUATEMALA - GUATEMALA

Details of tax revenue, in millions of quetzales

	1990	2000	2007	2008	2009	2010	2011	2012
Total tax revenue	2 801	16 531	36 320	38 117	37 566	41 048	46 874	48 435
1000 Taxes on income, profits and capital gains	507	3 295	8 654	9 698	9 706	10 319	12 696	13 445
1100 Of individuals	25	143	877	945	1 060	1 225	1 462	1 477
1110 On income and profits	25	143	877	945	1 060	1 225	1 462	1 477
Personal income tax	25	137	877	945	1 060	1 225	1 462	1 476
Income from financial products	-	6	0	0	0	0	0	1
1120 On capital gains	-	-	-	-	-	-	-	-
1200 Corporate	482	3 149	5 729	6 417	6 141	6 520	8 609	9 119
1210 On profits	482	3 149	5 729	6 417	6 141	6 520	8 609	9 119
Corporate income tax	482	1 610	5 408	6 085	5 768	6 132	8 198	8 656
Income from financial products	-	248	312	322	371	386	403	463
Commercial and agricultural enterprises	-	1 291	9	11	2	2	8	0
1220 On capital gains	-	-	-	-	-	-	-	-
1300 Unallocable between 1100 and 1200	-	2	2 048	2 336	2 505	2 574	2 625	2 849
Extraordinary and temporary solidarity tax in support of peace agreements		-	2 047	2 336	677	44	54	4
Solidarity tax		-	-	-	1 829	2 530	2 571	2 845
Extraordinary and temporary solidarity tax		2	1	0	0	0	0	0
2000 Social security contributions	436	2 569	5 069	5 427	5 706	6 267	7 014	6 048
2100 Employees	-	-	-	-	-	-	-	-
2110 On a payroll basis								
2120 On an income tax basis								
2200 Employers	-	-	-	-	-	-	-	-
2210 On a payroll basis								
2220 On an income tax basis								
2300 Self-employed or non-employed	-	-	-	-	-	-	-	-
2310 On a payroll basis								
2320 On an income tax basis								
2400 Unallocable between 2100, 2200 and 2300	436	2 569	5 069	5 427	5 706	6 267	7 014	6 048
2410 On a payroll basis	436	2 569	5 069	5 427	5 706	6 267	7 014	6 048
2420 On an income tax basis	-	-	-	-	-	-	-	-
3000 Taxes on payroll and workforce	-	-	-	-	-	-	-	-
4000 Taxes on property	45	165	440	496	578	631	648	566
4100 Recurrent taxes on immovable property	-	153	426	481	569	621	635	558
4110 Households		-	-	-	-	-	-	-
4120 Others		153	426	481	569	621	635	558
Property tax		6	1	1	1	1	1	1
Property tax (municipal)		147	426	480	568	620	634	557
4200 Recurrent taxes on net wealth	-	-	-	-	-	-	-	-
4210 Individual								
4220 Corporate								
4300 Estate, inheritance and gift taxes	-	-	-	-	-	-	-	-
4310 Estate and inheritance taxes								
4320 Gift taxes								
4400 Taxes on financial and capital transactions	45	12	14	15	9	10	13	8
4500 Non-recurrent taxes	-	-	-	-	-	-	-	-
4510 On net wealth								
4520 Other non-recurrent taxes								
4600 Other recurrent taxes on property	-	-	-	-	-	-	-	-

Table 19 - Cuadro 19 *(cont)*

GUATEMALA - GUATEMALA

Details of tax revenue, in millions of quetzales

	1990	2000	2007	2008	2009	2010	2011	2012
5000 Taxes on goods and services	1 709	10 317	21 764	22 118	20 980	23 259	25 877	27 499
5100 Taxes on production, sale, transfer, etc	1 681	10 131	21 411	21 716	20 513	22 754	25 318	26 595
5110 General taxes	762	6 259	15 382	16 155	15 015	16 980	19 472	20 913
5111 Value added taxes	762	6 259	15 382	16 155	15 015	16 980	19 472	20 913
5112 Sales tax	-	-	-	-	-	-	-	-
5113 Other	-	-	-	-	-	-	-	-
5120 Taxes on specific goods and services	919	3 872	6 029	5 561	5 497	5 773	5 846	5 682
5121 Excises	258	1 797	2 946	2 822	3 058	3 101	3 013	3 072
Tobacco and derivatives	76	205	355	342	340	347	259	312
Beer	-	97	144	147	143	159	176	191
Alcoholic beverages	-	77	87	91	90	98	101	100
Soft drinks	-	15	195	196	200	220	245	263
Other beverages	77	12	1	2	1	2	2	1
Cement	-	-	117	105	99	99	104	102
Oil and derivatives	105	1 389	2 047	1 938	2 184	2 179	2 125	2 103
5122 Profits of fiscal monopolies	-	-	-	-	-	-	-	-
5123 Customs and import duties	506	1 806	2 654	2 427	2 139	2 368	2 533	2 311
5124 Taxes on exports	-	-	-	-	-	-	-	-
5125 Taxes on investment goods	-	-	-	-	-	-	-	-
5126 Taxes on specific services	155	269	429	311	301	304	301	299
5127 Other taxes on internat trade and transactions	-	-	-	-	-	-	-	-
5128 Other taxes	-	-	-	-	-	-	-	-
5130 Unallocable between 5110 and 5120	-	-	-	-	-	-	-	-
5200 Taxes on use of goods and perform activities	28	186	353	402	468	505	558	904
5210 Recurrent taxes	28	186	353	402	468	505	558	904
5211 Paid by households: motor vehicles	-	-	-	-	-	-	-	331
5212 Paid by others: motor vehicles	28	186	353	402	468	505	558	573
5213 Paid in respect of other goods	-	-	-	-	-	-	-	-
5220 Non-recurrent taxes	-	-	-	-	-	-	-	-
5300 Unallocable between 5100 and 5200	-	-	-	-	-	-	-	-
6000 Other taxes	104	186	393	378	596	572	639	878
6100 Paid solely by business	-	-	-	-	-	-	-	-
6200 Other	104	186	393	378	596	572	639	878
Revenue stamps and stamped paper	104	182	392	376	595	572	638	877
Other indirect taxes	-	4	1	2	1	1	1	1
Total tax revenue on cash basis	2 801	16 531	36 320	38 117	37 566	41 048	46 874	48 435

Year ending 31st December.

The data are on cash basis.

The figures exclude some local government revenues as the data are not available. Revenues from the municipal property tax (IUSI) are included. The current law (Decree 15-98) states that the IUSI can be collected by those municipalities that have indicated the technical and administrative capacity to collect and administer the tax.

Heading 2000: Corresponds to social security contributions paid to the Guatemalan Social Security Institute (IGSS) and payments by public employees to the government's pension fund.

Headings 4120 and 4400: For years prior to 2000 the property tax under heading 4120 is included in the total under heading 4400.

Heading 5121: Up to 1999 "Other beverages" contains all alcoholic and non-alcoholic beverages.

Source: Superintendencia de Administración Tributaria, Ministry of Finance (for national and local taxes). Guatemalan Social Security Institute (IGSS) from 1990 to 1994 and Superintendencia de Administración Tributaria for subsequent years (for social security contribution figures).

StatLink http://dx.doi.org/10.1787/888932971349

Table 20 - Cuadro 20

HONDURAS - HONDURAS

Details of tax revenue, in millions of lempiras

	1990	2000	2007	2008	2009	2010	2011	2012
Total tax revenue	2 032	16 347	44 307	49 637	47 157	51 844	56 479	63 412
1000 Taxes on income, profits and capital gains	431	2 985	11 982	13 443	12 658	13 972	16 979	17 531
1100 Of individuals	157	991	3 919	4 259	4 067	4 528	5 232	5 745
1110 On income and profits	157	991	3 919	4 259	4 067	4 528	5 232	5 745
1120 On capital gains	-	-	-	-	-	-	-	-
1200 Corporate	274	1 916	7 915	8 904	8 424	8 705	11 437	11 556
1210 On profits	274	1 916	7 915	8 904	8 424	8 705	11 437	11 556
Corporate income tax	274	1 916	6 877	7 572	7 230	7 400	9 447	10 088
Income tax surcharge	-	-	1 038	1 332	1 194	1 305	1 990	1 468
1220 On capital gains	-	-	-	-	-	-	-	-
1300 Unallocable between 1100 and 1200	-	78	148	279	167	740	310	230
Tax on net assets	-	78	148	279	167	359	310	230
Revaluation of assets	-	-	0	-	-	381	-	-
2000 Social security contributions	179	1 727	6 037	7 308	8 122	8 671	6 955	10 934
2100 Employees	-	-	-	-	-	-	-	-
2110 On a payroll basis								
2120 On an income tax basis								
2200 Employers	-	-	-	-	-	-	-	-
2210 On a payroll basis								
2220 On an income tax basis								
2300 Self-employed or non-employed	-	-	-	-	-	-	-	-
2310 On a payroll basis								
2320 On an income tax basis								
2400 Unallocable between 2100, 2200 and 2300	179	1 727	6 037	7 308	8 122	8 671	6 955	10 934
2410 On a payroll basis	179	1 727	6 037	7 308	8 122	8 671	6 955	10 934
2420 On an income tax basis	-	-	-	-	-	-	-	-
3000 Taxes on payroll and workforce	-	-	-	-	-	-	-	-
4000 Taxes on property	16	189	291	265	224	254	290	327
4100 Recurrent taxes on immovable property	-	-	-	-	-	-	-	-
4110 Households	-	-	-	-	-	-	-	-
4120 Others	-	-	-	-	-	-	-	-
4200 Recurrent taxes on net wealth	-	-	-	-	-	-	-	-
4210 Individual			-	-	-	-	-	-
4220 Corporate			-	-	-	-	-	-
4300 Estate, inheritance and gift taxes	-	-	-	-	-	-	-	-
4310 Estate and inheritance taxes								
4320 Gift taxes								
4400 Taxes on financial and capital transactions	-	-	-	-	-	-	-	-
4500 Non-recurrent taxes	-	-	-	-	-	-	-	-
4510 On net wealth								
4520 Other non-recurrent taxes								
4600 Other recurrent taxes on property	16	189	291	265	224	254	290	327

Table 20 - Cuadro 20 *(cont)*

HONDURAS - HONDURAS

Details of tax revenue, in millions of lempiras

	1990	2000	2007	2008	2009	2010	2011	2012
5000 Taxes on goods and services	1 405	11 445	25 985	28 608	26 141	28 937	32 247	34 610
5100 Taxes on production, sale, transfer, etc	1 405	11 445	25 985	28 608	26 141	28 937	32 247	34 610
5110 General taxes	344	5 146	14 170	16 464	14 396	16 050	18 967	20 150
5111 Value added taxes	344	5 146	14 170	16 464	14 396	16 050	18 967	20 150
5112 Sales tax	-	-	-	-	-	-	-	-
5113 Other	-	-	-	-	-	-	-	-
5120 Taxes on specific goods and services	1 061	6 299	11 815	12 145	11 746	12 887	13 279	14 460
5121 Excises	256	3 600	7 606	7 581	8 022	8 458	8 670	9 490
Beer	71	376	358	373	344	376	466	503
Soft drinks	25	240	419	413	415	514	632	675
Liquors	32	48	80	79	76	121	164	165
Petroleum products	43	347	-	-	-	-	-	-
Cigarettes	57	369	582	568	646	607	660	633
Fuel tax	-	1 962	5 578	5 570	6 032	6 288	6 177	6 868
Other	28	258	589	577	509	551	572	646
5122 Profits of fiscal monopolies	-	-	-	-	-	-	-	-
5123 Customs and import duties	498	2 083	2 870	2 975	2 065	2 505	2 626	2 933
Petroleum	-	297	-	-	-	-	-	-
Other	498	1 786	2 870	2 975	2 065	2 505	2 626	2 933
5124 Taxes on exports	217	6	-	-	-	-	-	-
Bananas	39	5	-	-	-	-	-	-
Coffee	1	-	-	-	-	-	-	-
Temporary export tax	163	-	-	-	-	-	-	-
Other	15	1	-	-	-	-	-	-
5125 Taxes on investment goods	-	-	-	-	-	-	-	-
5126 Taxes on specific services	-	-	-	-	-	-	-	-
5127 Other taxes on internat trade and transactions	-	-	-	-	-	-	-	-
5128 Other taxes	90	610	1 340	1 589	1 659	1 924	1 983	2 038
5130 Unallocable between 5110 and 5120	-	-	-	-	-	-	-	-
5200 Taxes on use of goods and perform activities	-	-	-	-	-	-	-	-
5210 Recurrent taxes								
5211 Paid by households: motor vehicles								
5212 Paid by others: motor vehicles								
5213 Paid in respect of other goods								
5220 Non-recurrent taxes								
5300 Unallocable between 5100 and 5200	-	-	-	-	-	-	-	-
6000 Other taxes	1	2	12	13	12	9	9	10
6100 Paid solely by business	-	-	-	-	-	-	-	-
6200 Other	1	2	12	13	12	9	9	10
Total tax revenue on cash basis	2 032	16 347	44 307	49 637	47 157	51 844	56 479	63 412

Year ending 31st December.

The data are on cash basis.

Source: Secretaria de Finanzas.

StatLink http://dx.doi.org/10.1787/888932971368

Table 21 - Cuadro 21

MEXICO - MÉXICO

Details of tax revenue, in millions of mexican pesos

	1990	2000	2007	2008	2009	2010	2011	2012
Total tax revenue	127 959	1 014 625	2 002 846	2 539 615	2 071 854	2 458 249	2 830 055	2 923 564
1000 Taxes on income, profits and capital gains	34 673	276 548	554 099	629 135	591 942	683 604	772 704	803 071
1100 Of individuals	-	-	238 938	285 270	280 230	313 473	352 386	397 701
Tax on income of individuals			238 938	285 270	280 230	313 473	352 386	397 701
1110 On income and profits	-	-	-	-	-	-	-	-
1120 On capital gains	-	-	-	-	-	-	-	-
1200 Corporate	-	-	217 790	214 611	191 685	246 745	303 176	288 360
Tax on income of corporations			217 790	214 611	191 685	246 745	303 176	288 360
1210 On profits			-	-	-	-	-	-
1220 On capital gains			-	-	-	-	-	-
1300 Unallocable between 1100 and 1200	34 673	276 548	97 370	129 254	120 027	123 386	117 143	117 010
Tax on income of other individuals and corporations		244 841	54 785	61 208	64 816	66 937	66 004	74 042
Tax on asset		13 913	15 670	1 134	-2 540	-625	-1 120	-1 192
Credit on salary		17 794	23 177	15 886	12 113	9 708	2 076	1 387
Oil yields tax		-	3 738	4 441	921	2 296	3 019	573
IETU		-	-	46 586	44 718	45 069	47 165	42 199
2000 Social security contributions	17 165	167 292	307 026	321 843	346 031	378 006	411 289	454 778
2100 Employees	-	-	-	-	-	-	-	-
2110 On a payroll basis								
2120 On an income tax basis								
2200 Employers	-	-	-	-	-	-	-	-
2210 On a payroll basis								
2220 On an income tax basis								
2300 Self-employed or non-employed	-	-	-	-	-	-	-	-
2310 On a payroll basis								
2320 On an income tax basis								
2400 Unallocable between 2100, 2200 and 2300	17 165	167 292	307 026	321 843	346 031	378 006	411 289	454 778
2410 On a payroll basis	-	167 292	307 026	321 843	346 031	378 006	411 289	454 778
2420 On an income tax basis	-	-	-	-	-	-	-	-
3000 Taxes on payroll and workforce	1 797	11 217	28 071	31 123	31 965	36 911	41 980	-
Substitute tax on salary		-	-	-	-	-	-	
Payroll tax		11 101	20 277	22 919	23 530	27 813	31 817	
Tax on remuneration to the personal work		65	7 578	7 992	8 180	8 841	9 990	
Tax on professions and fees		36	68	72	70	71	58	
Tax on operations by contract		15	148	140	186	186	116	
4000 Taxes on property	1 914	13 964	33 161	35 847	35 484	38 955	41 186	-
4100 Recurrent taxes on immovable property	1 036	9 948	19 425	21 394	22 862	25 724	28 728	
4110 Households	-	-	-	-	-	-	-	
4120 Others	1 036	9 948	19 425	21 394	22 862	25 724	28 728	
Property tax		9 948	19 425	21 394	22 862	25 724	28 728	
4200 Recurrent taxes on net wealth	-	-	-	-	-	-	-	
4210 Individual								
4220 Corporate								
4300 Estate, inheritance and gift taxes	8	-	-	-	-	-	-	
4310 Estate and inheritance taxes	8							
4320 Gift taxes	-							
4400 Taxes on financial and capital transactions	870	4 017	13 736	14 452	12 622	13 231	12 458	
Alienation of immovable property		1 763	1 076	1 310	1 163	1 122	1 379	
Transfer of ownership of real estate		2 236	8 147	5 825	5 005	5 027	3 923	
Purchasing property		18	4 513	7 318	6 454	7 082	7 157	

Table 21 - Cuadro 21 *(cont)*

MEXICO - MÉXICO

Details of tax revenue, in millions of mexican pesos

	1990	2000	2007	2008	2009	2010	2011	2012
4500 Non-recurrent taxes	-	-	-	-	-	-	-	
4510 On net wealth								
4520 Other non-recurrent taxes								
4600 Other recurrent taxes on property	-	-	-	-	-	-	-	
5000 Taxes on goods and services	70 791	537 953	1 063 584	1 502 941	1 039 344	1 293 373	1 530 484	1 639 378
5100 Taxes on production, sale, transfer, etc	70 125	528 666	1 042 372	1 480 972	1 017 627	1 271 581	1 508 269	1 638 953
5110 General taxes	26 635	189 606	409 013	457 248	407 795	504 509	537 143	579 988
5111 Value added taxes	26 635	189 606	409 013	457 248	407 795	504 509	537 143	579 988
5112 Sales taxes	-	-	-	-	-	-	-	-
5113 Other general taxes on goods and services	-	-	-	-	-	-	-	-
5120 Taxes on specific goods and services	43 473	339 060	633 359	1 023 723	609 832	767 072	971 126	1 058 965
5121 Excises	10 072	86 163	47 008	60 462	69 770	86 098	94 623	98 490
Special tax on production and services		81 544	41 532	55 391	65 708	81 427	89 544	92 620
Tax on new automobiles		4 619	5 476	5 071	4 063	4 671	5 079	5 870
Tax on luxury goods and services		-	-	-	-	-	-	-
5122 Profits of fiscal monopolies	-	-	-	-	-	-	-	-
5123 Customs and import duties	6 998	33 285	33 344	37 831	31 732	26 602	29 946	31 161
Step customs officer		423	1 156	2 048	1 535	2 071	3 065	3 255
Import taxes		32 861	32 188	35 783	30 196	24 531	26 881	27 906
5124 Taxes on exports	75	4	3	1	1	0	2	1
Taxes on exports		4	3	1	1	0	2	1
5125 Taxes on investment goods	-	-	-	-	-	-	-	-
5126 Taxes on specific services	132	1 042	2 146	20 097	18 461	10 958	-5 610	2 786
IDE		-	-	17 700	15 888	8 022	-8 442	2 786
Tax on lodging		504	1 059	1 178	1 147	1 384	1 375	-
Public entertainment tax		240	365	383	486	462	360	-
Tax on lotteries, raffles and gambling		267	705	717	789	923	952	-
Tax on commercials		4	17	118	150	166	145	-
Various indirect taxes		28	0	0	0	1	0	-
5127 Other taxes on internat trade and transactions		-	-	-	-	-	-	-
5128 Other taxes	26 196	218 567	550 858	905 332	489 869	643 414	852 166	926 528
Ordinary fee on oil production		125 329	-	-	-	-	-	-
Extraordinary fee on oil production		68 235	-	-	-	-	-	-
Additional fee on oil production		2 576	3 233	3 715	149	-	-	-
Tax on oil yields		22 201	1 255	-	-	-	-	-
Mining fees		226	414	68	1 782	1 956	2 858	3 243
Ordinary		-	478 609	794 030	410 437	543 895	721 209	769 489
Stabilization Fund		-	55 402	71 536	63 839	77 071	81 247	106 151
Extraordinary on crude petroleum export		-	11 517	33 640	-556	6 644	24 152	19 594
Scientific research and technological Fund in the matter of energy		-	-	1 583	2 046	3 616	5 635	8 441
For oil control		-	24	37	23	29	35	42
Rights on the extraction of mineral oils		-	-	158	2 663	3 533	5 601	7 185
Special rights on mineral oils for fields in the "Paleoncanal icontepec"		-	-	565	7 676	2 494	6 117	7 521
Special rights on hydrocarbons		-	-	-	1 813	4 032	1 308	-
Special right on hydrocarbons in deep water fields		-	-	-	-	143	4 003	4 493
Right to register for exploration and exploitation of hydrocarbons		-	-	-	-	-	-	370

Table 21 - Cuadro 21 *(cont)*

MEXICO - MÉXICO

Details of tax revenue, in millions of mexican pesos

	1990	2000	2007	2008	2009	2010	2011	2012
5130 Unallocable between 5110 and 5120	17	-	-	-	-	-	-	-
5200 Taxes on use of goods and perform activities	666	9 287	21 212	21 970	21 717	21 792	22 215	425
5210 Recurrent taxes	666	9 287	21 212	21 970	21 717	21 792	22 215	425
5211 Paid by households in respect of motor vehicles	567	8 878	20 692	21 492	21 301	21 319	21 764	-
Tax on motor vehicules		8 878	20 692	21 492	21 301	21 319	21 764	-
5212 Paid by others in respect of motor vehicles	-	301	275	311	270	281	296	370
Tax on federal auto transport		301	275	311	270	281	296	370
5213 Other recurrent taxes	99	108	246	166	147	193	155	55
Sport fishing		40	98	85	68	59	50	55
Sport hunting		3	0	1	0	0	0	0
Tax on commercial activities		63	147	33	42	50	66	-
Trade in books and magazines		-	-	0	0	0	0	-
Tax on industrial activities		2	0	47	36	83	38	-
5220 Non-recurrent taxes	-	-	-	-	-	-	-	-
5300 Unallocable between 5100 and 5200	-	-	-	-	-	-	-	-
6000 Other taxes	1 619	7 651	16 906	18 726	27 087	27 399	32 412	26 337
6100 Paid solely by business	-	-	-	-	-	-	-	-
6200 Other	1 619	7 651	16 906	18 726	27 087	27 399	32 412	26 337
Accessories		5 504	12 403	13 744	21 710	22 206	24 059	24 077
Unallocable between 1000 and 5000 caused in exercices fiscal previous liquidation slopes or of payment		374	222	58	7	30	-118	2 260
Additional state and local taxes		1 773	4 280	4 924	5 361	5 162	8 471	-
Non-wastable tax credits against 1000		-	-	-	-	-	-	-
Tax expenditure component		-	-	-	-	-	-	-
Transfer component		-	-	-	-	-	-	-
Fees levied on hydrocarbon production	-26 196	-218 567	-550 858	-905 332	-489 869	-643 414	-852 166	-926 528
Total tax revenue (net of fees on hydrocarbons)	101 763	796 059	1 451 988	1 634 282	1 581 985	1 814 835	1 977 890	1 997 036

Year ending 31st December.

The data are on cash basis.

The 2012 data for revenues of the State and Local levels of government are not available. They comprise revenues in categories 3000, 4000, 5000, and 6000.

Heading 1000: In ECLAC data, income taxes are presented net of credit on salary figures.

Heading 2000: In ECLAC data, social security contributions are presented net of transfers from the Federal government for the payment of IMSS pensions.

Heading 5128: In ECLAC and CIAT data, fees levied on hydrocarbon production are treated as non tax revenues.

Source: Ministry of Finance, Economic Department.

StatLink http://dx.doi.org/10.1787/888932971387

Table 22 - Cuadro 22

NICARAGUA - NICARAGUA

Details of tax revenue, in millions of cordobas

	1990	2000	2007	2008	2009	2010	2011	2012
Total tax revenue		8 418	23 847	27 698	28 838	33 620	41 185	48 131
1000 Taxes on income, profits and capital gains		1 144	5 752	7 003	7 840	8 481	11 335	13 346
1100 Of individuals		-	-	-	-	-	-	-
1110 On income and profits		-	-	-	-	-	-	-
1120 On capital gains		-	-	-	-	-	-	-
1200 Corporate		-	-	-	-	-	-	-
1210 On profits		-	-	-	-	-	-	-
Income tax		1 144	5 752	7 003	7 840	8 481	11 335	13 346
1220 On capital gains		-	-	-	-	-	-	-
1300 Unallocable between 1100 and 1200		1 144	5 752	7 003	7 840	8 481	11 335	13 346
2000 Social security contributions		1 678	4 921	6 023	6 804	8 090	9 433	11 007
2100 Employees		-	-	-	-	-	-	-
2110 On a payroll basis								
2120 On an income tax basis								
2200 Employers		-	-	-	-	-	-	-
2210 On a payroll basis								
2220 On an income tax basis								
2300 Self-employed or non-employed		-	-	-	-	-	-	-
2310 On a payroll basis								
2320 On an income tax basis								
2400 Unallocable between 2100, 2200 and 2300		1 678	4 921	6 023	6 804	8 090	9 433	11 007
2410 On a payroll basis		1 678	4 921	6 023	6 804	8 090	9 433	11 007
2420 On an income tax basis		-	-	-	-	-	-	-
3000 Taxes on payroll and workforce		-	-	-	-	-	-	-
4000 Taxes on property		-	0	-	-	-	-	-
4100 Recurrent taxes on immovable property		-	-	-	-	-	-	-
4110 Households		-	-	-	-	-	-	-
4120 Others		-	-	-	-	-	-	-
4200 Recurrent taxes on net wealth		-	0	-	-	-	-	-
4210 Individual			0	-	-	-	-	-
4220 Corporate			-	-	-	-	-	-
4300 Estate, inheritance and gift taxes		-	-	-	-	-	-	-
4310 Estate and inheritance taxes								
4320 Gift taxes								
4400 Taxes on financial and capital transactions		-	-	-	-	-	-	-
4500 Non-recurrent taxes		-	-	-	-	-	-	-
4510 On net wealth								
4520 Other non-recurrent taxes								
4600 Other recurrent taxes on property		-	-	-	-	-	-	-
5000 Taxes on goods and services		5 584	13 153	14 650	14 170	17 029	20 395	23 754
5100 Taxes on production, sale, transfer, etc		5 584	13 153	14 650	14 170	17 029	20 395	23 754
5110 General taxes		2 931	8 025	9 009	8 871	10 353	12 876	15 151
5111 Value added taxes		2 931	8 025	9 009	8 871	10 353	12 876	15 151
5112 Sales tax		-	-	-	-	-	-	-
5113 Other		-	-	-	-	-	-	-
5120 Taxes on specific goods and services		2 653	5 128	5 641	5 299	6 676	7 519	8 603

Table 22 - Cuadro 22 *(cont)*

NICARAGUA - NICARAGUA

Details of tax revenue, in millions of cordobas

	1990	2000	2007	2008	2009	2010	2011	2012
5121 Excises		2 034	4 099	4 518	4 392	5 541	6 070	6 884
Liquor		84	144	189	147	198	240	214
Beer		203	480	561	556	645	781	915
Cigarettes		70	158	177	171	45	0	0
Soft drinks		123	146	194	188	248	292	351
Petroleum products		1 359	2 108	2 162	2 277	2 699	2 700	3 045
Excise taxes on imports		196	1 025	1 180	975	1 559	1 901	2 233
Other specific excises on consumption		-1	37	55	77	148	156	126
5122 Profits of fiscal monopolies		-	-	-	-	-	-	-
5123 Customs and import duties		619	1 030	1 123	908	1 135	1 449	1 719
Custom duties		452	1 004	1 093	870	1 094	1 400	1 661
Temporary protection duty		96	0	-	-	-	-	-
On products originating in Colombia or Honduras		72	26	29	38	41	49	58
5124 Taxes on exports		-	-	-	-	-	-	-
5125 Taxes on investment goods		-	-	-	-	-	-	-
5126 Taxes on specific services		-	-	-	-	-	-	-
5127 Other taxes on internat trade and transactions		-	-	-	-	-	-	-
5128 Other taxes		-	-	-	-	-	-	-
5130 Unallocable between 5110 and 5120		-	-	-	-	-	-	-
5200 Taxes on use of goods and perform activities		-	-	-	-	-	-	-
5210 Recurrent taxes								
5211 Paid by households: motor vehicles								
5212 Paid by others: motor vehicles								
5213 Paid in respect of other goods								
5220 Non-recurrent taxes								
5300 Unallocable between 5100 and 5200		-	-	-	-	-	-	-
6000 Other taxes		11	20	21	24	20	22	24
6100 Paid solely by business		-	-	-	-	-	-	-
6200 Other		11	20	21	24	20	22	24
Stamp tax		11	20	21	24	20	22	24
Total tax revenue on cash basis		8 418	23 847	27 698	28 838	33 620	41 185	48 131

Year ending 31st December.

The data are on cash basis.

Comparable statistics for 1990 cannot be shown due to the devaluation of the Nicaraguan cordoba.

Source: Ministry of Finance

StatLink http://dx.doi.org/10.1787/888932971406

Table 23 - Cuadro 23

PANAMA - PANAMÁ

Details of tax revenue, in thousands of balboas

	1990	2000	2007	2008	2009	2010	2011	2012
Total tax revenue	892 837	1 941 623	3 297 911	3 883 852	4 193 048	4 814 829	5 665 638	6 696 602
1000 Taxes on income, profits and capital gains	216 950	484 872	921 831	1 097 062	1 285 649	1 317 028	1 349 792	1 985 220
1100 Of individuals	14 155	20 343	27 927	30 098	38 811	35 456	28 458	37 825
1110 On income and profits								
1120 On capital gains								
1200 Corporate	72 413	186 351	459 321	544 752	731 493	749 818	701 364	1 257 178
1210 On profits	72 413	186 351	459 321	544 752	731 493	749 818	701 364	1 257 178
1220 On capital gains	-	-	-	-	-	-	-	-
1300 Unallocable between 1100 and 1200	130 382	278 178	434 583	522 212	515 345	531 754	619 970	690 217
Payroll	115 138	222 025	303 233	370 755	394 854	352 550	420 411	455 553
Panama Canal commission	10 225	52 774	62 068	62 899	62 109	52 398	65 377	60 246
Colón Free Zone	5 019	3 379	11 909	21 323	17 855	19 666	24 074	50 735
Other	-	-	57 373	67 235	40 527	107 140	110 108	123 682
2000 Social security contributions	271 300	742 000	1 104 000	1 330 200	1 383 300	1 637 100	2 041 500	2 168 500
2100 Employees	-	-	-	-	-	-	-	-
2110 On a payroll basis		-	-	-	-	-	-	-
2120 On an income tax basis								
2200 Employers	-	-	-	-	-	-	-	-
2210 On a payroll basis		-	-	-	-	-	-	-
2220 On an income tax basis		-	-	-	-	-	-	-
2300 Self-employed or non-employed	-	-	-	-	-	-	-	-
2310 On a payroll basis		-	-	-	-	-	-	-
2320 On an income tax basis		-	-	-	-	-	-	-
2400 Unallocable between 2100, 2200 and 2300	271 300	742 000	1 104 000	1 330 200	1 383 300	1 637 100	2 041 500	2 168 500
2410 On a payroll basis	-	-	-	-	-	-	-	-
2420 On an income tax basis	-	-	-	-	-	-	-	-
3000 Taxes on payroll and workforce	-	36 400	39 842	45 248	50 962	58 844	65 200	70 400
Education insurance	-	36 400	39 842	45 248	50 962	58 844	65 200	70 400
4000 Taxes on property	43 443	62 090	154 699	160 530	175 370	212 194	229 398	261 033
4100 Recurrent taxes on immovable property	28 330	33 898	74 092	80 919	104 522	107 791	109 986	119 964
4110 Households								
4120 Others								
4200 Recurrent taxes on net wealth	-	-	-	-	-	-	-	-
4210 Individual	-	-	-	-	-	-	-	-
4220 Corporate	-	-	-	-	-	-	-	-
4300 Estate, inheritance and gift taxes	154	-	-	-	-	-	-	-
4310 Estate and inheritance taxes								
4320 Gift taxes								
4400 Taxes on financial and capital transactions	3 419	9 343	45 383	40 528	24 456	29 810	36 195	40 998
4500 Non-recurrent taxes	-	-	-	-	-	-	-	-
4510 On net wealth								
4520 Other non-recurrent taxes								
4600 Other recurrent taxes on property	11 540	18 849	35 224	39 083	46 392	74 593	83 218	100 071
Commercial licences	11 540	18 849	35 224	39 083	46 392	74 593	83 218	100 071
5000 Taxes on goods and services	335 470	573 374	1 021 558	1 212 812	1 261 432	1 513 066	1 893 533	2 067 189
5100 Taxes on production, sale, transfer, etc	331 758	530 329	960 450	1 143 757	1 191 097	1 472 515	1 845 207	2 067 189
5110 General taxes	80 303	69 013	205 080	526 710	557 166	766 154	1 042 213	1 183 878
5111 Value added taxes	80 303	69 013	205 080	526 710	557 166	766 154	1 042 213	1 183 878
5112 Sales tax	-	-	-	-	-	-	-	-
5113 Other	-	-	-	-	-	-	-	-

Table 23 - Cuadro 23 *(cont)*

PANAMA - PANAMÁ

Details of tax revenue, in thousands of balboas

	1990	2000	2007	2008	2009	2010	2011	2012
5120 Taxes on specific goods and services	138 623	461 316	755 370	617 047	633 931	706 360	802 993	883 311
5121 Excises	-	141 348	140 362	158 821	188 411	238 728	310 441	355 717
Gasoline products	-	108 783	89 584	85 824	111 404	96 518	90 136	100 903
Beer	-	18 249	25 272	28 459	30 635	31 025	32 715	34 572
Wine and liquor	-	11 971	11 124	12 279	11 071	10 775	10 769	10 486
Soft drinks	-	2 292	3 753	4 404	4 951	5 646	6 207	6 622
Various products	-	-	10 580	27 760	30 302	94 726	170 595	45 285
Automobiles	-	-	-	-	-	-	-	132 880
Other	-	53	49	95	48	38	19	24,969
5122 Profits of fiscal monopolies	-	-	-	-	-	-	-	-
5123 Customs and import duties	124 914	298 323	573 841	411 586	390 129	390 024	393 668	420 448
5124 Taxes on exports	12 621	158	-	283	104	104	-	-
5125 Taxes on investment goods	-	-	-	-	-	-	-	-
5126 Taxes on specific services	-	16 637	32 543	37 492	45 323	65 110	80 484	86 146
Insurance premiums	-	16 637	23 577	26 929	34 514	47 056	51 664	54 188
Cable and telecommunications	-	-	8 306	9 645	9 870	17 015	27 827	30 507
Gambling	-	-	660	918	939	1 039	993	1 451
5127 Other taxes on international trade and transactions	1 088	4 850	8 624	8 865	9 964	12 395	18 400	21 000
Banks, financial institutions, and currency exchange	-	2 005	8 623	8 865	9 964	12 395	18 400	21 000
Other	1 088	2 845	1	-	-	-	-	-
5128 Other taxes	-	-	-	-	-	-	-	-
5130 Unallocable between 5110 and 5120	112 832	-	-	-	-	-	-	-
5200 Taxes on use of goods and perform activities	3 712	43 045	61 108	69 055	70 335	40 551	48 327	-
5210 Recurrent taxes	-	38 758	48 000	53 373	55 807	40 551	48 327	-
5211 Paid by households: motor vehicles	-	7 042	10 327	10 863	11 332	-	-	-
5212 Paid by others: motor vehicles	-	4 682	4 731	4 924	5 173	-	-	-
5213 Paid in respect of other goods	-	27 033	32 942	37 586	39 302	40 551	48 327	-
On commercial activities	-	25 405	31 052	35 547	37 184	38 367	45 723	-
On industrial activities	-	1 628	1 891	2 039	2 118	2 184	2 604	-
5220 Non-recurrent taxes	3 712	4 287	13 107	15 682	14 528	-	-	-
Building and construction	-	-	-	-	-	-	-	-
Ship registration	-	-	-	-	-	-	-	-
5300 Unallocable between 5100 and 5200	-	-	-	-	-	-	-	-
6000 Other taxes	25 674	42 887	55 981	38 000	36 336	76 597	86 214	144 261
6100 Paid solely by business	-	11	-	27	-	-	-	-
6200 Other	25 674	42 876	55 981	37 973	36 336	76 597	86 214	144 261
Legal services	16 691	42 330	37 689	37 912	36 278	41 064	47 000	44 900
Total tax revenue on cash basis	892 837	1 941 623	3 297 911	3 883 852	4 193 048	4 814 829	5 665 638	6 696 602

Year ending 31st December.

The data are on cash basis.

Heading 3000: In ECLAC data, Education insurance is classified as "Other taxes" (6000).

Heading 5127: In CIAT and ECLAC data, the tax on banks, financial institutions, and currency exchange is classified as a property tax.

Heading 6000: The 2012 figure for local government taxes has been estimated and is included in heading 6200. It includes some revenues that would otherwise be shown under 4000 and 5000.

Source: Contraloría General de la Republica.

StatLink http://dx.doi.org/10.1787/888932971425

Table 24 - Cuadro 24

PARAGUAY - PARAGUAY

Details of tax revenue, in millions of guaranies

	1990	2000	2007	2008	2009	2010	2011	2012
Total tax revenue	348 889	3 587 451	9 669 213	11 749 612	12 725 017	15 637 675	14 503 774	13 836 418
1000 Taxes on income, profits and capital gains	73 726	470 388	1 228 454	1 571 467	2 187 607	2 096 498	2 607 282	2 902 614
1100 Of individuals	-	-	766	318	574	1 150	154	507
1110 On income and profits								
1120 On capital gains								
1200 Corporate	-	4 238	14 432	11 535	11 315	13 405	8 855	10 542
1210 On profits	-	4 238	14 432	11 535	11 315	13 405	8 855	10 542
Income tax on small businesses	-	-	4 620	9 128	8 838	9 380	5 129	5 760
Simplified tax on small businesses	-	4 238	8 411	1 181	644	715	544	317
Simplified tax on maquiladoras	-	-	1 401	1 226	1 833	3 310	3 182	4 465
1220 On capital gains	-	-	-	-	-	-	-	-
1300 Unallocable between 1100 and 1200	73 726	466 150	1 213 256	1 559 614	2 175 718	2 081 943	2 598 273	2 891 565
Income tax on agricultural activities	-	15 042	11 200	16 227	22 651	30 113	59 788	66 106
Tax on industrial, commercial, and service activities	-	451 108	1 202 056	1 543 387	2 153 067	2 051 830	2 538 485	2 825 459
Other	73 726	-	-	-	-	-	-	-
2000 Social security contributions	28 882	919 533	2 265 097	2 784 731	3 118 645	3 552 640	1 323 447	-
2100 Employees	-	-	-	-	-	-	-	-
2110 On a payroll basis		-	-	-	-	-	-	-
2120 On an income tax basis								
2200 Employers	-	-	-	-	-	-	-	-
2210 On a payroll basis		-	-	-	-	-	-	-
2220 On an income tax basis		-	-	-	-	-	-	-
2300 Self-employed or non-employed	-	-	-	-	-	-	-	-
2310 On a payroll basis		-	-	-	-	-	-	-
2320 On an income tax basis		-	-	-	-	-	-	-
2400 Unallocable between 2100, 2200 and 2300	28 882	919 533	2 265 097	2 784 731	3 118 645	3 552 640	1 323 447	-
2410 On a payroll basis	28 882	919 533	2 265 097	2 784 731	3 118 645	3 552 640	1 323 447	-
2420 On an income tax basis	-	-	-	-	-	-	-	-
3000 Taxes on payroll and workforce	-	-	-	-	-	-	-	-
4000 Taxes on property	17 162	-	203 605	255 333	253 821	272 385	-	-
4100 Recurrent taxes on immovable property	17 162	-	194 246	239 680	240 217	254 306	-	-
4110 Households	17 162	-	194 246	239 680	240 217	254 306	-	-
Real estate tax	-	-	190 796	230 570	233 423	249 697	-	-
Tax on vacant lots	-	-	2 046	3 855	2 953	2 925	-	-
Other	17 162	-	1 404	5 256	3 841	1 684	-	-
4120 Others								
4200 Recurrent taxes on net wealth	-	-	-	-	-	-	-	-
4210 Individual	-	-	-	-	-	-	-	-
4220 Corporate	-	-	-	-	-	-	-	-
4300 Estate, inheritance and gift taxes	-	-	-	-	-	-	-	-
4310 Estate and inheritance taxes								
4320 Gift taxes								
4400 Taxes on financial and capital transactions	-	-	9 294	15 170	13 391	16 316	-	-
Real estate transfer tax	-	-	6 412	11 275	9 675	11 766	-	-
Other	-	-	2 882	3 895	3 716	4 551	-	-
4500 Non-recurrent taxes	-	-	-	-	-	-	-	-
4510 On net wealth								
4520 Other non-recurrent taxes								
4600 Other recurrent taxes on property	-	-	65	482	213	1 762	-	-

Table 24 - Cuadro 24 *(cont)*

PARAGUAY - PARAGUAY

Details of tax revenue, in millions of guaranies

	1990	2000	2007	2008	2009	2010	2011	2012
5000 Taxes on goods and services	179 312	2 080 878	5 808 675	7 039 349	7 068 556	9 460 962	10 477 217	10 827 231
5100 Taxes on production, sale, transfer, etc	179 312	2 080 878	5 687 532	6 887 675	6 928 055	9 249 698	10 477 217	10 827 231
5110 General taxes	-	1 150 496	3 496 787	4 409 140	4 399 503	5 991 694	6 887 685	7 126 623
5111 Value added taxes	-	1 150 496	3 496 787	4 409 140	4 399 503	5 991 694	6 887 685	7 126 623
5112 Sales tax	-	-	-	-	-	-	-	-
5113 Other	-	-	-	-	-	-	-	-
5120 Taxes on specific goods and services	179 312	930 382	2 190 745	2 478 535	2 528 552	3 258 004	3 589 532	3 700 608
5121 Excises	41 087	456 561	1 335 033	1 411 846	1 532 365	1 710 531	1 892 587	2 063 020
Fuels	41 087	316 694	1 000 727	1 027 042	1 093 058	1 126 143	1 328 213	1 455 820
Other excises	-	136 194	309 383	347 467	399 940	537 887	564 374	607 200
Animal health and quality service	-	3 673	24 923	37 337	39 367	46 501	-	-
Livestock trade	-	-	-	-	-	-	-	-
5122 Profits of fiscal monopolies	-	-	-	-	-	-	-	-
5123 Customs and import duties	138 225	473 821	838 494	1 045 788	975 487	1 524 252	1 696 945	1 637 588
5124 Taxes on exports	-	-	-	-	-	-	-	-
5125 Taxes on investment goods	-	-	-	-	-	-	-	-
5126 Taxes on specific services	-	-	17 218	20 900	20 700	23 221	-	-
Advertising	-	-	3 613	5 109	4 555	5 249	-	-
Public transport	-	-	4 173	4 508	4 245	4 363	-	-
Other	-	-	9 432	11 284	11 900	13 609	-	-
5127 Other taxes on internat trade and transactions	-	-	-	-	-	-	-	-
5128 Other taxes	-	-	-	-	-	-	-	-
5130 Unallocable between 5110 and 5120	-	-	-	-	-	-	-	-
5200 Taxes on use of goods and perform activities	-	-	119 834	151 211	140 466	211 027	-	-
5210 Recurrent taxes	-	-	119 834	151 211	140 466	211 027	-	-
5211 Paid by households: motor vehicles	-	-	-	-	-	-	-	-
5212 Paid by others: motor vehicles	-	-	28 343	27 174	41 701	52 365	-	-
Motor vehicle licences	-	-	28 343	27 174	41 701	52 365	-	-
5213 Paid in respect of other goods	-	-	91 492	124 037	98 765	158 662	-	-
Tax on construction	-	-	16 168	20 362	24 476	31 696	-	-
Licencing fees	-	-	75 323	103 675	74 289	126 965	-	-
5220 Non-recurrent taxes	-	-	16 168	20 362	24 476	31 696	-	-
5300 Unallocable between 5100 and 5200	-	-	1 309	463	35	237	-	-
6000 Other taxes	49 807	116 652	163 383	98 733	96 388	255 190	95 828	106 573
6100 Paid solely by business	-	-	-	-	-	-	-	-
6200 Other	49 807	116 652	163 383	98 733	96 388	255 190	95 828	106 573
Registration and stamp duties	-	71 777	70 954	6 825	319	332	159	168
Luxury automobile tax	-	-	2 750	839	118	91	129	153
Other	49 807	44 875	89 679	91 069	95 951	254 767	95 540	106 252
Total tax revenue on cash basis	348 889	3 587 451	9 669 213	11 749 612	12 725 017	15 637 675	14 503 774	13 836 418

Year ending 31st December.

The data are on cash basis.

The figures for years up to and including 2004, as well as for 2011 and 2012, exclude local government revenues as the data are not available. This affects data in categories 4000, 5000, and 6000.

Heading 2000: Data on social security contributions collected by the central government are not available for 2012. Data on social security contributions collected by decentralized institutions are not available for 2011 and 2012.

Heading 5121: Data for Animal health and quality service are not available for 2011 and 2012.

Source: Ministry of Finance.

StatLink http://dx.doi.org/10.1787/888932971463

Table 25 - Cuadro 25

PERU - PERÚ

Details of tax revenue, in millions of new soles

	1990	2000	2007	2008	2009	2010	2011	2012
Total tax revenue	645	25 851	59 800	67 533	62 198	75 647	86 627	95 364
1000 Taxes on income, profits and capital gains	37	5 130	24 357	26 464	22 645	28 357	36 640	40 650
1100 Of individuals	3	2 117	4 671	6 141	6 438	7 286	8 869	9 943
First category		167	217	241	145	160	196	243
Second category		7	611	712	661	869	1 291	1 136
Fourth category		234	408	437	473	521	567	637
Fifth category		1 641	3 241	3 966	4 329	4 735	5 877	7 054
Solidarity contribution for pension plan		-	26	557	577	768	661	491
Tax debt payments		68	168	228	254	233	277	382
1110 On income and profits								
1120 On capital gains								
1200 Corporate	32	3 012	19 685	20 322	16 207	21 071	27 712	30 265
1210 On profits	32	3 012	19 685	20 322	16 207	21 071	27 712	30 265
Third category		2 023	13 258	14 921	10 691	14 652	19 321	20 744
Income tax on non-residents		487	961	1 204	1 391	1 511	1 735	2 244
Income tax special regime		47	60	79	89	118	153	202
Other incomes corporate		18	95	110	98	148	224	239
Tax debt payments		438	3 829	2 248	2 216	2 856	3 987	4 397
Temporary tax on net assets		-	1 483	1 761	1 722	1 788	2 293	2 439
1220 On capital gains	-	-	-	-	-	-	-	-
1300 Unallocable between 1100 and 1200	1	-	-	-	-	-	59	442
2000 Social security contributions	50	3 184	5 219	6 211	6 667	7 189	8 319	9 694
2100 Employees	-	541	914	1 209	1 401	1 618	1 997	2 389
2110 On a payroll basis		541	914	1 209	1 401	1 618	1 997	2 389
2120 On an income tax basis								
2200 Employers	-	2 447	4 092	4 774	5 015	5 283	6 099	7 075
2210 On a payroll basis		2 447	4 092	4 774	5 015	5 283	6 099	7 075
2220 On an income tax basis		-	-	-	-	-	-	-
2300 Self-employed or non-employed	-	95	34	38	38	42	46	51
2310 On a payroll basis		95	34	38	38	42	46	51
2320 On an income tax basis		-	-	-	-	-	-	-
2400 Unallocable between 2100, 2200 and 2300	50	102	178	190	213	246	177	179
2410 On a payroll basis	50	102	178	190	213	246	177	179
2420 On an income tax basis	-	-	-	-	-	-	-	-
3000 Taxes on payroll and workforce	-	1 038	9	7	6	3	1	2
4000 Taxes on property	99	0	1 929	2 173	2 042	2 237	1 876	1 897
4100 Recurrent taxes on immovable property	-	-	552	615	676	864	856	958
4110 Households								
4120 Others								
4200 Recurrent taxes on net wealth	61	0	0	-	-	-	-	-
4210 Individual	60	0	0	-	-	-	-	-
4220 Corporate	1	-	-	-	-	-	-	-
Revaluation of fixed assets	1		-	-	-	-	-	-
4300 Estate, inheritance and gift taxes	-	-	-	-	-	-	-	-
4310 Estate and inheritance taxes								
4320 Gift taxes								
4400 Taxes on financial and capital transactions	38	-	1 377	1 559	1 366	1 373	1 020	939
Financial transactions tax	-		1 031	1 138	968	944	395	126
Real Estate Transfer Tax	-		347	421	398	429	625	813
Tax Law Decree 519	38		-	-	-	-	-	-

Table 25 - Cuadro 25 *(cont)*

PERU - PERÚ

Details of tax revenue, in millions of new soles

	1990	2000	2007	2008	2009	2010	2011	2012
4500 Non-recurrent taxes	-	-	-	-	-	-	-	-
4510 On net wealth								
4520 Other non-recurrent taxes								
4600 Other recurrent taxes on property	-	-	-	-	-	-	0	0
5000 Taxes on goods and services	423	15 739	26 235	30 456	28 172	34 855	37 802	40 420
5100 Taxes on production, sale, transfer, etc	423	15 739	26 235	30 456	28 172	34 855	37 802	40 420
5110 General taxes	78	9 519	19 865	25 109	22 918	28 694	31 533	33 779
5111 Value added taxes	78	9 472	19 865	25 109	22 918	28 694	31 533	33 779
5112 Sales tax	-	-	-	-	-	-	-	-
5113 Other	-	47	0	-	0	0	-	0
5120 Taxes on specific goods and services	345	6 220	6 370	5 347	5 254	6 161	6 269	6 641
5121 Excises	232	3 521	4 465	3 682	4 288	4 879	5 001	5 243
Fuels	151	2 120	2 419	1 457	2 255	2 410	2 231	2 149
Gasoline sales tax	3	97	174	222	143	210	282	325
Other	78	1 304	1 872	2 003	1 890	2 258	2 487	2 769
5122 Profits of fiscal monopolies	-	-	-	-	-	-	-	-
5123 Customs and import duties	64	2 698	1 625	1 281	576	855	810	901
5124 Taxes on exports	2	-	-	-	-	-	-	-
5125 Taxes on investment goods	-	-	-	-	-	-	-	-
5126 Taxes on specific services	-	-	281	385	390	428	459	497
Casinos and slot machines	-	-	109	170	163	187	195	219
Tourism tax	-	-	87	93	104	105	116	115
Municipal taxes on services	-	-	85	122	123	136	148	163
5127 Other taxes on internat trade and transactions	48	-	-	-	-	-	-	-
5128 Other taxes	-	-	-	-	-	-	-	-
5130 Unallocable between 5110 and 5120	-	-	-	-	-	-	-	-
5200 Taxes on use of goods and perform activities	-	-	-	-	-	-	-	-
5210 Recurrent taxes								
5211 Paid by households: motor vehicles								
5212 Paid by others: motor vehicles								
5213 Paid in respect of other goods								
5220 Non-recurrent taxes								
5300 Unallocable between 5100 and 5200	-	-	-	-	-	-	-	-
6000 Other taxes	36	761	2 051	2 223	2 665	3 005	1 989	2 701
6100 Paid solely by business	-	84	82	91	98	108	118	133
Single simplified regime		84	82	91	98	108	118	133
University Development Fund		-	-	-	-	-	-	-
6200 Other	36	678	1 969	2 131	2 567	2 897	1 872	2 568
Tax debt payments	9	543	510	515	735	714	709	857
Penalties	-	114	263	268	287	330	453	937
Municipal fees	-	-	1 021	1 166	1 260	1 562	710	775
Other national level	28	20	148	146	234	238	-	-
Other local level	-	-	27	36	51	54	-	-
Total tax revenue on cash basis	645	25 851	59 800	67 533	62 198	75 647	86 627	95 364

Year ending 31st December.

The data are on cash basis.

The figures for years up to and including 2004 exclude local government revenues as the data are not available.

Source: Central Reserve Bank of Peru and National Superintendency of Tax Administration.

StatLink http://dx.doi.org/10.1787/888932971444

Table 26 - Cuadro 26

URUGUAY - URUGUAY

Details of tax revenue, in millions of uruguayan pesos

	1990	2000	2007	2008	2009	2010	2011	2012
Total tax revenue	2 352	59 656	137 545	166 284	184 547	210 191	244 433	266 149
1000 Taxes on income, profits and capital gains	114	5 620	18 683	34 366	38 457	44 573	50 957	58 291
1100 Of individuals	-	-	4 869	14 823	16 431	19 654	24 429	30 071
1110 On income and profits			607	2 441	3 990	5 011	6 007	7 537
First category			581	1 781	1 921	2 358	2 946	3 764
Social security assistance			-	660	2 066	2 651	3 061	3 773
1120 On capital gains			4 262	12 381	12 441	14 643	18 422	22 534
Second category			4 262	12 381	12 441	14 643	18 422	22 534
1200 Corporate	114	5 620	13 464	18 518	20 240	23 257	23 940	26 166
1210 On profits	114	5 620	13 464	18 518	20 240	23 257	23 940	26 166
Corporate income tax (IRAE)	-	-	709	11 724	16 512	21 280	21 719	23 937
Corporate income tax (IRIC)	97	5 096	11 055	5 313	2 355	491	469	414
Small firms (minimum VAT)	-	296	563	573	596	586	600	631
Other	17	228	1 138	907	777	900	1 151	1 185
1220 On capital gains	-	-	-	-	-	-	-	-
1300 Unallocable between 1100 and 1200	-	-	349	1 025	1 785	1 662	2 588	2 053
Non resident taxpayers			349	1 025	1 785	1 662	2 588	2 053
2000 Social security contributions	717	17 679	28 473	34 778	42 922	49 742	59 930	72 601
2100 Employees	-	-	-	-	-	-	-	-
2110 On a payroll basis								
2120 On an income tax basis								
2200 Employers	-	-	-	-	-	-	-	-
2210 On a payroll basis	-	-	-	-	-	-	-	-
2220 On an income tax basis	-	-	-	-	-	-	-	-
2300 Self-employed or non-employed	-	-	-	-	-	-	-	-
2310 On a payroll basis								
2320 On an income tax basis								
2400 Unallocable between 2100, 2200 and 2300	717	17 679	28 473	34 778	42 922	49 742	59 930	72 601
2410 On a payroll basis	717	17 679	28 473	34 778	42 922	49 742	59 930	72 601
2420 On an income tax basis	-	-	-	-	-	-	-	-
3000 Taxes on payroll and workforce	-	-	-	-	-	-	-	-
4000 Taxes on property	197	6 077	13 966	15 213	16 581	16 935	18 960	12 947
4100 Recurrent taxes on immovable property	72	2 521	6 098	6 780	6 622	6 308	6 941	-
4110 Households								
4120 Others								
4200 Recurrent taxes on net wealth	94	2 076	5 392	6 939	8 634	8 948	10 030	11 067
4210 Individual	64	108	340	325	371	382	422	445
4220 Corporate	30	1 968	5 052	6 614	8 263	8 567	9 607	10 622
Corporate wealth	28	1 661	4 805	6 380	8 056	8 354	9 413	10 609
Other	1	307	247	234	207	213	194	13
4300 Estate, inheritance and gift taxes	-	-	-	-	-	-	-	-
4310 Estate and inheritance taxes								
4320 Gift taxes								
4400 Taxes on financial and capital transactions	-	372	1 455	1 206	1 027	1 350	1 545	1 414
Capital transfers		372	1 268	1 202	1 027	1 347	1 545	1 413
Capital transfers (additional)		-	137	-	-	-	-	-
4500 Non-recurrent taxes	-	-	-	-	-	-	-	-
4510 On net wealth								
4520 Other non-recurrent taxes								
4600 Other recurrent taxes on property	31	1 107	1 021	288	299	328	445	466

Table 26 - Cuadro 26 *(cont)*

URUGUAY - URUGUAY

Details of tax revenue, in millions of uruguayan pesos

	1990	2000	2007	2008	2009	2010	2011	2012
5000 Taxes on goods and services	1 334	30 877	76 359	81 919	86 505	98 942	114 586	122 310
5100 Taxes on production, sale, transfer, etc	1 270	28 301	72 607	77 784	82 657	94 990	110 473	122 310
5110 General taxes	660	18 009	50 943	58 277	61 469	69 365	79 672	88 338
5111 Value added taxes	660	17 995	50 923	58 277	61 469	69 365	79 672	88 338
5112 Sales tax	1	14	20	0	0	0	0	-
5113 Other	-	-	-	-	-	-	-	-
5120 Taxes on specific goods and services	610	10 291	21 664	19 507	21 188	25 625	30 801	33 972
5121 Excises	393	7 673	12 336	11 560	13 312	16 401	19 401	21 417
Fuels	203	4 067	5 694	4 437	5 462	6 551	8 447	9 147
Tobacco products	80	1 741	3 085	2 948	3 248	4 236	4 925	4 768
Alcoholic beverages	24	229	448	533	657	602	622	800
Beer	8	205	372	402	480	602	895	895
Non-alcoholic beverages	19	464	804	990	1 240	1 172	1 451	1 518
Motor vehicles	20	656	1 333	1 616	1 662	2 289	2 710	3 025
Sales of agricultural goods (MEVIR and INIA)	4	76	323	417	414	451	538	648
Other	35	235	277	217	148	497	-188	616
5122 Profits of fiscal monopolies	-	-	-	-	-	-	-	-
5123 Customs and import duties	214	1 967	7 077	7 103	7 042	8 478	10 543	11 670
5124 Taxes on exports	1	92	311	371	349	371	446	432
5125 Taxes on investment goods	-	-	-	-	-	-	-	-
5126 Taxes on specific services	3	293	1 419	472	484	376	411	454
5127 Other taxes on international trade and transactions	-	265	520	-	-	-	-	0
5128 Other taxes	-	-	-	-	-	-	-	-
5130 Unallocable between 5110 and 5120	-	-	-	-	-	-	-	-
5200 Taxes on use of goods and perform activities	64	2 576	3 753	4 135	3 848	3 952	4 113	-
5210 Recurrent taxes	64	2 576	3 753	4 135	3 848	3 952	4 113	-
5211 Paid by households: motor vehicles								
5212 Paid by others: motor vehicles	64	2 576	3 753	4 135	3 848	3 952	4 113	-
5213 Paid in respect of other goods								
5220 Non-recurrent taxes								
5300 Unallocable between 5100 and 5200	-	-	-	-	-	-	-	-
6000 Other taxes	-10	-596	63	8	82	0	0	0
6100 Paid solely by business	-10	-596	63	8	82	0	0	0
6200 Other	-	-	-	-	-	-	-	-
Total tax revenue on cash basis	2 352	59 656	137 545	166 284	184 547	210 191	244 433	266 149

Year ending 31st December.

The data are on cash basis.

Data on the following taxes are not available for 2012: Property tax (municipal), Rural property tax, Vehicle licences (municipal), Primary education tax. This affects data in categories 4100 and 5200.

Heading 2000: Figures for 1990-1998 are reconstructed estimates, as the current methodology used to calculate social security contributions was not employed until 1999.

Headings 4000 and 5000: In ECLAC data, the tax on sales in public auctions is classified in category 4000.

Heading 5112: In ECLAC data, the tax on the sale of goods by public auction is classified in category 4000.

Source: Dirección General Impositiva, Ministry of Economy and Finance, Banco de Previsión Social, National Institute of Statistics and Contaduría General de la Nación.

StatLink http://dx.doi.org/10.1787/888932971482

Table 27 - Cuadro 27

VENEZUELA - VENEZUELA

Details of tax revenue, in millions of bolivares

	1990	2000	2007	2008	2009	2010	2011	2012
Total tax revenue	412	10 849	83 163	95 791	101 014	116 311	169 603	216 518
1000 Taxes on income, profits and capital gains	344	4 686	37 564	39 632	38 966	36 836	53 280	70 739
1100 Of individuals	-	-	-	-	-	-	-	-
1110 On income and profits								
1120 On capital gains								
1200 Corporate	315	3 368	19 959	17 834	12 944	8 700	16 510	22 879
1210 On profits	315	3 368	19 959	17 834	12 944	8 700	16 510	22 879
Oil	315	3 368	19 959	17 834	12 944	8 700	16 510	22 879
1220 On capital gains	-	-	-	-	-	-	-	-
1300 Unallocable between 1100 and 1200	30	1 317	17 606	21 798	26 022	28 137	36 770	47 859
2000 Social security contributions	20	591	4 218	5 085	6 740	5 547	-	-
2100 Employees	-	-	-	-	-	-	-	-
2110 On a payroll basis								
2120 On an income tax basis								
2200 Employers	-	-	-	-	-	-	-	-
2210 On a payroll basis								
2220 On an income tax basis								
2300 Self-employed or non-employed	-	-	-	-	-	-	-	-
2310 On a payroll basis								
2320 On an income tax basis								
2400 Unallocable between 2100, 2200 and 2300	20	591	4 218	5 085	6 740	5 547	-	-
2410 On a payroll basis								
2420 On an income tax basis								
3000 Taxes on payroll and workforce	-	-	-	-	-	-	-	-
4000 Taxes on property	1	400	2 715	6 250	175	222	273	346
4100 Recurrent taxes on immovable property	-	-	-	-	-	-	-	-
4110 Households								
4120 Others								
4200 Recurrent taxes on net wealth	-	-	-	-	-	-	-	-
4210 Individual								
4220 Corporate								
4300 Estate, inheritance and gift taxes	1	19	105	119	175	222	273	346
4310 Estate and inheritance taxes								
4320 Gift taxes								
4400 Taxes on financial and capital transactions	-	381	2 610	6 132	-	-	-	-
Bank debits		292	2 610	6 132	-	-	-	-
Registration of immovable property rights		89	-	-	-	-	-	-
4500 Non-recurrent taxes	-	-	-	-	-	-	-	-
4510 On net wealth								
4520 Other non-recurrent taxes								
4600 Other recurrent taxes on property	-	-	-	-	-	-	-	-

Table 27 - Cuadro 27 *(cont)*

VENEZUELA - VENEZUELA

Details of tax revenue, in millions of bolivares

	1990	2000	2007	2008	2009	2010	2011	2012
5000 Taxes on goods and services	46	5 173	38 667	44 824	55 134	73 707	108 268	141 505
5100 Taxes on production, sale, transfer, etc	46	5 173	38 667	44 824	55 134	73 707	108 268	141 505
5110 General taxes	-	3 272	27 895	31 396	41 611	56 101	84 348	111 102
5111 Value added taxes	-	3 272	27 895	31 396	41 611	56 101	84 348	111 102
5112 Sales tax		-	-	-	-	-	-	-
5113 Other		-	-	-	-	-	-	-
5120 Taxes on specific goods and services	46	1 901	10 772	13 428	13 523	17 606	23 920	30 403
5121 Excises	16	774	2 978	5 744	6 727	8 872	8 774	11 247
Oil	6	468	704	1 174	766	1 280	-	-
Alcoholic beverages	6	85	908	1 323	1 765	2 192	2 762	3 542
Tobacco	4	220	1 364	3 246	4 205	5 401	6 011	7 706
Matches	-	1	2	1	2	-	-	-
5122 Profits of fiscal monopolies	-	-	-	-	-	-	-	-
5123 Customs and import duties	30	972	7 573	7 267	6 409	8 504	15 017	19 052
5124 Taxes on exports	-	-	-	-	-	-	-	-
5125 Taxes on investment goods	-	-	-	-	-	-	-	-
5126 Taxes on specific services	0	155	220	417	386	230	129	104
Telecommunications	0	151	166	247	183	-	-	-
Casinos, bingo and slot machines	-	5	55	171	203	230	129	104
5127 Other taxes on internat trade and transactions	-	-	-	-	-	-	-	-
5128 Other taxes	-	-	-	-	-	-	-	-
5130 Unallocable between 5110 and 5120	-	-	-	-	-	-	-	-
5200 Taxes on use of goods and perform activities	-	-	-	-	-	-	-	-
5210 Recurrent taxes								
5211 Paid by households: motor vehicles								
5212 Paid by others: motor vehicles								
5213 Paid in respect of other goods								
5220 Non-recurrent taxes								
5300 Unallocable between 5100 and 5200	-	-	-	-	-	-	-	-
6000 Other taxes	-	-	-	-	-	-	7 781	3 928
6100 Paid solely by business	-	-	-	-	-	-	-	-
6200 Other	-	-	-	-	-	-	7 781	3 928
Total tax revenue on cash basis	412	10 849	83 163	95 791	101 014	116 311	169 603	216 518

Year ending 31st December

The data are on cash basis

The figures exclude state and local government revenues as the data are not available.

Heading 2000: The data on social security contributions are unavailable for 2011 and 2012.

Source: Ministry of Finance, SENIAT.

StatLink http://dx.doi.org/10.1787/888932971501

PART IV

Tax Revenues by Sub-sectors of General Government

Revenues of both the Latin American and the OECD countries have been attributed to the different levels of government according to the revised guidelines set out in to the final version of the 2008 System of National Accounts (SNA). Under this, revenues are generally attributed to the level of government that exercises the authority to impose the tax or has the final discretion to set and vary the tax rate.

PARTE IV

Ingresos tributarios por sub-sectores de gobierno general

Los ingresos de los países latinoamericanos y de los países de la OCDE se han atribuido a los diferentes niveles de gobierno de acuerdo con lo recogido en la versión final 2008 del Sistema de Cuentas Nacionales (SCN), según el cual, los ingresos se atribuyen por lo general al nivel de gobierno que ejerce la facultad de aplicar el impuesto o que puede a su discreción establecer y modificar la tasa del impuesto.

Table 28 - Cuadro 28

Attribution of tax revenues to sub-sectors of general government as percentage of total tax revenue[1]

Atribución de los ingresos tributarios en los sub-sectores del gobierno general como porcentaje del ingreso tributario total[1]

	Central government			State or Regional government			Local government			Social Security Funds			
	1995	2000	2011	1995	2000	2011	1995	2000	2011	1995	2000	2011	
Federal countries													**Países federales**
Argentina	59.0	66.4	64.0	17.5	17.8	14.5				23.4	15.8	21.5	Argentina
Brazil	44.7	47.8	45.9	26.8	25.3	23.8	3.7	3.4	5.2	24.8	23.5	25.2	Brasil
Mexico	80.1	80.7	81.9	2.1	2.0	2.5	1.1	0.8	1.1	16.6	16.5	14.5	México
Venezuela	94.6	94.6	96.6							5.4	5.4	3.4	Venezuela
OECD[2,3]	53.3	56.5	54.5	15.9	15.3	16.3	7.7	6.9	7.7	22.9	21.1	21.3	OCDE[2,3]
Regional countries													**Países regionales**
Colombia[4]	58.9	64.4	71.7	5.5	5.6	4.7	8.6	9.4	11.0	27.0	20.6	12.6	Colombia[4]
OECD[5]	50.4	49.0	29.9	4.8	7.6	23.1	8.5	9.1	9.6	35.8	33.8	36.9	OECD[5]
Unitary countries													**Países unitarios**
Bolivia	100.0	91.3	94.0								8.7	6.0	Bolivia
Chile	89.9	87.8	88.5				6.5	7.9	6.6	3.6	4.4	4.9	Chile
Costa Rica	66.2	65.3	63.3					2.1	2.9	33.8	32.6	33.8	Costa Rica
Dominican Republic	99.3	99.0	99.5							0.7	1.0	0.5	República Dominicana
Ecuador	73.9	87.7	71.1							26.1	12.3	28.9	Ecuador
El Salvador	85.9	83.6	88.8							14.1	16.4	11.2	El Salvador
Guatemala	83.8	83.6	83.7				0.6	0.9	1.4	15.6	15.5	15.0	Guatemala
Honduras	90.1	89.4	87.7							9.9	10.6	12.3	Honduras
Nicaragua	84.1	80.1	77.1							15.9	19.9	22.9	Nicaragua
Panama	62.0	59.6	62.4					2.2	1.5	38.0	38.2	36.0	Panamá
Paraguay[6]	100.0	82.7	76.7								17.3	23.3	Paraguay
Peru	88.2	87.7	87.5						2.9	11.8	12.3	9.6	Perú
Uruguay	62.0	62.5	71.4				7.8	7.9	4.1	30.1	29.6	24.5	Uruguay
OECD[2,6]	65.8	66.4	63.0				10.7	11.0	12.0	23.2	22.3	24.7	OCDE[2,6]

1. The figures exclude local government revenues for Argentina (but include provincial revenues), Bolivia, Costa Rica (up to 1997), Dominican Republic, Ecuador, El Salvador, Honduras, Nicaragua, Panama (up to 1998), Paraguay, Peru (up to 2004) and Venezuela as the data are not available.

1. Las cifras excluyen los ingresos de gobiernos locales en Argentina (pero incluye ingresos de las provincias), Bolivia, Costa Rica (hasta 1997), República Dominicana, Ecuador, El Salvador, Honduras, Nicaragua, Panamá (hasta 1998), Paraguay, Perú (hasta 2004) y Venezuela dado que los datos no están disponibles.

2. Chile and Mexico are also part of the OECD group. / 2. Chile y México son también parte del grupo OCDE.

3. Represents the unweighted average for OECD federal member countries. / 3. Representa el promedio no ponderado para los países federales miembros de la OCDE.

4. Colombia is constitutionally a unitary country with a decentralised political structure. / 4. Colombia es constitucionalmente un país unitario con una estructura política descentralizada.

5. Includes Spain, which is constitutionally a non-federal country with a highly decentralised political structure. / 5. Incluye España, que es constitucionalmente un país no federal con una estructura política altamente descentralizada.

6. Data estimated for 2011. / 6. Datos estimados para el 2011.

7. Represents the unweighted average for OECD unitary countries. / 7. Representa el promedio no ponderado para los países unitarios miembros de la OCDE.

StatLink http://dx.doi.org/10.1787/888932971520

Argentina **Argentina**

Table 29 - Cuadro 29

Tax revenues by sub-sectors of government

Ingresos tributarios por sub-sector de administración

Millions of argentinean pesos — Millones de pesos argentinos

	Federal government / Gobierno federal					State/Regional / Estado/Regional					Local government[1] / Gobierno local[1]					Social security funds / Fondos de seguridad social				
	1990	2000	2005	2010	2012	1990	2000	2005	2010	2012	1990	2000	2005	2010	2012	1990	2000	2005	2010	2012
1000 Taxes on income, profits and capital gains	382	11 303	29 203	78 427	140 108	-	-	-	-	-						-	-	-	-	-
2000 Social security contributions	-	-	-	-	-	-	-	-	-	-						2 583	9 670	17 400	102 460	179 776
3000 Taxes on payroll and workforce	-	-	-	-	-	-	-	-	-	-						-	-	-	-	-
4000 Taxes on property	499	1 254	11 439	32 674	52 061	803	2 643	4 558	10 864	20 371						-	-	-	-	-
4100 Recurrent taxes on immovable property	-	-	-	-	-	412	1 809	2 836	5 035	9 814										
4200 Recurrent taxes on net wealth	3	1 084	1 867	5 248	7 408	-	-	-	-	-										
4300 Estate, inheritance and gift taxes	-	-	-	-	-	-	-	-	-	-										
4400 Taxes on financial and capital transactions	496	100	9 550	27 423	44 652	160	833	1 722	5 829	10 556										
4500 Non-recurrent taxes	-	70	21	3	1	-	-	-	-	-										
4600 Other recurrent taxes on property	-	-	-	-	-	231	-	-	-	-										
5000 Taxes on goods and services	4 713	27 592	62 057	198 346	309 417	979	6 918	15 903	54 746	98 245						-	-	-	-	-
5100 Taxes on production, sale, transfer, etc	4 713	27 592	62 057	198 346	309 417	846	6 114	14 613	51 148	91 789										
5110 General taxes	1 591	18 426	34 968	113 330	188 509	846	6 114	14 613	51 148	91 789										
5120 Taxes on specific goods and services	3 122	9 166	27 089	85 016	120 908	-	-	-	-	-										
5130 Unallocable between 5110 and 5120	-	-	-	-	-	-	-	-	-	-										
5200 Taxes on use of goods and perform activities[2]	-	-	-	-	-	133	804	1 289	3 598	6 456										
5300 Unallocable between 5100 and 5200	-	-	-	-	-	-	-	-	-	-										
6000 Other taxes	215	389	869	2 386	4 759	43	1 309	1 469	3 110	3 316						-	-	-	-	-
TOTAL TAX REVENUE	5 809	40 538	103 568	311 833	506 345	1 825	10 870	21 930	68 719	121 932						2 583	9 670	17 400	102 460	179 776

1. The figures exclude local government revenues as the data are not available.

1. Las cifras excluyen los ingresos de gobiernos locales ya que los datos no están disponibles.

2. In ECLAC data, property tax on motor vehicles is classified in category 4000.

2. En los datos de CEPAL el impuesto sobre propiedad de vehículos automotores es clasificado en la categoría 4000.

StatLink http://dx.doi.org/10.1787/888932971539

Bolivia **Bolivia**

Table 30 - Cuadro 30

Tax revenues by sub-sectors of government

Ingresos tributarios por sub-sector de administración

Millions of bolivianos Millones de bolivianos

	Central government Gobierno central					Local government[1] Gobierno local[1]					Social security funds[2] Fondos de seguridad social[2]				
	1990	2000	2005	2010	2012	1990	2000	2005	2010	2012	1990	2000	2005	2010	2012
1000 Taxes on income, profits and capital gains	123	967	2 058	5 326	7 556						-	-	-	-	-
2000 Social security contributions	-	-	-	-	-						-	666	936	1 645	2 878
3000 Taxes on payroll and workforce	-	-	-	-	-						-	-	-	-	-
4000 Taxes on property	208	946	2 094	2 541	3 603						-	-	-	-	-
4100 Recurrent taxes on immovable property		-	-	-	-										
4200 Recurrent taxes on net wealth		-	-	-	-										
4300 Estate, inheritance and gift taxes		3	7	20	23										
4400 Taxes on financial and capital transactions		943	2 087	2 521	3 580										
4500 Non-recurrent taxes		-	-	-	-										
4600 Other recurrent taxes on property		-	-	-	-										
5000 Taxes on goods and services	786	5 206	9 674	20 011	31 782						-	-	-	-	-
5100 Taxes on production, sale, transfer, etc	786	5 206	9 674	20 011	31 782										
5110 General taxes	497	2 649	4 574	9 293	14 245										
5120 Taxes on specific goods and services	289	2 557	5 100	10 718	17 537										
5130 Unallocable between 5110 and 5120	-	-	-	-	-										
5200 Taxes on use of goods and perform activities	-	-	-	-	-										
5300 Unallocable between 5100 and 5200	-	-	-	-	-										
6000 Other taxes	-9	-135	-31	-1 029	6 732						-	-	-	-	-
TOTAL TAX REVENUE	1 108	6 984	13 794	26 850	49 673							666	936	1 645	2 878

1. The figures exclude local government revenues as the data are not available.

1. Las cifras excluyen los ingresos de gobiernos locales ya que los datos no están disponibles.

2. The data for social security contributions are available from the year 2000 only.

2. Las cifras sobre las contribuciones de seguridad social están disponibles desde el año 2000.

StatLink http://dx.doi.org/10.1787/888932971558

Brazil **Brasil**

Table 31 - Cuadro 31

Tax revenues by sub-sectors of government

Ingresos tributarios por sub-sector de administración

Millions of reais Millones de reales

	Federal government[1] Gobierno federal					State/Regional Estado/Regional					Local government Gobierno local					Social security funds Fondos de seguridad social				
	1990	2000	2005	2010	2012	1990	2000	2005	2010	2012[2]	1990	2000	2005	2010	2012[3]	1990	2000	2005	2010	2012
1000 Taxes on income, profits and capital gains	1	68 667	149 309	258 505	321 670	-	-	-	-	-	-	-	-	-	-	-	-	-	-	-
2000 Social security contributions	-	-	-	-	-	-	-	-	-	-	-	-	-	-	-	1	83 469	168 226	315 476	427 680
3000 Taxes on payroll and workforce	0	6 749	14 469	33 038	-	-	-	-	-	-	-	-	-	-	-	-	-	-	-	-
4000 Taxes on property	0	17 726	35 282	27 036	31 450	0	5 623	11 282	23 878	-	0	5 469	9 710	23 073	-	-	-	-	-	-
4100 Recurrent taxes on immovable property	0	234	288	483	680	-	-	-	-	-	0	4 519	8 117	17 154	-					
4200 Recurrent taxes on net wealth	-	-	-	-	-	-	-	-	-	-	-	-	-	-	-					
4300 Estate, inheritance and gift taxes	-	-	-	-	-	0	329	821	2 517	-	-	-	-	-	-					
4400 Taxes on financial and capital transactions	0	17 492	34 994	26 553	30 770	-	-	-	-	-	0	950	1 593	5 919	-					
4500 Non-recurrent taxes	-	-	-	-	-	-	-	-	-	-	-	-	-	-	-					
4600 Other recurrent taxes on property	-	-	-	-	-	0	5 294	10 460	21 361	-	-	-	-	-	-					
5000 Taxes on goods and services	1	74 190	147 819	241 229	300 470	1	83 848	158 809	284 606	329 780	0	6 106	11 247	32 839	-	-	-	-	-	-
5100 Taxes on production, sale, transfer, etc	1	74 190	147 819	241 229	300 470	1	82 279	153 437	267 977	329 780	0	6 106	11 247	32 839	-					
5110 General taxes	1	65 745	129 567	196 975	266 620	1	82 279	153 437	267 977	329 780	0	6 106	11 247	32 839	-					
5120 Taxes on specific goods and services	-	8 445	18 252	44 254	33 850	-	-	-	-	-	-	-	-	-	-					
5130 Unallocable between 5110 and 5120	-	-	-	-	-	-	-	-	-	-	-	-	-	-	-					
5200 Taxes on use of goods and perform activities	-	-	-	-	-	0	1 569	5 372	16 629	-	-	-	-	-	-					
5300 Unallocable between 5100 and 5200	-	-	-	-	-	-	-	-	-	-	-	-	-	-	-					
6000 Other taxes	0	2 337	2 039	3 353	58 360	0	322	1 551	-	49 520	0	377	1 404	8 642	78 090	-	-	-	-	-
TOTAL TAX REVENUE	1	169 669	348 918	563 160	711 950	1	89 793	171 641	308 484	379 300	0	11 952	22 360	64 554	78 090	1	83 469	168 226	315 476	427 680

1. For years prior to 2000, as well as for 2012, the PASEP contributions under heading 3000 are included in the total for PIS contributions under heading 5110. For 2012, revenue from the other taxes under heading 3000 is included in category 6000.

1. Para los años antes del 2000, así como para el año 2012, las contribuciones PASEP bajo la categoría 3000 son incluidas en el total para las contribuciones PIS bajo la categoría 5110. Para el 2012, ingresos provenientes de otros impuestos bajo la categoría 3000 son incluidos en la categoría 6000.

2. For 2012, category 6000 includes IPVA, ITCD, and Taxas Estaduais. / 2. Para 2012, la categoría 6000 incluye el IPVA, el ITCD, y las "Taxas Estaduais".

3. For 2012, category 6000 includes ISS, IPTU, and ITBI. / 3. Para 2012, la categoría 6000 incluye el ISS, el IPTU, y el ITI.

StatLink http://dx.doi.org/10.1787/888932971577

Chile

Table 32 - Cuadro 32

Tax revenues by sub-sectors of government

Ingresos tributarios por sub-sector de administración

Millions of chilean pesos

Millones de pesos chilenos

	Central government Gobierno central					Local government Gobierno local					Social security funds Fondos de seguridad social				
	1990	2000	2005	2010	2012	1990	2000	2005	2010	2012	1990	2000	2005	2010	2012
1000 Taxes on income, profits and capital gains	412 974	1 841 630	5 171 293	8 329 060	10 803 031	-	-	-	-	-	-	-	-	-	-
2000 Social security contributions	66 738	232 728	287 422	371 386	-	-	-	-	-	-	92 821	344 030	644 295	1 122 601	1 422 554
3000 Taxes on payroll and workforce	-	-	-	-	-	-	-	-	-	-	-	-	-	-	-
4000 Taxes on property	59 682	255 371	490 120	245 044	409 596	49 637	298 666	411 656	540 320	728 466	-	-	-	-	-
4100 Recurrent taxes on immovable property	10 331	3 578	4 909	8 805	18 208	49 637	298 666	411 656	540 320	728 466					
4200 Recurrent taxes on net wealth	-	-	-	-	-	-	-	-	-	-					
4300 Estate, inheritance and gift taxes	3 444	10 906	23 184	39 338	66 719	-	-	-	-	-					
4400 Taxes on financial and capital transactions	45 907	240 886	462 027	196 901	324 669	-	-	-	-	-					
4500 Non-recurrent taxes	-	-	-	-	-	-	-	-	-	-					
4600 Other recurrent taxes on property	-	-	-	-	-	-	-	-	-	-					
5000 Taxes on goods and services	1 063 677	4 719 255	6 831 421	10 330 378	12 798 158	55 045	322 514	514 952	800 810	979 200	-	-	-	-	-
5100 Taxes on production, sale, transfer, etc	1 060 304	4 684 525	6 811 328	10 294 165	12 750 259	13 705	105 302	140 703	220 657	285 878					
5110 General taxes	664 421	3 306 350	5 391 285	8 399 926	10 447 374	-	-	-	-	-					
5120 Taxes on specific goods and services[1]	395 883	1 378 175	1 420 043	1 894 239	2 302 885	13 705	105 302	140 703	220 657	285 878					
5130 Unallocable between 5110 and 5120	-	-	-	-	-	-	-	-	-	-					
5200 Taxes on use of goods and perform activities	3 374	34 730	20 094	36 213	47 899	41 340	217 212	374 249	580 153	693 322					
5300 Unallocable between 5100 and 5200	-	-	-	-	-	-	-	-	-	-					
6000 Other taxes	-23 356	-112 195	-85 954	-61 117	55 355	-	-	-	-	-	-	-	-	-	-
TOTAL TAX REVENUE	1 579 715	6 936 788	12 694 301	19 214 751	24 066 140	104 682	621 180	926 608	1 341 129	1 707 666	92 821	344 030	644 295	1 122 601	1 422 554

1. In ECLAC data, figures from the Oil Prices Stabilisation Fund (FEPP) are considered as non tax revenues.

1. En los datos de CEPAL, las cifras del Fondo de Estabilización de Precios del Petróleo (FEPP) son tratadas como ingresos no tributarios.

StatLink http://dx.doi.org/10.1787/888932971596

Colombia **Colombia**

Table 33 - Cuadro 33

Tax revenues by sub-sectors of government

Ingresos tributarios por sub-sector de administración

Millions of colombian pesos / Millones de pesos colombianos

	Central government Gobierno central					State/Regional[1] Estado/Regional[1]					Local government[1] Gobierno local[1]					Social security funds Fondos de seguridad social				
	1990	2000	2005	2010	2012	1990	2000	2005	2010	2012	1990	2000	2005	2010	2012	1990	2000	2005	2010	2012
1000 Taxes on income, profits and capital gains	771 694	7 103 525	17 348 618	26 190 739	43 649 796	-	-	-	-	-	-	-	-	-	-	-	-	-	-	-
2000 Social security contributions	-	-	-	-	-	-	-	-	-	-	-	-	-	-	-	203 596	6 275 803	10 024 842	15 500 589	16 145 691
3000 Taxes on payroll and workforce	-	-	-	-	-	-	-	-	-	-	-	-	-	-	-	-	-	-	-	-
4000 Taxes on property	-	1 036 584	2 863 946	5 196 303	9 651 645	-	-	-	-	-	56 160	991 070	1 974 213	3 163 084	3 917 577	-	-	-	-	-
4100 Recurrent taxes on immovable property		-	-	-	-						56 160	991 070	1 974 213	3 163 084	3 917 577					
4200 Recurrent taxes on net wealth		-	462 720	1 970 530	4 183 293						-	-	-	-	-					
4300 Estate, inheritance and gift taxes		-	-	-	-						-	-	-	-	-					
4400 Taxes on financial and capital transactions		1 036 584	2 401 226	3 225 773	5 468 352						-	-	-	-	-					
4500 Non-recurrent taxes		-	-	-	-						-	-	-	-	-					
4600 Other recurrent taxes on property		-	-	-	-						-	-	-	-	-					
5000 Taxes on goods and services	1 035 934	11 022 878	21 393 776	34 882 447	41 567 647	263 429	1 204 940	1 966 325	2 874 375	3 271 180	89 290	1 140 090	2 506 452	4 306 620	5 407 497	-	-	-	-	-
5100 Taxes on production, sale, transfer, etc	1 035 934	11 022 878	21 393 776	34 882 447	41 567 647	263 429	1 204 940	1 966 325	2 874 375	3 271 180	89 290	1 140 090	2 506 452	4 306 620	5 407 497					
5110 General taxes	583 078	8 445 776	17 427 948	28 811 682	36 291 054	-	-	-	-	-	89 290	1 140 090	2 506 452	4 306 620	5 407 497					
5120 Taxes on specific goods and services	452 856	2 577 102	3 965 828	6 070 765	5 276 593	263 429	1 204 940	1 966 325	2 874 375	3 271 180	-	-	-	-	-					
5130 Unallocable between 5110 and 5120	-	-	-			-	-	-	-	-	-	-	-	-	-					
5200 Taxes on use of goods and perform activities	-	-	-	-	-	-	-	-	-	-	-	-	-	-	-					
5300 Unallocable between 5100 and 5200	-	-	-	-	-	-	-	-	-	-	-	-	-	-	-					
6000 Other taxes	78 306	480 784	682 084	482 848	209 240	-	518 253	1 117 016	2 005 277	2 247 160	81 017	738 983	1 578 573	3 403 883	4 134 163	-	-	-	-	-
TOTAL TAX REVENUE	1 885 934	19 643 771	42 288 424	66 752 337	95 078 328	263 429	1 723 193	3 083 341	4 879 652	5 518 340	226 467	2 870 144	6 059 238	10 873 586	13 459 237	203 596	6 275 803	10 024 842	15 500 589	16 145 691

1. Corresponds to the reported consolidated revenues of the territorial entities (departments and municipalities). / 1. Corresponde al reporte de los ingresos consolidados de las entidades territoriales consolidadas (departamentos y municipios).

StatLink http://dx.doi.org/10.1787/888932971615

Costa Rica **Costa Rica**

Table 34 - Cuadro 34

Tax revenues by sub-sectors of government

Ingresos tributarios por sub-sector de administración

Millions of colones Millones de colones

	Central government Gobierno central					Local government[1] Gobierno local[1]					Social security funds Fondos de seguridad social				
	1990	2000	2005	2010	2012	1990	2000	2005	2010	2012	1990	2000	2005	2010	2012
1000 Taxes on income, profits and capital gains	11 820	128 805	324 224	748 093	891 669		-	-	-	-	-	-	-	-	-
2000 Social security contributions[2]	-	-	-	-	-		-	-	-	-	29 065	249 886	503 651	1 148 663	1 414 755
3000 Taxes on payroll and workforce	-	-	-	-	-		-	-	-	-	7 054	41 918	73 954	165 443	205 971
4000 Taxes on property	366	7 291	10 846	18 270	23 588		5 390	14 264	45 393	58 280	-	-	-	-	-
4100 Recurrent taxes on immovable property	-	-	-	3 527	2 638		5 310	14 245	44 080	58 280					
4200 Recurrent taxes on net wealth	-	4 284	-	-	-		-	-	-	-					
4300 Estate, inheritance and gift taxes	-	-	-	-	-		-	-	-	-					
4400 Taxes on financial and capital transactions	366	3 007	10 846	14 743	20 950		-	-	-	-					
4500 Non-recurrent taxes	-	-	-	-	-		-	-	-	-					
4600 Other recurrent taxes on property	-	-	-	-	-		80	19	1 313	-					
5000 Taxes on goods and services	52 360	444 726	920 160	1 696 729	2 040 758		11 981	26 810	65 862	81 831	-	-	-	-	-
5100 Taxes on production, sale, transfer, etc	49 980	425 353	887 390	1 598 790	1 934 078		11 981	26 810	65 862	81 831					
5110 General taxes	21 326	222 775	485 168	920 298	1 122 978		-	-	-	-					
5120 Taxes on specific goods and services[3]	28 654	202 887	399 192	678 492	811 100		10 612	24 294	61 002	1 913					
5130 Unallocable between 5110 and 5120	-	-308	3 031	-	-		1 369	2 515	4 860	79 918					
5200 Taxes on use of goods and perform activities	2 380	19 357	32 758	97 803	106 557		-	-	-	-					
5300 Unallocable between 5100 and 5200	-	15	12	136	123		-	-	-	-					
6000 Other taxes[4]	6 113	2 573	7 009	12 864	35 778		1 242	3 207	4 366	5 285	-	-	-	-	-
TOTAL TAX REVENUE	70 660	583 395	1 262 240	2 475 956	2 991 793		18 613	44 280	115 621	145 396	36 119	291 804	577 605	1 314 106	1 620 726

1. The figures for years up to and including 1997 exclude local government revenues as the data are not available.
1. Las cifras para los años hasta 1997 inclusive excluyen los ingresos de gobiernos locales ya que los datos no están disponibles.
2. In ECLAC data, social security contributions include INA, IMAS, and FODESAF.
2. En las estadísticas de CEPAL, las Contribuciones a la Seguridad Social incluye INA, IMAS y FODESAF.
3. In ECLAC data, the Property tax on vehicles, aircraft and boats is classified in category 4000.
3. Las estadísticas de CEPAL consideran el impuesto sobre la propiedad de vehículos, aeronaves y embarcaciones Ley No 7088 en la categoría de Impuestos sobre la Propiedad (4000).
4. In ECLAC data, the tax on the transfer of used vehicles Law No. 7088 of 30/11/87 is classified as a property tax (4000).
4. Las estadísticas de CEPAL consideran el impuesto traspaso de vehículos usados Ley No 7088 de 30-11-87 en la categoría de Impuestos sobre la Propiedad (4000).

StatLink http://dx.doi.org/10.1787/888932971634

Dominican Republic | **República Dominicana**

Table 35 - Cuadro 35

Tax revenues by sub-sectors of government

Ingresos tributarios por sub-sector de administración

Millions of dominican pesos | Millones de pesos dominicanos

	Central government Gobierno central					Local government[1] Gobierno local[1]					Social security funds[2] Fondos de seguridad social[2]				
	1990	2000	2005	2010	2012	1990	2000	2005	2010	2012	1990	2000	2005	2010	2012
1000 Taxes on income, profits and capital gains	1 670	7 060	24 102	40 496	76 315						-	-	-	-	-
2000 Social security contributions	-	-	-	-	-						53	490	35	1 845	1 250
3000 Taxes on payroll and workforce	-	3 722	5 940	13 147	15 959						-	-	-	-	-
4000 Taxes on property	46	505	6 555	12 738	18 867						-	-	-	-	-
4100 Recurrent taxes on immovable property	9	115	1 710	3 004	8 351										
4200 Recurrent taxes on net wealth	-	-	-	-	-										
4300 Estate, inheritance and gift taxes	11	96	84	231	227										
4400 Taxes on financial and capital transactions	22	217	4 546	8 125	8 723										
4500 Non-recurrent taxes	3	32	89	488	609										
4600 Other recurrent taxes on property	1	45	127	891	957										
5000 Taxes on goods and services	4 488	36 038	111 344	175 716	199 673						-	-	-	-	-
5100 Taxes on production, sale, transfer, etc	4 410	35 281	109 602	173 403	196 473										
5110 General taxes	976	9 940	41 033	82 012	-										
5120 Taxes on specific goods and services[3]	3 396	22 590	67 736	91 356	-										
5130 Unallocable between 5110 and 5120	-	-	-	-	-										
5200 Taxes on use of goods and perform activities	77	757	1 742	2 313	3 199										
5300 Unallocable between 5100 and 5200	-	-	-	-	-										
6000 Other taxes[4]	159	495	1 661	-	0						-	-	-	-	-
TOTAL TAX REVENUE	6 362	47 820	149 602	242 097	310 814						53	490	35	1 845	1 250

1. The figures exclude local government revenues as the data are not available.
1. Las cifras excluyen los ingresos de gobiernos locales ya que los datos no están disponibles.
2. The figures exclude social secuirty contributions to general government managed by the private sector.
2. Estos datos excluyen contribuciones a la seguridad social hacia el gobierno central administradas por el sector privado.
3. In ECLAC data, the tax on transfer of movable goods is classified as a property tax (4000).
3. Las estadísticas de CEPAL consideran el Sobre Transferencias de Bienes Inmuebles (Actos Traslativos) en la categoría de Impuestos sobre la Propiedad (4000).
4. In ECLAC data, the Vehicle transfer tax is classified as a property tax (4000).
4. Las estadísticas de CEPAL consideran el Transacciones de Vehículos de Motor en la categoría de Impuestos sobre la Propiedad (4000).

StatLink http://dx.doi.org/10.1787/888932971653

Ecuador **Ecuador**

Table 36 - Cuadro 36

Tax revenues by sub-sectors of government

Ingresos tributarios por sub-sector de administración

Millions of USD Millones de USD

	Central government Gobierno central					Local government[1] Gobierno local[1]					Social security funds Fondos de seguridad social				
	1990	2000	2005	2010	2012	1990	2000	2005	2010	2012	1990	2000	2005	2010	2012
1000 Taxes on income, profits and capital gains	138	293	937	2 353	3 313						-	-	-	-	-
2000 Social security contributions	-	-	-	-	-						243	228	1 109	2 549	4 752
3000 Taxes on payroll and workforce	-	-	-	-	-						-	-	-	-	-
4000 Taxes on property	-	-	-	-	-						-	-	-	-	-
4100 Recurrent taxes on immovable property															
4200 Recurrent taxes on net wealth															
4300 Estate, inheritance and gift taxes															
4400 Taxes on financial and capital transactions															
4500 Non-recurrent taxes															
4600 Other recurrent taxes on property															
5000 Taxes on goods and services	668	1 330	2 802	6 152	8 830						-	-	-	-	-
5100 Taxes on production, sale, transfer, etc	665	1 319	2 742	5 997	8 636										
5110 General taxes	302	836	1 975	3 886	5 415										
5120 Taxes on specific goods and services	363	483	767	2 110	3 221										
5130 Unallocable between 5110 and 5120	-	-	-	-	-										
5200 Taxes on use of goods and perform activities[2]	3	11	60	156	194										
5300 Unallocable between 5100 and 5200	-	-	-	-	-										
6000 Other taxes	27	-	2	289	111						-	-	-	-	-
TOTAL TAX REVENUE	833	1 623	3 741	8 794	12 255						243	228	1 109	2 549	4 752

1. The figures exclude local government revenues as the data are not available.

1. Las cifras excluyen los ingresos de gobiernos locales ya que los datos no están disponibles.

2. In ECLAC data, the annual tax on motor vehicles is classified as a property tax (4000).

2. Las estadísticas de CEPAL consideran el A la propiedad (vehículos) en la categoría de Impuestos sobre la Propiedad (4000).

StatLink http://dx.doi.org/10.1787/888932971672

El Salvador **El Salvador**

Table 37 - Cuadro 37

Tax revenues by sub-sectors of government

Ingresos tributarios por sub-sector de administración

Millions of USD Millones de USD

	Central government Gobierno central					Local government[1] Gobierno local[1]					Social security funds[2] Fondos de seguridad social[2]				
	1990	2000	2005	2010	2012	1990	2000	2005	2010	2012	1990	2000	2005	2010	2012
1000 Taxes on income, profits and capital gains	95	429	668	940	1 184						-	-	-	-	-
2000 Social security contributions	-	-	-	-	-						67	263	282	369	404
3000 Taxes on payroll and workforce	-	-	-	-	-						-	-	-	-	-
4000 Taxes on property	26	12	16	16	20						-	-	-	-	-
4100 Recurrent taxes on immovable property	-	-	-	-	-										
4200 Recurrent taxes on net wealth	16	-	-	-	-										
4300 Estate, inheritance and gift taxes	-	-	-	-	-										
4400 Taxes on financial and capital transactions	10	12	16	16	20										
4500 Non-recurrent taxes	-	-	-	-	-										
4600 Other recurrent taxes on property	-	-	-	-	-										
5000 Taxes on goods and services	259	903	1 447	1 855	2 118						-	-	-	-	-
5100 Taxes on production, sale, transfer, etc	259	903	1 447	1 855	2 118										
5110 General taxes	133	714	1 104	1 433	1 677										
5120 Taxes on specific goods and services	127	189	344	422	441										
5130 Unallocable between 5110 and 5120	-	-	-	-	-										
5200 Taxes on use of goods and perform activities	-	-	-	-	-										
5300 Unallocable between 5100 and 5200	-	-	-	-	-										
6000 Other taxes	58	0	-	-	-						-	-	-	-	-
TOTAL TAX REVENUE	438	1 344	2 131	2 810	3 322						67	263	282	369	404

1. The figures exclude local government revenues as the data are not available.

1. Las cifras excluyen los ingresos de gobiernos locales ya que los datos no están disponibles.

2. Corresponds to social security contributions paid to the Salvadoran Institute of Social Security.

2. Corresponde a contribuciones de seguridad social pagadas al Instituto Salvadoreño del Seguro Social.

StatLink http://dx.doi.org/10.1787/888932971691

Guatemala **Guatemala**

Table 38 - Cuadro 38

Tax revenues by sub-sectors of government

Ingresos tributarios por sub-sector de administración

Millions of quetzales / Millones de quetzales

	Central government Gobierno central					Local government[1] Gobierno local[1]					Social security funds[2] Fondos de seguridad social[2]				
	1990	2000	2005	2010	2012	1990	2000	2005	2010	2012	1990	2000	2005	2010	2012
1000 Taxes on income, profits and capital gains	507	3 295	6 049	10 319	13 445	-	-	-	-	-	-	-	-	-	-
2000 Social security contributions	-	-	-	-	-	-	-	-	-	-	436	2 569	4 072	6 267	6 048
3000 Taxes on payroll and workforce	-	-	-	-	-	-	-	-	-	-	-	-	-	-	-
4000 Taxes on property	45	17	9	11	9	-	147	341	620	557	-	-	-	-	-
4100 Recurrent taxes on immovable property	-	6	1	1	1		147	341	620	557					
4200 Recurrent taxes on net wealth	-	-	-	-	-		-	-	-	-					
4300 Estate, inheritance and gift taxes	-	-	-	-	-		-	-	-	-					
4400 Taxes on financial and capital transactions	45	12	8	10	8		-	-	-	-					
4500 Non-recurrent taxes	-	-	-	-	-		-	-	-	-					
4600 Other recurrent taxes on property	-	-	-	-	-		-	-	-	-					
5000 Taxes on goods and services	1 709	10 317	16 402	23 259	27 499	-	-	-	-	-	-	-	-	-	-
5100 Taxes on production, sale, transfer, etc	1 681	10 131	16 083	22 754	26 595										
5110 General taxes	762	6 259	10 753	16 980	20 913										
5120 Taxes on specific goods and services	919	3 872	5 330	5 773	5 682										
5130 Unallocable between 5110 and 5120	-	-	-	-	-										
5200 Taxes on use of goods and perform activities	28	186	319	505	904										
5300 Unallocable between 5100 and 5200	-	-	-	-	-										
6000 Other taxes	104	186	315	572	878	-	-	-	-	-	-	-	-	-	-
TOTAL TAX REVENUE	2 365	13 816	22 775	34 161	41 831	-	147	341	620	557	436	2 569	4 072	6 267	6 048

1. The figures exclude some local government revenues as the data are not available. Revenues from the municipal property tax (IUSI) are included. The current law (Decree 15-98) states that the IUSI can be collected by those municipalities that have indicated the technical and administrative capacity to collect and administer the tax.

1. Las cifras excluyen los ingresos de gobiernos locales ya que los datos no están disponibles. Los ingresos provenientes del Impuesto Único Sobre Inmuebles (IUSI) están incluídos. La legislación vigente (Decreto 15-98) establece que el IUSI pueden ser recaudado por los municipios que han indicado la capacidad técnica y administrativa para recaudar y administrar el impuesto.

2. Corresponds to social security contributions to the Guatemalan Social Security Institute (IGSS) and payments by public employees to the government's pension fund.

2. Corresponde a las contribuciones de seguridad social pagadas al Instituto Guatemalteco de Seguridad Social (IGSS) y pagos de empleados públicos al Fondo de pensiones del Estado.

StatLink http://dx.doi.org/10.1787/888932971710

Honduras **Honduras**

Table 39 - Cuadro 39

Tax revenues by sub-sectors of government

Ingresos tributarios por sub-sector de administración

Millions of lempiras — Millones de lempiras

	Central government Gobierno central					Local government[1] Gobierno local[1]					Social security funds Fondos de seguridad social				
	1990	2000	2005	2010	2012	1990	2000	2005	2010	2012	1990	2000	2005	2010	2012
1000 Taxes on income, profits and capital gains	431	2 985	7 498	13 972	17 531						-	-	-	-	-
2000 Social security contributions	-	-	-	-	-						179	1 727	4 416	8 671	10 934
3000 Taxes on payroll and workforce	-	-	-	-	-						-	-	-	-	-
4000 Taxes on property	16	189	170	254	327						-	-	-	-	-
4100 Recurrent taxes on immovable property		-	-	-	-										
4200 Recurrent taxes on net wealth		-	-	-	-										
4300 Estate, inheritance and gift taxes		-	-	-	-										
4400 Taxes on financial and capital transactions		-	-	-	-										
4500 Non-recurrent taxes		-	-	-	-										
4600 Other recurrent taxes on property		189	170	254	327										
5000 Taxes on goods and services	1 405	11 445	19 032	28 937	34 610						-	-	-	-	-
5100 Taxes on production, sale, transfer, etc	1 405	11 445	19 032	28 937	34 610										
5110 General taxes	344	5 146	9 565	16 050	20 150										
5120 Taxes on specific goods and services	1 061	6 299	9 468	12 887	14 460										
5130 Unallocable between 5110 and 5120	-	-	-	-	-										
5200 Taxes on use of goods and perform activities	-	-	-	-	-										
5300 Unallocable between 5100 and 5200	-	-	-	-	-										
6000 Other taxes	1	2	7	9	10						-	-	-	-	-
TOTAL TAX REVENUE	1 853	14 620	26 708	43 173	52 478						179	1 727	4 416	8 671	10 934

1. The figures exclude local government revenues as the data are not available.

1. Las cifras excluyen los ingresos de gobiernos locales ya que los datos no están disponibles.

StatLink http://dx.doi.org/10.1787/888932971729

Mexico **México**

Table 40 - Cuadro 40

Tax revenues by sub-sectors of government

Ingresos tributarios por sub-sector de administración

Millions of mexican pesos

Millones de pesos mexicanos

	Federal government Gobierno federal					State/Regional Estado/Regional					Local government Gobierno local					Social security funds Fondos de seguridad social				
	1990	2000	2005	2010	2012	1990	2000	2005	2010	2012 [2]	1990	2000	2005	2010	2012 [2]	1990	2000	2005	2010	2012
1000 Taxes on income, profits and capital gains	34 668	276 548	402 036	683 604	803 071	3	-	-	-	-	2	-	-	-	-	-	-	-	-	-
2000 Social security contributions	-	-	-	-	-	-	-	-	-	-	-	-	-	-	-	17 165	167 292	261 673	378 006	454 778
3000 Taxes on payroll and workforce	818	-	-	-	-	972	11 215	20 429	36 818		7	2	32	93		-	-	-	-	-
4000 Taxes on property	3	-	-	-	-	894	7 018	10 905	13 137		1 017	6 946	15 891	25 818		-	-	-	-	-
4100 Recurrent taxes on immovable property	-					482	5 238	6 544	8 522		554	4 710	10 098	17 202						
4200 Recurrent taxes on net wealth	-					-	-	-	-		-	-	-	-						
4300 Estate, inheritance and gift taxes	-					7	-	-	-		1	-	-	-						
4400 Taxes on financial and capital transactions	3					405	1 781	4 361	4 615		462	2 236	5 793	8 616						
4500 Non-recurrent taxes	-					-	-	-	-		-	-	-	-						
4600 Other recurrent taxes on property	-					-	-	-	-		-	-	-	-						
5000 Taxes on goods and services	70 559	536 406	942 354	1 287 081	1 639 378	118	1 346	2 124	5 805		114	202	288	487		-	-	-	-	-
5100 Taxes on production, sale, transfer, etc	69 983	527 624	927 401	1 268 645	1 638 953	45	910	1 364	2 470		97	133	214	466						
5110 General taxes	26 635	189 606	318 432	504 509	579 988	-	-	-	-		-	-	-	-						
5120 Taxes on specific goods and services	43 348	338 018	608 969	764 136	1 058 965	30	910	1 364	2 470		95	133	214	466						
5130 Unallocable between 5110 and 5120	-	-	-	-	-	15	-	-	-		2	-	-	-						
5200 Taxes on use of goods and perform activities	576	8 782	14 953	18 436	425	73	436	760	3 335		17	69	74	21						
5300 Unallocable between 5100 and 5200	-	-	-	-	-	-	-	-	-		-	-	-	-						
6000 Other taxes	1 340	5 878	8 616	22 236	26 337	165	907	1 537	2 547		114	866	1 539	2 616		-	-	-	-	-
TOTAL TAX REVENUE	107 388	818 832	1 353 007	1 992 921	2 468 787	2 152	20 485	34 995	58 307		1 254	8 016	17 750	29 014		17 165	167 292	261 673	378 006	454 778
Fees levied on hydrocarbon production[1]	-26 196	-218 567	-526 171	-643 414	-926 528	-	-	-	-		-	-	-	-		-	-	-	-	-
Total tax revenue (net of fees on hydrocarbons)	81 192	600 265	826 836	1 349 507	1 542 258	2 152	20 485	34 995	58 307		1 254	8 016	17 750	29 014		17 165	167 292	261 673	378 006	454 778

1. In ECLAC and CIAT data, fees levied on hydrocarbon production are treated as non tax revenues.

1. En los datos de CEPAL y CIAT, los derechos sobre la producción de hidrocarbonos son tratados como ingresos no tributarios.

2. The 2012 data for revenues of the State and Local levels of government are not available. They comprise revenues in categories 3000, 4000, 5000, and 6000.

2. Los datos del año 2012 de los ingresos a nivel estatal y local del gobierno no se encuentran disponibles. Incluyen los ingresos de las siguientes categorías 3000, 4000, 5000 y 6000.

StatLink http://dx.doi.org/10.1787/888932971748

Nicaragua **Nicaragua**

Table 41 - Cuadro 41

Tax revenues by sub-sectors of government

Ingresos tributarios por sub-sector de administración

Millions of cordobas Millones de córdobas

	Central government Gobierno central					Local government[1] Gobierno local[1]					Social security funds Fondos de seguridad social				
	1990[2]	2000	2005	2010	2012	1990[2]	2000	2005	2010	2012	1990[2]	2000	2005	2010	2012
1000 Taxes on income, profits and capital gains		1 144	3 902	8 481	13 346							-	-	-	-
2000 Social security contributions		-	-	-	-							1 678	3 363	8 090	11 007
3000 Taxes on payroll and workforce		-	-	-	-							-	-	-	-
4000 Taxes on property		-	2	-	-							-	-	-	-
4100 Recurrent taxes on immovable property		-	-	-	-										
4200 Recurrent taxes on net wealth		-	2	-	-										
4300 Estate, inheritance and gift taxes		-	-	-	-										
4400 Taxes on financial and capital transactions		-	-	-	-										
4500 Non-recurrent taxes		-	-	-	-										
4600 Other recurrent taxes on property		-	-	-	-										
5000 Taxes on goods and services		5 584	9 725	17 029	23 754							-	-	-	-
5100 Taxes on production, sale, transfer, etc		5 584	9 725	17 029	23 754										
5110 General taxes		2 931	5 599	10 353	15 151										
5120 Taxes on specific goods and services		2 653	4 126	6 676	8 603										
5130 Unallocable between 5110 and 5120		-	-	-	-										
5200 Taxes on use of goods and perform activities		-	-	-	-										
5300 Unallocable between 5100 and 5200		-	-	-	-										
6000 Other taxes		11	17	20	24							-	-	-	-
TOTAL TAX REVENUE		6 739	13 646	25 530	37 124							1 678	3 363	8 090	11 007

1. The figures exclude local government revenues as the data are not available.

1. Las cifras excluyen los ingresos de gobiernos locales ya que los datos no están disponibles.

2. Comparable statistics for 1990 cannot be shown due to the devaluation of the Nicaraguan cordoba.

2. No se pueden presentar estadísticas comparables para el año 1990, debido a la devaluación del córdoba nicaragüense.

StatLink http://dx.doi.org/10.1787/888932971767

Panama | **Panamá**

Table 42 - Cuadro 42

Tax revenues by sub-sectors of government
Ingresos tributarios por sub-sector de administración

Thousands of balboas | Miles de balboas

	Central government Gobierno central					Local government[1] Gobierno local[1]					Social security funds Fondos de seguridad social				
	1990	2000	2005	2010	2012	1990	2000	2005	2010	2012[2]	1990	2000	2005	2010	2012
1000 Taxes on income, profits and capital gains	216 950	484 872	562 852	1 317 028	1 985 220		-	-	-	-	-	-	-	-	-
2000 Social security contributions	-	-	-	-	-		-	-	-	-	271 300	742 000	827 300	1 637 100	2 168 500
3000 Taxes on payroll and workforce	-	36 400	36 243	58 844	70 400		-	-	-	-	-	-	-	-	-
4000 Taxes on property	43 443	62 090	109 086	212 194	261 033		0	0	-	-	-	-	-	-	-
4100 Recurrent taxes on immovable property	28 330	33 898	56 424	107 791	119 964		0	0	-						
4200 Recurrent taxes on net wealth	-	-	-	-	-		-	-	-						
4300 Estate, inheritance and gift taxes	154	-	-	-	-		-	-	-						
4400 Taxes on financial and capital transactions	3 419	9 343	21 049	29 810	40 998		-	-	-						
4500 Non-recurrent taxes	-	-	-	-	-		-	-	-						
4600 Other recurrent taxes on property	11 540	18 849	31 613	74 593	100 071		-	-	-						
5000 Taxes on goods and services	335 470	530 276	641 708	1 472 515	2 067 189		43 098	50 631	40 551	-	-	-	-	-	-
5100 Taxes on production, sale, transfer, etc	331 758	530 276	641 708	1 472 515	2 067 189		53	5	-						
5110 General taxes	80 303	69 013	137 585	766 154	1 183 878		-	-	-						
5120 Taxes on specific goods and services[3]	138 623	461 263	504 123	706 360	883 311		53	5	-						
5130 Unallocable between 5110 and 5120	112 832	-	-	-	-		-	-	-						
5200 Taxes on use of goods and perform activities	3 712	-	-	-	-		43 045	50 626	40 551						
5300 Unallocable between 5100 and 5200	-	-	-	-	-		-	-	-						
6000 Other taxes	25 674	42 876	28 784	41 064	44 900		11	0	35 533	99 361	-	-	-	-	-
TOTAL TAX REVENUE	621 537	1 156 514	1 378 673	3 101 645	4 428 741		43 109	50 631	76 084	99 361	271 300	742 000	827 300	1 637 100	2 168 500

1. The figures for years up to and including 1998 exclude local government revenues as the data are not available.
1. Las cifras para los años hasta 1998 inclusive excluyen los ingresos de gobiernos locales ya que los datos no están disponibles.
2. The 2012 figure for local government taxes has been estimated as shown under heading 6000. It includes some revenues that would otherwise be shown under 4000 and 5000.
2. Las cifras del 2012 para impuestos de gobiernos locales han sido estimadas bajo la categoría 6000. Incluye ingresos que normalmente serian mostrados bajo las categorías 4000 y 5000.
3. In CIAT and ECLAC data, the tax on banks, financial institutions, and currency exchange is classified as a property tax.
3. Las estadísticas de CIAT y CEPAL consideran el Bancos y Casa de Cambios en la categoría de Impuestos sobre la Propiedad (4000).

StatLink http://dx.doi.org/10.1787/888932971786

Paraguay **Paraguay**

Table 43 - Cuadro 43

Tax revenues by sub-sectors of government

Ingresos tributarios por sub-sector de administración

Millions of guaranies

Millones de guaranies

	Central government[1] Gobierno central[1]					Local government[2] Gobierno local[2]					Social security funds[3] Fondos de seguridad social[3]				
	1990	2000	2005	2010	2012	1990	2000	2005	2010	2012	1990	2000	2005	2010	2012
1000 Taxes on income, profits and capital gains	73 726	470 388	938 886	2 096 498	2 902 614			-	-	-	-	-	-	-	-
2000 Social security contributions	28 882	300 451	541 310	1 140 654				-	-	-	-	619 082	1 050 670	2 411 987	
3000 Taxes on payroll and workforce	-	-	-	-	-			-	-	-	-	-	-	-	-
4000 Taxes on property	17 162	-	-	-	-			-	272 385		-	-	-	-	-
4100 Recurrent taxes on immovable property	17 162							-	254 306						
4200 Recurrent taxes on net wealth	-							-	-						
4300 Estate, inheritance and gift taxes	-							-	-						
4400 Taxes on financial and capital transactions	-							-	16 316						
4500 Non-recurrent taxes	-							-	-						
4600 Other recurrent taxes on property	-							-	1 762						
5000 Taxes on goods and services	179 312	2 080 878	4 309 832	9 226 477	10 827 231			-	234 485		-	-	-	-	-
5100 Taxes on production, sale, transfer, etc	179 312	2 080 878	4 309 832	9 226 477	10 827 231			-	23 221						
5110 General taxes	-	1 150 496	2 478 998	5 991 694	7 126 623			-	-						
5120 Taxes on specific goods and services	179 312	930 382	1 830 834	3 234 783	3 700 608			-	23 221						
5130 Unallocable between 5110 and 5120	-	-	-	-	-			-	-						
5200 Taxes on use of goods and perform activities	-	-	-	-	-			-	211 027						
5300 Unallocable between 5100 and 5200	-	-	-	-	-			-	237						
6000 Other taxes	49 807	116 652	238 134	109 424	106 573			355 192	145 766		-	-	-	-	-
TOTAL TAX REVENUE	348 889	2 968 370	6 028 162	12 573 052	13 836 418	-	-	355 192	652 636			619 082	1 050 670	2 411 987	

1. The figures for 2012 exclude social security contributions to central government as the data are not available.

1. Las cifras para 2012 excluyen las contribuciones de seguridad social al gobierno central ya que los datos no están disponibles.

2. The figures for years up to and including 2004, as well as 2011 and 2012, exclude local government revenues as the data are not available.

2. Las cifras para los años hasta 2004 inclusive, además de 2011 y 2012, excluyen los ingresos de gobiernos locales ya que los datos no están disponibles.

3. The figures for years up to and including 1998, as well as 2011 and 2012, exclude decentralized institutions as the data are not available.

3. Las cifras para los años hasta 1998 inclusive, además de 2011 y 2012, excluyen los ingresos de organismos descentralizados ya que los datos no están disponibles.

StatLink http://dx.doi.org/10.1787/888932971824

Peru **Perú**

Table 44 - Cuadro 44

Tax revenues by sub-sectors of government

Ingresos tributarios por sub-sector de administración

Millions of new soles | Millones de nuevos soles

	Central government Gobierno central					Local government[1] Gobierno local[1]					Social security funds Fondos de seguridad social				
	1990	2000	2005	2010	2012	1990	2000	2005	2010	2012	1990	2000	2005	2010	2012
1000 Taxes on income, profits and capital gains	37	5 130	12 283	28 357	40 650			-	-	-	-	-	-	-	-
2000 Social security contributions	-	-	-	-	-			-	-	-	50	3 184	4 000	7 189	9 694
3000 Taxes on payroll and workforce	-	1 038	27	3	2			-	-	-	-	-	-	-	-
4000 Taxes on property	99	0	783	944	126			549	1 293	1 771	-	-	-	-	-
4100 Recurrent taxes on immovable property	-	-	-	-	-			453	864	958					
4200 Recurrent taxes on net wealth	61	0	0	-	-			-	-	-					
4300 Estate, inheritance and gift taxes	-	-	-	-	-			-	-	-					
4400 Taxes on financial and capital transactions	38	-	706	944	126			96	429	813					
4500 Non-recurrent taxes	-	-	-	-	-			-	-	-					
4600 Other recurrent taxes on property	-	-	76	-	0			-	-	-					
5000 Taxes on goods and services	423	15 739	21 748	34 566	40 061			104	290	359	-	-	-	-	-
5100 Taxes on production, sale, transfer, etc	423	15 739	21 748	34 566	40 061			104	290	359					
5110 General taxes	78	9 519	14 779	28 694	33 779			-	-	-					
5120 Taxes on specific goods and services	345	6 220	6 969	5 871	6 282			104	290	359					
5130 Unallocable between 5110 and 5120	-	-	-	-	-			-	-	-					
5200 Taxes on use of goods and perform activities	-	-	-	-	-			-	-	-					
5300 Unallocable between 5100 and 5200	-	-	-	-	-			-	-	-					
6000 Other taxes	36	761	800	1 389	1 926			989	1 616	775	-	-	-	-	-
TOTAL TAX REVENUE	595	22 667	35 640	65 259	82 765			1 642	3 199	2 905	50	3 184	4 000	7 189	9 694

1. The figures for years up to and including 2004 exclude local government revenues as the data are not available.

1. Las cifras para los años hasta 2004 inclusive excluyen los ingresos de gobiernos locales ya que los datos no están disponibles.

StatLink http://dx.doi.org/10.1787/888932971805

Uruguay **Uruguay**

Table 45 - Cuadro 45

Tax revenues by sub-sectors of government
Ingresos tributarios por sub-sector de administración

Millions of uruguayan pesos — Millones de pesos uruguayos

	Central government Gobierno central					Local government[1] Gobierno local[1]					Social security funds Fondos de seguridad social				
	1990	2000	2005	2010	2012	1990	2000	2005	2010	2012	1990	2000	2005	2010	2012
1000 Taxes on income, profits and capital gains	114	5 620	11 969	44 573	58 291	-	-	-	-		-	-	-	-	-
2000 Social security contributions	-	-	-	-	-	-	-	-	-		717	17 679	21 425	49 742	72 601
3000 Taxes on payroll and workforce	-	-	-	-	-	-	-	-	-		-	-	-	-	-
4000 Taxes on property	125	3 935	8 252	11 690	12 947	72	2 142	3 787	5 245		-	-	-	-	-
4100 Recurrent taxes on immovable property	-	378	852	1 064	-	72	2 142	3 787	5 245						
4200 Recurrent taxes on net wealth	94	2 076	4 943	8 948	11 067	-	-	-	-						
4300 Estate, inheritance and gift taxes	-	-	-	-	-	-	-	-	-						
4400 Taxes on financial and capital transactions	-	372	933	1 350	1 414	-	-	-	-						
4500 Non-recurrent taxes	-	-	-	-	-	-	-	-	-						
4600 Other recurrent taxes on property	31	1 107	1 524	328	466	-	-	-	-						
5000 Taxes on goods and services	1 270	28 301	52 727	94 990	122 310	64	2 576	3 071	3 952		-	-	-	-	-
5100 Taxes on production, sale, transfer, etc	1 270	28 301	52 727	94 990	122 310	-	-	-	-						
5110 General taxes	660	18 009	34 641	69 365	88 338	-	-	-	-						
5120 Taxes on specific goods and services	610	10 291	18 086	25 625	33 972	-	-	-	-						
5130 Unallocable between 5110 and 5120	-	-	-	-	-	-	-	-	-						
5200 Taxes on use of goods and perform activities	-	-	-	-	-	64	2 576	3 071	3 952						
5300 Unallocable between 5100 and 5200	-	-	-	-	-	-	-	-	-						
6000 Other taxes	-10	-596	76	0	0	-	-	-	-		-	-	-	-	-
TOTAL TAX REVENUE	1 500	37 259	73 023	151 253	193 548	136	4 718	6 858	9 196		717	17 679	21 425	49 742	72 601

1. The figures exclude local government revenues for 2012 as the data are not available.

1. Las cifras excluyen los ingresos de gobiernos locales para 2012 ya que los datos no están disponibles.

2. In ECLAC data, the tax on the sale of goods by public auction is classified in category 4000.

2. Las estadísticas de CEPAL consideran el impuesto a la compraventa de bienes muebles en remate público en la categoría de Impuestos sobre la Propiedad (4000).

StatLink http://dx.doi.org/10.1787/888932971843

Venezuela **Venezuela**

Table 46 - Cuadro 46

Tax revenues by sub-sectors of government

Ingresos tributarios por sub-sector de administración

Millions of bolivares Millones de bolívares

	Federal government Gobierno federal					State/Regional[1] Estado/Regional[1]					Local government[1] Gobierno local[1]					Social security funds Fondos de seguridad social				
	1990	2000	2005	2010	2012	1990	2000	2005	2010	2012	1990	2000	2005	2010	2012	1990	2000	2005	2010	2012[2]
1000 Taxes on income, profits and capital gains	344	4 686	18 529	36 836	70 739											-	-	-	-	-
2000 Social security contributions	-	-	-	-	-											20	591	1 890	5 547	
3000 Taxes on payroll and workforce	-	-	-	-	-											-	-	-	-	-
4000 Taxes on property	1	400	2 834	222	346											-	-	-	-	-
4100 Recurrent taxes on immovable property	-	-	-	-	-															
4200 Recurrent taxes on net wealth	-	-	-	-	-															
4300 Estate, inheritance and gift taxes	1	19	55	222	346															
4400 Taxes on financial and capital transactions	-	381	2 779	-	-															
4500 Non-recurrent taxes	-	-	-	-	-															
4600 Other recurrent taxes on property	-	-	-	-	-															
5000 Taxes on goods and services	46	5 173	25 032	73 707	141 505											-	-	-	-	-
5100 Taxes on production, sale, transfer, etc	46	5 173	25 032	73 707	141 505															
5110 General taxes	-	3 272	19 513	56 101	111 102															
5120 Taxes on specific goods and services	46	1 901	5 519	17 606	30 403															
5130 Unallocable between 5110 and 5120	-	-	-	-	-															
5200 Taxes on use of goods and perform activities	-	-	-	-	-															
5300 Unallocable between 5100 and 5200	-	-	-	-	-															
6000 Other taxes	-	-	-	-	3 928											-	-	-	-	-
TOTAL TAX REVENUE	391	10 258	46 395	110 765	216 518											20	591	1 890	5 547	

1. The figures exclude state and local government revenues as the data are not available.
1. Las cifras excluyen los ingresos de gobiernos estatales y locales ya que los datos no están disponibles.
2. The data on social security contributions are unavailable for 2012.
2. Las cifras para 2012 sobre las contribuciones de seguridad social no están disponibles.

StatLink http://dx.doi.org/10.1787/888932971862

Chart 3. **Attribution of tax revenues to sub-sectors of general government, 2011**

Receipts as percentage of total tax revenue

Gráfico 3. **Atribución de los ingresos tributarios en los sub-sectores del gobierno general, 2011**

Ingresos como porcentaje de los ingresos tributarios totales

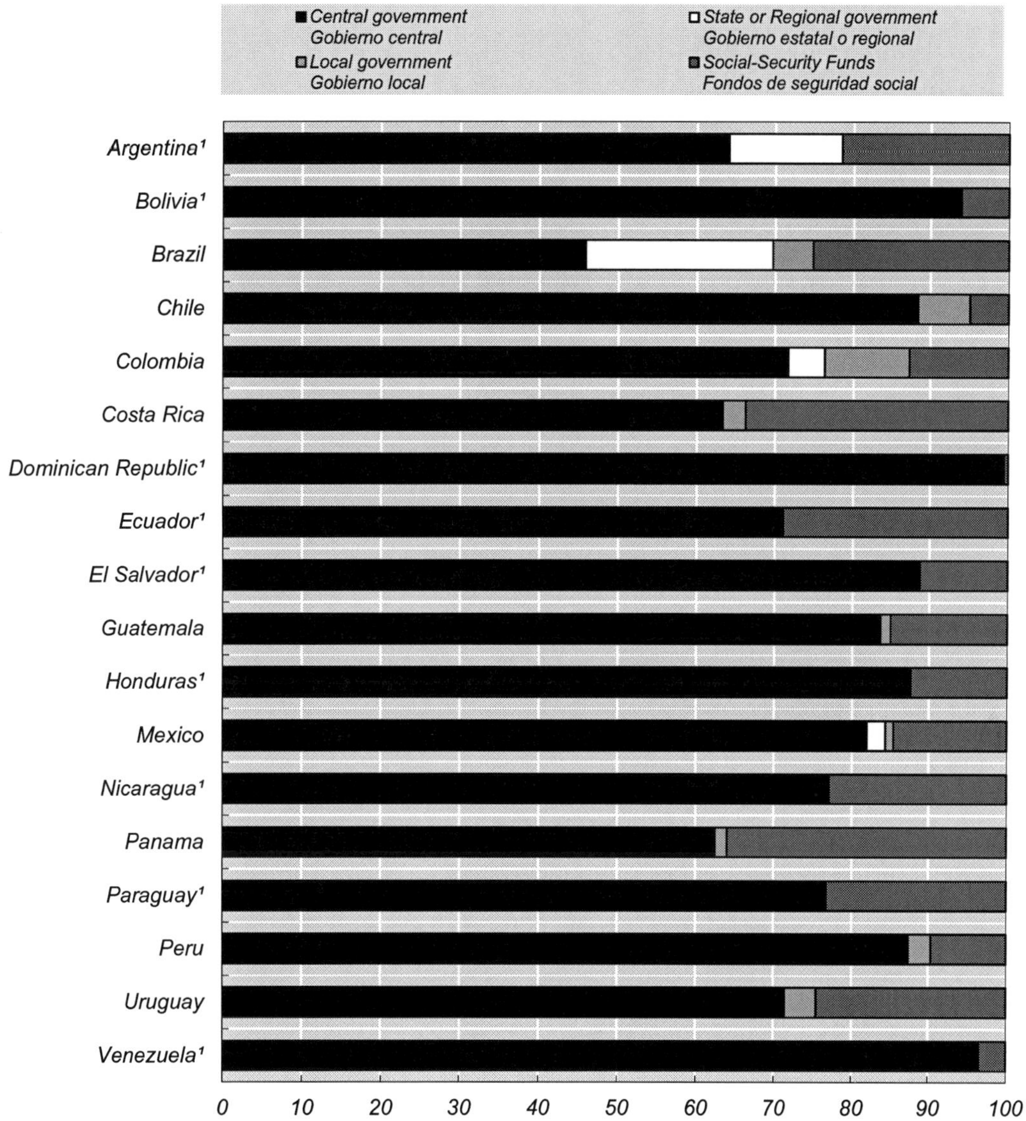

1. The figures exclude local government revenues for Argentina, Bolivia, Dominican Republic, Ecuador, El Salvador, Honduras, Nicaragua, Paraguay and Venezuela as the data are not available.

1. Las cifras excluyen los ingresos de gobiernos locales en Argentina, Bolivia, República Dominicana, Ecuador, El Salvador, Honduras, Nicaragua, Paraguay y Venezuela dado que los datos no están disponibles.

Source: Table 28 in Part IV/Cuadro 28 en Parte IV.

StatLink http://dx.doi.org/10.1787/888932970836

ANNEX A

The OECD Classification of Taxes and Interpretative Guide

Table of Contents

Page

The OECD Classification of Taxes

1000 *Taxes on income, profits and capital gains*

- 1100 Individuals
  - 1110 Income and profits
  - 1120 Capital gains
- 1200 Corporates
  - 1210 Income and profits
  - 1220 Capital gains
- 1300 Unallocable as between 1100 and 1200

2000 *Social security contributions*

- 2100 Employees
- 2200 Employers
- 2300 Self-employed, non-employed
- 2400 Unallocable as between 2100, 2200 and 2300

3000 *Taxes on payroll and workforce*

4000 *Taxes on property*

- 4100 Recurrent taxes on immovable property
  - 4110 Households
  - 4120 Other
- 4200 Recurrent net wealth taxes
  - 4210 Individuals
  - 4220 Corporates
- 4300 Estate, inheritance and gift taxes
  - 4310 Estate and inheritance taxes
  - 4320 Gift taxes
- 4400 Taxes on financial and capital transactions
- 4500 Other non-recurrent taxes on property
- 4600 Other recurrent taxes on property

5000 *Taxes on goods and services*

5100 Taxes on production, sale and transfer of goods and services

5110 General sales taxes

5111 Value-added taxes

5112 Sales taxes

5113 Other general taxes

5120 Taxes on specific goods and services

5121 Excises

5122 Profits of fiscal monopolies

5123 Customs and import duties

5124 On exports

5125 On investment goods

5126 On specific services

5127 Other taxes on international trade and transactions

5128 Other taxes on specific goods and services

5130 Unallocable as between 5110 and 5120

5200 Taxes on use of goods

5210 Recurrent taxes

5211 Motor vehicles taxes households

5212 Motor vehicles taxes others

5213 Other recurrent taxes

5220 Non-recurrent taxes

5300 Unallocable as between 5100 and 5200

6000 *Other taxes*

6100 Paid solely by business

6200 Paid by other than business, or unidentifiable

The OECD Interpretative Guide

A. Coverage

General criteria

1. In the OECD classification the term "taxes" is confined to compulsory unrequited payments to general government. Taxes are unrequited in the sense that benefits provided by government to taxpayers are not normally in proportion to their payments.

2. The term 'tax' does not include fines unrelated to tax offences and compulsory loans paid to government. Borderline cases between tax and non-tax revenues in relation to certain fees and charges are discussed in §9–13.

3. General government consists of the central administration, agencies whose operations are under its effective control, state and local governments and their administrations, certain social security schemes and autonomous governmental entities, excluding public enterprises. This definition of government follows that of the 2008 *System of National Accounts* (SNA).[1] In that publication, the general government sector and its sub-sectors are defined in chapter 4, section F, pages 80-84.

4. Compulsory payments to supra-national bodies and their agencies are no longer included as taxes as from 1998, with some exceptions. However, custom duties collected by EU member states on behalf of the European Union are still identified as memorandum items and included in overall tax revenue amounts in the country tables (Part III) of the country in which they are collected. (See §95). In countries where the church forms part of general government church taxes are included, provided they meet the criteria set out in §1 above. As the data refer to receipts of general government, levies paid to non-government bodies, welfare agencies or social insurance schemes outside general government, trade unions or trade associations, even where such levies are compulsory, are excluded. Compulsory payments to general government earmarked for such bodies are, however, included, provided that the government is not simply acting in an agency capacity.[2] Profits from fiscal monopolies are distinguished from those of other public enterprises and are treated as taxes because they reflect the exercise of the taxing power of the state by the use of monopoly powers (see §62–64), as are profits received by the government from the purchase and sale of foreign exchange at different rates (see §70).

5. Taxes paid by governments (e.g. social security contributions and payroll taxes paid by governments in their capacity as an employer, consumption taxes on their purchases or taxes on their property) are not excluded from the data provided. However, where it is possible to identify the amounts of revenue involved,[3] they are shown in Section III.C of this Report.

6. The relationship between this classification and that of the System of National Accounts (SNA) is set out in Sections H and J below. Because of the differences between the two classifications, the data shown in national accounts are sometimes calculated or classified differently from the practice set out in this guide. These and other differences are

mentioned where appropriate (e.g. in §13 and §26 below) but it is not possible to refer to all of them. There may also be some differences between this classification and that employed domestically by certain national administrations (e.g. see §10 below), so that OECD and national statistics data may not always be consistent: any such differences, however, are likely to be very slight in terms of amounts of revenues involved.

Social security contributions

7. Compulsory social security contributions, as defined in §35 below, paid to general government, are treated here as tax revenues. Being compulsory payments to general government they clearly resemble taxes. They may, however, differ from other taxes in that the receipt of social security benefits depends, in most countries, upon appropriate contributions having been made, although the size of the benefits is not necessarily related to the amount of the contributions. Better comparability between countries is obtained by treating social security contributions as taxes, but they are listed under a separate heading so that they can be distinguished in any analysis.

8. Social security contributions which are either voluntary or not payable to general government (see §1) are not treated as taxes, though in some countries, as indicated in the country footnotes, there are difficulties in eliminating voluntary contributions and certain compulsory payments to the private sector.

Fees, user charges and licence fees

9. Apart from vehicle licence fees, which are universally regarded as taxes, it is not easy to distinguish between those fees and user charges which are to be treated as taxes and those which are not, since, whilst a fee or charge is levied in connection with a specific service or activity, the strength of the link between the fee and the service provided may vary considerably, as may the relation between the amount of the fee and the cost of providing the service. Where the recipient of a service pays a fee clearly related to the cost of providing the service, the levy may be regarded as requited and under the definition of §1 would not be considered as a tax. In the following cases, however, a levy could be considered as 'unrequited':

a) where the charge greatly exceeds the cost of providing the service;

b) where the payer of the levy is not the receiver of the benefit (e.g. a fee collected from slaughterhouses to finance a service which is provided to farmers);

c) where government is not providing a specific service in return for the levy which it receives even though a licence may be issued to the payer (e.g. where the government grants a hunting, fishing or shooting licence which is not accompanied by the right to use a specific area of government land);

d) where benefits are received only by those paying the levy but the benefits received by each individual are not necessarily in proportion to his payments (e.g. a milk marketing levy paid by dairy farmers and used to promote the consumption of milk).

10. In marginal cases, however, the application of the criteria set out in §1 can be particularly difficult. The solution adopted – given the desirability of international uniformity and the relatively small amounts of revenue usually involved – is to follow the

predominant practice among tax administrations rather than to allow each country to adopt its own view as to whether such levies are regarded as taxes or as non-tax revenue.[4]

11. A list of the main fees and charges in question and their normal[5] treatment in this publication is as follows:

Non-tax revenues:	court fees; driving licence fees; harbour fees; passport fees; radio and television licence fees where public authorities provide the service.
Taxes within heading 5200:	permission to perform such activities as distributing films; hunting, fishing and shooting; providing entertainment or gambling facilities; selling alcohol or tobacco; permission to own dogs or to use or own motor vehicles or guns; severance taxes.

12. In practice it may not always be possible to isolate tax receipts from non-tax revenue receipts when they are recorded together. If it is estimated that the bulk of the receipts derive from non-tax revenues, the whole amount involved is treated as a non-tax revenue; otherwise, such government receipts are included and classified according to the rules provided in §28 below.

13. Two differences between the OECD classification and SNA regarding the borderline between tax and non-tax revenues are:

a) SNA classifies a number of levies as indirect taxes if paid by enterprises, but as non-tax revenues if paid by households, a distinction which is regarded as irrelevant in this classification for distinguishing between tax and non-tax revenues.[6]

b) Predominant practice among most OECD tax administrations, which is occasionally used in this classification for distinguishing between tax and non-tax revenues, is not a relevant criterion for SNA purposes.

Royalties

14. Royalty payments for the right to extract oil and gas or to exploit other mineral resources are normally regarded as non-tax revenues since they are property income from government-owned land or resources.

Fines and penalties

15. Receipts from fines and penalties paid for infringement of regulations identified as relating to a particular tax and interest on payments overdue in respect of a particular tax are recorded together with receipts from that tax. Other kinds of fines identifiable as relating to tax offences are classified in the residual heading 6000. Fines not relating to tax offences (e.g. for parking offences), or not identifiable as relating to tax offences, are not treated as taxes.

B. Basis of reporting

Accrual reporting

16. The data reported in this publication for recent years are predominantly recorded on an accrual basis, i.e. recorded at the time that the tax liability was created. Further information is provided in the footnotes to the country table in Part III of the Report.

17. However, data for earlier years are still predominantly recorded on a cash basis, i.e. at the time at which the payment was received by government. Thus, for example, taxes withheld by employers in one year but paid to the government in the following year and taxes due in one year but actually paid in the following year are both included in the receipts of the second year. Corrective transactions, such as refunds, repayments and drawbacks, are deducted from gross revenues of the period in which they are made.

18. Data on tax revenues are recorded without offsets for the administrative expenses connected with tax collection. Similarly, where the proceeds of tax are used to subsidise particular members of the community, the subsidy is not deducted from the yield of the tax, though the tax may be shown net of subsidies in the national records of some countries.

19. As regards fiscal monopolies (heading 5122), only the amount actually transferred to the government is included in government revenues. However, if any expenditures of fiscal monopolies are considered to be government expenditures (e.g. social expenditures undertaken by fiscal monopolies at the direction of the government) they are added back for the purpose of arriving at tax revenue figures (see §62 below).

The distinction between tax and expenditure provisions[7]

20. Because this publication is concerned only with the revenue side of government operations, no account being taken of the expenditure side, a distinction has to be made between tax and expenditure provisions. Normally there is no difficulty in making this distinction as expenditures are made outside the tax system and the tax accounts and under legislation separate from the tax legislation. In borderline cases, cash flow is used to distinguish between tax provisions and expenditure provisions. Insofar as a provision affects the flow of tax payments from the taxpayer to the government, it is regarded as a tax provision and is taken into account in the data shown in this publication. A provision which does not affect this flow is seen as an expenditure provision and is disregarded in the data recorded in this publication.

21. Tax allowances, exemptions and deductions against the tax base clearly affect the amount of tax paid to the government and are therefore considered as tax provisions. At the other extreme, those subsidies which cannot be offset against tax liability and which are clearly not connected with the assessment process, do not reduce tax revenues as recorded in this publication. Tax credits are amounts deductible from tax payable (as distinct from deductions from the tax base). Two types of tax credits are distinguished, those (referred to here as wastable tax credits) which are limited to the amount of the tax liability and therefore cannot give rise to a payment by the authorities to the taxpayer, and those (referred to as non-wastable tax credits) which are not so limited, so that the excess of the credit over the tax liability can be paid to the taxpayer.[8] A wastable tax credit, like a tax allowance, clearly affects the amount of tax paid to the government, and is therefore considered as a tax provision. The practice followed for non-wastable tax credits[9] is to distinguish between the 'tax expenditure component',[10] which is that portion of the credit that is used to reduce or eliminate a taxpayer's liability, and the 'transfer component', which is the portion that exceeds the taxpayer's liability and is paid to that taxpayer. Reported tax revenues should be reduced by the amount of the tax expenditure component but not by the amount of the transfer component. In addition, the amounts of the tax expenditure and transfer components should be reported as memorandum items in the country tables. Countries that are unable to distinguish between the tax expenditure and transfer components should indicate whether or not the tax revenues have been reduced by the total of these components, and provide any available estimates of the amounts of the two components. Further information is given in

section C of Part I of the Report, which illustrates the effect of alternative treatments of non-wastable tax credits on Tax to GDP.

Calendar and fiscal years

22. National authorities whose fiscal years do not correspond to the calendar year show data, where possible, on a calendar year basis to permit maximum comparability with the data of other countries. There remain a few countries where data refer to fiscal years. For these the GDP data used in the comparative tables also correspond to the fiscal years.

C. General classification criteria

The main classification criteria

23. The classification of receipts among the main headings (1000, 2000, 3000, 4000, 5000 and 6000) is generally governed by the base on which the tax is levied: 1000 income, profits and capital gains; 2000 and 3000 earnings, payroll or number of employees; 4000 property; 5000 goods and services; 6000 multiple bases, other bases or unidentifiable bases. Where a tax is calculated on more than one base, the receipts are, where possible, split among the various headings (see §28 and §78). The headings 4000 and 5000 cover not only taxes where the tax base is the property, goods or services themselves but also certain related taxes. Thus, taxes on the transfer of property are included in 4400[11] and taxes on the use of goods or on permission to perform activities in 5200. In headings 4000 and 5000 a distinction is made in certain sub-headings between recurrent and non-recurrent taxes: recurrent taxes are defined as those levied at regular intervals (usually annually) and non-recurrent taxes are levied once and for all (see also §43 to §46, §49, §50 and §76 for particular applications of this distinction).

24. Earmarking of a tax for specific purposes does not affect the classification of tax receipts. However, as explained in §35 on the classification of social security contributions, the conferment of an entitlement to social benefits is crucial to the definition of the 2000 main heading.

25. The way that a tax is levied or collected (e.g., by use of stamps) does not affect classification.

Classification of taxpayers

26. In certain sub-headings distinctions are made between different categories of taxpayers. These distinctions vary from tax to tax:

a) Between individuals and corporations in relation to income and net wealth taxes

The basic distinction is that corporation income taxes, as distinct from individual income taxes, are levied on the corporation as an entity, not on the individuals who own it, and without regard to the personal circumstances of these individuals. The same distinction applies to net wealth taxes on corporations and those on individuals. Taxes paid on the profits of partnerships and the income of institutions, such as life insurance or pension funds, are classified according to the same rule. They are classified as corporate taxes (1200) if they are charged on the partnership or institution as an entity without regard to the personal circumstances of the owners. Otherwise, they are treated as individual taxes (1100). Usually, there is different legislation for the corporation taxes and for the individual taxes.[12] The distinction made here between individuals and corporations does not follow the sector classification between households, enterprises, and so on of the System of National Accounts for income and outlay accounts. The SNA classification requires certain unincorporated businesses[13] to be excluded from the household sector and included with non-financial enterprises and financial institutions. The tax on the profits of these businesses, however, cannot always be separated from the tax on the other income of their owners, or can be separated only on an arbitrary basis. No attempt at this separation is made here and the whole of the individual income tax is shown together without regard to the nature of the income chargeable.

b) Between households and others in relation to taxes on immovable property

Here the distinction is that adopted by the SNA for the production and consumption expenditure accounts. The distinction is between households as consumers (i.e. excluding non-incorporated business) on the one hand and producers on the other hand. However, taxes on dwellings occupied by households, whether paid by owner-occupiers, tenants or landlords, are classified under households. This follows the common distinction made between taxes on domestic property versus taxes on business property. Some countries are not, however, in a position to make this distinction.

c) Between households and others in relation to motor vehicle licences

Here the distinction is between households as consumers on the one hand and producers on the other, as in the production and consumption expenditure accounts of the SNA.

d) Between business and others in relation to the residual taxes (6000)

The distinction is the same as in c) above between producers on the one hand and households as consumers on the other hand. Taxes which are included under the heading 6000 because they involve more than one tax base or because the tax base does not fall within any of the previous categories but which are identifiable as levyable only on producers and not on households are included under 'business'. The rest of the taxes which are included under the heading 6000 are shown as 'other' or non-identified.

Surcharges

27. Receipts from surcharges in respect of particular taxes are usually classified with the receipts from the relevant tax whether or not the surcharge is temporary. If, however, the surcharge has a characteristic which would render it classifiable in a different heading of the OECD list, receipts from the surcharge are classified under that heading separately from the relevant tax.

Unidentifiable tax receipts and residual sub-headings

28. A number of cases arise where taxes cannot be identified as belonging entirely to a heading or sub-heading of the OECD classification and the following practices are applied in such cases:

a) The heading is known, but it is not known how receipts should be allocated between sub-headings: receipts are classified in the appropriate residual sub-heading (1300, 2400, 4520, 4600, 5130, 5300 or 6200).

b) It is known that the bulk of receipts from a group of taxes (usually local taxes) is derived from taxes within a particular heading or sub-heading, but some of the taxes in the group whose amount cannot be precisely ascertained may be classifiable in other headings or sub-headings: receipts are shown in the heading or sub-heading under which most of the receipts fall.

c) Neither the heading nor sub-heading of a tax (usually local) can be identified: the tax is classified in 6200 unless it is known that it is a tax on business in which case it is classified in 6100.

D. Commentaries on items of the list

1000 – *Taxes on income, profits and capital gains*

29. This heading covers taxes levied on the net income or profits (i.e. gross income minus allowable tax reliefs) of individuals and enterprises. Also covered are taxes levied on the capital gains of individuals and enterprises, and gains from gambling.

30. Included in the heading are:

a) taxes levied predominantly on income or profits, though partially on other bases. Taxes on various bases which are not predominantly income or profits are classified according to the principles laid down in §28 and §78;

b) taxes on property, which are levied on a presumed or estimated income as part of an income tax (see also §43(a), (c) and (d));

c) compulsory payments to social security fund contributions that are levied on income but do not confer an entitlement to social benefits. When such contributions do confer an entitlement to social benefits, they are included in heading 2000 (see §35);

d) receipts from integrated scheduler income tax systems are classified as a whole in this heading, even though certain of the scheduler taxes may be based upon gross income and may not take into account the personal circumstances of the taxpayer.

31. The main subdivision of this heading is between levies on individuals (1100) and those on corporate enterprises (1200). Under each subdivision a distinction is made between taxes on income and profits (1110 and 1210), and taxes on capital gains (1120 and 1220). If certain receipts cannot be identified as appropriate to either 1100 or 1200, or if in practice this distinction cannot be made (e.g., because there are no reliable data on the recipients of payments from which withholding taxes are deducted) they are classified in 1300 as not-allocable.

Treatment of credits under imputation systems

32. Under imputation systems of corporate income tax, a company's shareholders are wholly or partly relieved of their liability to income tax on dividends paid by the company out of income or profits liable to corporate income tax. In countries with such systems,[14] part of the tax on the company's profits is available to provide relief against the shareholders' own tax liability. The relief to the shareholder takes the form of a tax credit, the amount of which may be less than, equal to, or more than the shareholder's overall tax liability. If the tax credit exceeds this tax liability the excess may be payable to the shareholder. As this type of tax credit is an integral part of the imputation system of corporate income tax, any payment to the shareholders is treated as a repayment of tax and not as expenditure (compare the treatment of other tax credits described in §21).

33. As the tax credit under imputation systems (even when exceeding tax liability) is to be regarded as a tax provision, the question arises whether it should be deducted from

individual income tax receipts (1110) or corporate income tax receipts (1210). In this Report, the full amount of corporate income tax paid is shown under 1210 and no imputed tax is included under 1110. Thus, the full amount of the credit reduces the amount of 1110 whether the credit results in a reduction of personal income tax liability or whether an actual refund is made because the credit exceeds the income tax liability. (Where, however, such tax credits are deducted from corporation tax in respect of dividends paid to corporations the amounts are deducted from the receipts of 1210.)

1120 and 1220 – *Taxes on capital gains*

34. These sub-headings comprise taxes imposed on capital gains, 1120 covering those levied on the gains of individuals and 1220 those levied on the gains of corporate enterprises, where receipts from such taxes can be separately identified. In many countries this is not the case and the receipts from such taxes are then classified with those from the income tax. Heading 1120 also includes taxes on gains from gambling.

2000 – *Social security contributions*

35. Classified here are all compulsory payments that confer an entitlement to receive a (contingent) future social benefit. Such payments are usually earmarked to finance social benefits and are often paid to institutions of general government that provide such benefits. However, such earmarking is not part of the definition of social security contributions and is not required for a tax to be classified here. However, conferment of an entitlement is required for a tax to be classified under this heading. So, levies on income or payroll that are earmarked for social security funds but do not confer an entitlement to benefit are excluded from this heading and shown under personal income taxes (1100) or taxes on payroll and workforce (3000). Taxes on other bases, such as goods and services, which are earmarked for social security benefits are not shown here but are classified according to their respective bases because they generally confer no entitlement to social security benefits.

36. Contributions for the following types of social security benefits would, *inter alia*, be included: unemployment insurance benefits and supplements, accident, injury and sickness benefits, old-age, disability and survivors' pensions, family allowances, reimbursements for medical and hospital expenses or provision of hospital or medical services. Contributions may be levied on both employees and employers.

37. Contributions may be based on earnings or payroll ('on a payroll basis') or on net income after deductions and exemptions for personal circumstances ('on an income tax basis'), and the revenues from the two bases should be separately identified if possible. However, where contributions to a general social security scheme are on a payroll basis, but the contributions of particular groups (such as the self-employed) cannot be assessed on this basis and net income is used as a proxy for gross earnings, the receipts may still be classified as being on a payroll basis. In principle, this heading excludes voluntary contributions paid to social security schemes. When separately identifiable these are shown in the memorandum item on the financing of social security benefits. In practice, however, they cannot always be separately identified from compulsory contributions, in which case they are included in this heading.

38. Contributions to social insurance schemes which are not institutions of general government and to other types of insurance schemes, provident funds, pension funds, friendly societies or other saving schemes are not considered as social security contributions. Provident funds are arrangements under which the contributions of each employee and of the

corresponding employer on his/her behalf are kept in a separate account earning interest and withdrawable under specific circumstances. Pension funds are separately organised schemes negotiated between employees and employers and carry provisions for different contributions and benefits, sometimes more directly tied to salary levels and length of service than under social security schemes. When contributions to these schemes are compulsory or quasi-compulsory (e.g. by virtue of agreement with professional and union organisations) they are shown in the memorandum item (refer to Section III.B of the Report).

39. Contributions by government employees and by governments in respect of their employees, to social security schemes classified within general government are included in this heading. Contributions to separate schemes for government employees, which can be regarded as replacing general social security schemes, are also regarded as taxes.[15] Where, however, a separate scheme is not seen as replacing a general scheme and has been negotiated between the government, in its role as an employer, and its employees, it is not regarded as social security and contributions to it are not regarded as taxes, even though the scheme may have been established by legislation.

40. This heading excludes 'imputed' contributions, which correspond to social benefits paid directly by employers to their employees or former employees or to their representatives (e.g. when employers are legally obliged to pay sickness benefits for a certain period).

41. Contributions are divided into those of employees (2100), employers (2200), and self-employed or non-employed (2300), and then further sub-divided according to the basis on which they are levied. Employees are defined for this purpose as all persons engaged in activities of business units, government bodies, private non-profit institutions, or other paid employment, except the proprietors and their unpaid family members in the case of unincorporated businesses. Members of the armed forces are included, irrespective of the duration and type of their service, if they contribute to social security schemes. The contributions of employers are defined as their payments on account of their employees to social security schemes. Where employees or employers are required to continue the payment of social security contributions when the employee becomes unemployed these contributions, data permitting, are shown in 2100 and 2200 respectively. Accordingly, the sub-heading 2300 is confined to contributions paid by the self-employed and by those outside of the labour force (e.g. disabled or retired individuals).

3000 – *Taxes on payroll and workforce*

42. This heading covers taxes paid by employers, employees or the self-employed either as a proportion of payroll or as a fixed amount per person, and which do not confer entitlement to social benefits. Examples of taxes classified here are the United Kingdom national insurance surcharge (introduced in 1977), the Swedish payroll tax (1969–1979), and the Austrian Contribution to the Family Burden Equalisation Fund and Community Tax.

4000 – *Taxes on property*

43. This heading covers recurrent and non-recurrent taxes on the use, ownership or transfer of property. These include taxes on immovable property or net wealth, taxes on the change of ownership of property through inheritance or gift and taxes on financial and capital transactions. The following kinds of tax are excluded from this heading:

a) taxes on capital gains resulting from the sale of a property (1120 or 1220);

b) taxes on the use of goods or on permission to use goods or perform activities (5200); see §73;

c) taxes on immovable property levied on the basis of a presumed net income which take into account the personal circumstances of the taxpayer. They are classified as income taxes along with taxes on income and capital gains derived from property (1100);

d) taxes on the use of property for residence, where the tax is payable by either proprietor or tenant and the amount payable is a function of the user's personal circumstances (pay, dependants, and so on). They are classified as taxes on income (1100);

e) taxes on building in excess of permitted maximum density, taxes on the enlargement, construction or alteration of certain buildings beyond a permitted value and taxes on building construction. They are classified as taxes on permission to perform activities (5200);

f) taxes on the use of one's own property for special trading purposes like selling alcohol, tobacco, meat or for exploitation of land resources (e.g. United States severance taxes). They are classified as taxes on permission to perform activities (5200).

4100 – *Recurrent taxes on immovable property*

44. This sub-heading covers taxes levied regularly in respect of the use or ownership of immovable property.

- these taxes are levied on land and buildings;
- they can be in the form of a percentage of an assessed property value based on a national rental income, sales price, or capitalised yield; or in terms of other characteristics of real property (for example size or location), from which a presumed rent or capital value can be derived.
- such taxes can be levied on proprietors, tenants, or both. They can also be paid by one level of government to another level of government in respect of property under the jurisdiction of the latter.
- debts are not taken into account in the assessment of these taxes, and they differ from taxes on net wealth in this respect.

45. Taxes on immovable property are further sub-divided into those paid by households (4110) and those paid by other entities (4120), according to the criteria set out in §26(*b*) above.

4200 – *Recurrent taxes on net wealth*

46. This sub-heading covers taxes levied regularly (in most cases annually) on net wealth, i.e. taxes on a wide range of movable and immovable property, net of debt. It is sub-divided into taxes paid by individuals (4210) and taxes paid by corporate enterprises (4220) according to the criteria set out in §26(*a*) above. If separate figures exist for receipts paid by institutions, the tax payments involved are added to those paid by corporations.

4300 – *Estate, inheritance and gift taxes*

47. This sub-heading is divided into taxes on estates and inheritances (4310) and taxes on gifts (4320).[16] Estate taxes are charged on the amount of the total estate whereas inheritance

taxes are charged on the shares of the individual recipients; in addition the latter may take into account the relationship of the individual recipients to the deceased.

4400 – *Taxes on financial and capital transactions*

48. This sub-heading comprises, *inter alia*, taxes on the issue, transfer, purchase and sale of securities, taxes on cheques, and taxes levied on specific legal transactions such as validation of contracts and the sale of immovable property. The heading does not include:

a) taxes on the use of goods or property or permission to perform certain activities (5200);

b) fees paid to cover court charges, charges for birth, marriage or death certificates, which are normally regarded as non-tax revenues (see §9);

c) taxes on capital gains (1000);

d) recurrent taxes on immovable property (4100);

e) recurrent taxes on net wealth (4200);

f) once-and-for-all levies on property or wealth (4500).

4500 – *Other non-recurrent taxes on property*[16]

49. This sub-heading covers once-and-for-all, as distinct from recurrent, levies on property. It is divided into taxes on net wealth (4510) and other non-recurrent taxes on property (4520). Heading 4510 would include taxes levied to meet emergency expenditures, or for redistribution purposes. Heading 4520 would cover taxes levied to take account of increases in land value due to permission given to develop or provision of additional local facilities by general government, any taxes on the revaluation of capital and once-and-for-all taxes on particular items of property.

4600 – *Other recurrent taxes on property*

50. These rarely exist in OECD member countries, but the heading would include taxes on goods such as cattle, jewellery, windows, and other external signs of wealth.

5000 – *Taxes on goods and services*

51. All taxes and duties levied on the production, extraction, sale, transfer, leasing or delivery of goods, and the rendering of services (5100), or in respect of the use of goods or permission to use goods or to perform activities (5200) are included here. The heading thus covers:

a) multi-stage cumulative taxes;

b) general sales taxes – whether levied at manufacture/production, wholesale or retail level;

c) value-added taxes;

d) excises;

e) taxes levied on the import and export of goods;

f) taxes levied in respect of the use of goods and taxes on permission to use goods, or perform certain activities;

g) taxes on the extraction, processing or production of minerals and other products.

52. Borderline cases between this heading and heading 4000 (taxes on property) and 6100 (other taxes on business) are referred to in §43, §48 and §75. Residual sub-headings (5300)

and (5130) cover tax receipts which cannot be allocated between 5100 and 5200 and between 5110 and 5120, respectively; see §28.

5100 – *Taxes on the production, sale, transfer, leasing and delivery of goods and rendering of services*

53. This sub-heading consists of all taxes, levied on transactions in goods and services on the basis of their intrinsic characteristics (e.g. value, weight of tobacco, strength of alcohol, and so on) as distinct from taxes imposed on the use of goods, or permission to use goods or perform activities, which fall under 5200.

5110 – *General taxes on goods and services*

54. This sub-heading includes all taxes, other than import and export duties (5123 and 5124), levied on the production, leasing, transfer, delivery or sales of a wide range of goods and/or the rendering of a wide range of services, irrespective of whether they are domestically produced or imported and irrespective of the stage of production or distribution at which they are levied. It thus covers value-added taxes, sales taxes and multi-stage cumulative taxes. Receipts from border adjustments in respect of such taxes when goods are imported are added to gross receipts for this category, and repayments of such taxes when goods are exported are deducted. These taxes are subdivided into 5111 value-added taxes, 5112 sales taxes, 5113 other general taxes on goods and services.

55. Borderline cases arise between this heading and taxes on specific goods (5120) when taxes are levied on a large number of goods, for example, the United Kingdom purchase tax (repealed in 1973) and the Japanese commodity tax (repealed in 1988). In conformity with national views, the former United Kingdom purchase tax is classified as a general tax (5112) and the former Japanese commodity tax as excises (5121).

5111 – *Value-added taxes*

56. All general consumption taxes charged on value-added are classified in this sub-heading, irrespective of the method of deduction and the stages at which the taxes are levied. In practice, all OECD countries with value-added taxes normally allow immediate deduction of taxes on purchases by all but the final consumer and impose tax at all stages. In some countries the heading may include certain taxes, such as those on financial and insurance activities, either because receipts from them cannot be identified separately from those from the value-added tax, or because they are regarded as an integral part of the value-added tax, even though similar taxes in other countries might be classified elsewhere (e.g. 5126 as taxes on services or 4400 as taxes on financial and capital transactions).

5112 – *Sales taxes*

57. All general taxes levied at one stage only, whether at manufacturing or production, wholesale or retail stage are classified here.

5113 – *Other general taxes on goods and services*

58. This sub-heading covers multi-stage cumulative taxes (also known as 'cascade taxes') where tax is levied each time a transaction takes place without deduction for tax paid on inputs, and also those general consumption taxes where elements of value-added, sales or cascade taxes are combined.

5120 – *Taxes on specific goods and services*

59. Excises, profits generated and transferred from fiscal monopolies, and customs and imports duties as well as taxes on exports, foreign exchange transactions, investment goods

and betting stakes and special taxes on services, which do not form part of a general tax of 5110, are included in this category.

5121 – *Excises*

60. Excises are taxes levied on particular products, or on a limited range of products, which are not classifiable under 5110 (general taxes), 5123 (import duties) and 5124 (export duties). They may be imposed at any stage of production or distribution and are usually assessed by reference to the weight or strength or quantity of the product, but sometimes by reference to value. Thus, special taxes on, for example, sugar, beetroot, matches, chocolates, and taxes at varying rates on a certain range of goods, as well as those levied in most countries on tobacco goods, alcoholic drinks and hydrocarbon oils and other energy sources, are included in this sub-heading.

61. Excises are distinguished from:

a) 5110 (general taxes). This is discussed in §54-55;

b) 5123 (import duties). If a tax collected principally on imported goods also applies, or would apply, under the law by which the tax is imposed to comparable home-produced goods, the receipts there from would be classified as excises (5121). This principle applies even if there is no comparable home production or no possibility of it (see also §65);

c) 5126 (taxes on services). The problem here arises in respect of taxes on electricity, gas and energy. All of these are regarded as taxes on goods and are included under 5121.

5122 – *Profits of fiscal monopolies*

62. This sub-heading covers that part of the profits of fiscal monopolies which is transferred to general government or which is used to finance any expenditures considered to be government expenditures (see §19). Amounts are shown when they are transferred to general government or used to make expenditures considered to be government expenditures

63. Fiscal monopolies reflect the exercise of the taxing power of government by the use of monopoly powers. Fiscal monopolies are non-financial public enterprises exercising a monopoly in most cases over the production or distribution of tobacco, alcoholic beverages, salt, matches, playing cards and petroleum or agricultural products (i.e. on the kind of products which are likely to be, alternatively or additionally, subject to the excises of 5121), to raise the government revenues which in other countries are gathered through taxes on dealings in such commodities by private business units. The government monopoly may be at the production stage or, as in the case of government-owned and controlled liquor stores, at the distribution stage.

64. Fiscal monopolies are distinguished from public utilities such as rail transport, electricity, post offices, and other communications, which may enjoy a monopoly or quasi-monopoly position but where the primary purpose is normally to provide basic services rather than to raise revenue for government. Transfers from such other public enterprises to the government are considered as non-tax revenues. The traditional concept of fiscal monopoly has not been extended to include state lotteries, the profits of which are accordingly regarded as non-tax revenues. Fiscal monopoly profits are distinguished from export and import monopoly profits (5127) transferred from marketing boards or other enterprises dealing with international trade.

5123 – *Customs and other import duties*

65. Taxes, stamp duties and surcharges restricted by law to imported products are included here. Also included are levies on imported agricultural products which are imposed in member countries of the European Union and amounts paid by certain of these countries under the Monetary Compensation Accounts (MCA) system.[17] Starting from 1998, customs duties collected by European Union member states on behalf of the European Union are no longer reported under this heading in the country tables (in Part III of the Report). Excluded here are taxes collected on imports as part of a general tax on goods and services, or an excise applicable to both imported and domestically produced goods.

5124 – *Taxes on exports*

66. In the 1970s, export duties were levied in Australia, Canada and Portugal as a regular measure and they have been used in Finland for counter-cyclical purposes. Some member countries of the European Union pay, as part of the MCA system, a levy on exports (see note 18 to §65). Where these amounts are identifiable, they are shown in this heading. This heading does not include repayments of general consumption taxes or excises or customs duties on exported goods, which should be deducted from the gross receipts under 5110, 5121 or 5123, as appropriate.

5125 – *Taxes on investment goods*

67. This sub-heading covers taxes on investment goods, such as machinery. These taxes may be imposed for a number of years or temporarily for counter-cyclical purposes. Taxes on industrial inputs which are also levied on consumers [e.g. the Swedish energy tax which is classified under (5121)] are not included here.

5126 – *Taxes on specific services*

68. All taxes assessed on the payment for specific services, such as taxes on insurance premiums, banking services, gambling and betting stakes (e.g. from horse races, football pools, lottery tickets), transport, entertainment, restaurant and advertising charges, fall into this category. Taxes levied on the gross income of companies providing the service (e.g. gross insurance premiums or gambling stakes received by the company) are also classified under this heading. Tax revenues from bank levies and payments to deposit insurance and financial stability schemes are provisionally included here for the 2012 edition. The detailed classification is set out in paragraph 105.

69. Excluded from this sub-heading are:

a) taxes on services forming part of a general tax on goods and services (5110);

b) taxes on electricity, gas and energy (5121 as excises);

c) taxes on individual gains from gambling (1120 as taxes on capital gains of individuals and non-corporate enterprises) and lump-sum taxes on the transfer of private lotteries or on the permission to set up lotteries (5200);[18]

d) taxes on cheques and on the issue, transfer or redemption of securities (4400 as taxes on financial and capital transactions).

5127 – *Other taxes on international trade and transactions*

70. This sub-heading covers revenue received by the government from the purchase and sale of foreign exchange at different rates. When the government exercises monopoly powers to extract a margin between the purchase and sales price of foreign exchange, other

than to cover administrative costs, the revenue derived constitutes a compulsory levy exacted in indeterminate proportions from both purchaser and seller of foreign exchange. It is the common equivalent of an import duty and export duty levied in a single exchange rate system or of a tax on the sale or purchase of foreign exchange. Like the profits of fiscal monopolies and import or export monopolies transferred to government, it represents the exercise of monopoly powers for tax purposes and is included in tax revenues.

71. The sub-heading covers also the profits of export or import monopolies, which do not however exist in OECD countries, taxes on purchase or sale of foreign exchange, and any other taxes levied specifically on international trade or transactions.

5128 – *Other taxes on specific goods and services*

72. This item includes taxes on the extraction of minerals, fossil fuels and other exhaustible resources from deposits owned privately or by another government together with any other unidentifiable receipts from taxes on specific goods and services. Taxes on the extraction of exhaustible resources are usually a fixed amount per unit of quality or weight, but can be a percentage of value. The taxes are recorded when the resources are extracted. Payments from the extraction of exhaustible resources from deposits owned by the government unit receiving the payment are classified as rent.

5200 – *Taxes on use of goods or on permission to use goods or perform activities*

73. This sub-heading covers taxes which are levied in respect of the use of goods as distinct from taxes on the goods themselves. Unlike the latter taxes – reported under 5100 –, they are not assessed on the value of the goods but usually as fixed amounts. Taxes on permission to use goods or to perform activities are also included here, as are pollution taxes not based upon the value of particular goods. It is sometimes difficult to distinguish between compulsory user charges and licence fees which are regarded as taxes and those which are excluded as non-tax revenues. The criteria which are employed are noted in §9–10.

74. Although the sub-heading refers to the 'use' of goods, registration of ownership rather than use may be what generates liability to tax, so that the taxes of this heading may apply to the ownership of animals or goods rather than their use (e.g. race horses, dogs and motor vehicles) and may apply even to unusable goods (e.g. unusable motor vehicles or guns).

75. Borderline cases arise with:

a) taxes on the permission to perform business activities which are levied on a combined income, payroll or turnover base and, accordingly, are classified following the rules in §78;

b) taxes on the ownership or use of property of headings 4100, 4200 and 4600. The heading 4100 is confined to taxes on the ownership or tenancy of immovable property and – unlike the taxes of 5200 – they are related to the value of the property. The net wealth taxes and taxes on chattels of 4200 and 4600 respectively are confined to the ownership rather than the use of assets, apply to groups of assets rather than particular goods and again are related to the value of the assets

5210 – *Recurrent taxes on use of goods and on permission to use goods or perform activities*

76. The principal characteristic of taxes classified here is that they are levied at regular intervals and that they are usually fixed amounts. The most important item in terms of revenue receipts is vehicle licence taxes. This sub-heading also covers taxes on permission

to hunt, shoot, fish or to sell certain products and taxes on the ownership of dogs and on the performance of certain services, provided that they meet the criteria set out in §9–10. The sub-divisions of 5210 are user taxes on motor vehicles paid by households (5211) and those paid by others (5212).[19] Sub-heading 5213 covers dog licences and user charges for permission to perform activities such as selling meat or liquor when the levies are on a recurring basis. It also covers recurrent general licences for hunting, shooting and fishing where the right to carry out these activities is not granted as part of a normal commercial transaction (e.g. the granting of the licence is not accompanied by the right to use a specific area which is owned by government).

5220 – *Non-recurrent taxes on use of goods and on permission to use goods or perform activities*

77. This section covers non-recurrent taxes levied on the use of goods or on permission to use goods or perform activities and taxes levied each time goods are used. It includes taxes levied on the emission or discharge into the environment of noxious gases, liquids or other harmful substances.

- Payments for tradable emission permits issued by governments under cap and trade schemes should be recorded here at the time the emissions occur. No revenue should be recorded for permits that governments issue free of charge. The accrual basis of recording means that there can be a timing difference between the cash being received by government for the permits and the time the emission occurs. In the national accounts, this timing gives rise to a financial liability for government during the period.

- Payments made for the collection and disposal of waste or noxious substances by public authorities should be excluded as they constitute a sale of services to enterprises.

78. Other taxes falling under heading 5200 that are not levied recurrently are also included here. Thus, once-and-for-all payments for permission to sell liquor or tobacco or to set up betting shops are included provided they meet the criteria set out in §9–10.

6000 – *Other taxes*

79. Taxes levied on a base, or bases, other than those described under headings 1000, 3000, 4000 and 5000, or on bases of which none could be regarded as being predominantly the same as that of any one of these headings, are covered here. As regards taxes levied on a multiple base, if it is possible to estimate receipts related to each base (e.g. the Austrian and German 'Gewerbesteuer') this is done and the separate amounts included under the appropriate headings. If the separate amounts cannot be estimated, but it is known that most of the receipts are derived from one base, the whole of the receipts are classified according to that base. If neither of these procedures can be followed, they are classified here. The sub-headings may also include receipts from taxes which governments are unable to identify or isolate (see §28). Included here also are fines and penalties paid for infringement of regulations relating to taxes but not identifiable as relating to a particular category of taxes (see §15). A subdivision is made between taxes levied wholly or predominantly on business (6100) and those levied on others (6200).

E. Conciliation with National Accounts

80. This section of the tables provides a re-conciliation between the OECD calculation of total tax revenues and the total of all taxes and social contributions paid to general government as recorded in the country's National Accounts. Where the country is a member of the European Union (EU), the comparison is between the OECD calculation of total tax revenues and the sum of tax revenues and social contributions recorded in the combination of the general government and the institutions of the EU sectors of the National Accounts.

F. Memorandum item on the financing of social security benefits

81. In view of the varying relationship between taxation and social security contributions and the cases referred to in §35 to §41, a memorandum item collects together all payments earmarked for social security-type benefits, other than voluntary payments to the private sector. Data are presented as follows (refer section III.B of the Report):

a) Taxes of 2000 series.

b) Taxes earmarked for social security benefits.

c) Voluntary contributions to the government.

d) Compulsory contributions to the private sector.

Guidance on the breakdown of (a) to (d) above is provided in §35 to §41.

G. Memorandum item on identifiable taxes paid by government

82. Identifiable taxes actually paid by government are presented in a memorandum item classified by the main headings of the OECD classification of taxes. In the vast majority of countries, only social security contributions and payroll taxes paid by government can be identified. These are, however, usually the most important taxes paid by governments (refer section III.C of the Report).

H. Relation of OECD classification of taxes to national accounting systems

83. A system of national accounts (SNA) seeks to provide a coherent framework for recording and presenting the main flows relating respectively to production, consumption, accumulation and external transactions of a given economic area, usually a country or a major region within a country. Government revenues are an important part of the transactions recorded in SNA. The final version of the 2008 SNA was jointly published by five international organisations: the United Nations, the International Monetary Fund, the European Union, the Organisation for Economic Co-operation and Development, and the World Bank in August 2009. The *System* is a comprehensive, consistent and flexible set of macroeconomic accounts. It is designed for use in countries with market economies, whatever their stage of economic development, and also in countries in transition to market economies. The important parts of the SNA's conceptual framework and its definitions of the various sectors of the economy have been reflected in the OECD's classification of taxes.

84. There are, however, some differences between the OECD classification of taxes and SNA concepts that are listed below. They arise because the aim of the former is to provide

the maximum disaggregation of statistical data on what are generally regarded as taxes by tax administrations.

a) OECD includes social security contributions in total tax revenues (§7 and §8 above);

b) there are different points of view on whether or not some levies and fees are classified as taxes (§9 and §10 above);

c) OECD excludes imputed taxes or subsidies resulting from the operation of official multiple exchange rates;

d) there are differences in the treatment of non-wastable tax credits

85. As noted in §1 and §2, headings 1000 to 6000 of the OECD list of taxes cover all unrequited payments to general government, other than compulsory loans and fines. Such unrequited payments including fines, but excluding compulsory loans can be obtained from adding together the following figures in the 2008 SNA

- value-added type taxes (D.211);
- taxes and duties on imports, excluding VAT (D.212);
- export taxes (D.213);
- taxes on products, excluding VAT, import and export taxes (D.214);
- other taxes on production (D.29);
- taxes on income (D.51);
- other current taxes (D.59);
- social contributions (D.61), excluding voluntary contributions;
- capital taxes (D.91).

I. The OECD classification of taxes and the International Monetary Fund (GFS) system

86. The coverage and valuation of tax revenues in the GFS system and the 2008 SNA are very similar. Therefore, with the exception of the treatment of non-wastable tax credits, the differences between the OECD classification and that of the 2008 SNA (see §84 above) also apply to the GFS. In addition the International Monetary Fund subdivides the OECD 5000 heading into section IV (Domestic Taxes on Goods and Services) and section V (Taxes on International Trade and Transactions). This reflects the fact that while the latter usually yield insignificant amounts of revenue in OECD countries, this is not the case in many non-OECD countries.

J. Comparison of the OECD classification of taxes with other international classifications

87. The table below describes an item by item comparison of the OECD classification of taxes and the classifications used in the following:

i) System of National Accounts (2008 SNA);
ii) European System of Accounts (1995 ESA);
iii) IMF *Government Finance Statistics Manual* (GFSM2001).

OECD Classification		2008 SNA	1995 ESA	GFSM2001
1000	Taxes on income, profits and capital gains			
	1100 Individuals			
	1110 Income/profits	D51-8.61a	D51A	1111
	1120 Capital gains	D51-8.61c,d	D51C,D	1111
	1200 Corporations			
	1210 Income/profits	D51-8.61b	D51B	1112
	1220 Capital gains	D51-8.61c	D51C	1112
	1300 Unallocable as between 1100 and 1200			1113
2000	Social security contributions			
	2100 Employees	D613-8.85	D61111	1211
	2200 Employers	D611-8.83	D61121	1212
	2300 Self-employed, non-employed	D613-8.85	D61131	1213
	2400 Unallocable as between 2100, 2200 and 2300			1214
3000	Taxes on payroll and workforce	D29-7.97a	D29C	112
4000	Taxes on property			
	4100 Recurrent taxes on immovable property			
	4110 Households	D59-8.63a	D59A	1131
	4120 Other	D29-7.97b	D29A	1131
	4200 Recurrent net wealth taxes			
	4210 Individual	D59-8.63b	D59A	1132
	4220 Corporations	D59-8.63b	D59A	1132
	4300 Estate, inheritance and gift taxes			
	4310 Estate and inheritance taxes	D91-10.207b	D91A	1133
	4320 Gift taxes	D91-10.207b	D91A	1133
	4400 Taxes on financial and capital transactions	D59-7.96d; D29-7.97e	D214B,C	1134:1161
	4500 Other non-recurrent taxes on property	D91-10.207a	D91B	1135
	4600 Other recurrent taxes on property	D59-8.63c	D59A	1136
5000	Taxes on goods and services			
	5100 Taxes on production, sale and transfer of goods and services			
	5110 General sales taxes			
	5111 Value-added taxes	D211-7.89	D211; D29G	11411
	5112 Sales taxes	D2122-7.94a; D214-7.96a	D2122D; D214I	11412
	5113 Other general taxes	D214-7.96a	D214I	11413
	5120 Taxes on specific goods and services			
	5121 Excises	D2122-7.94b; D214-7.96b	D2122C; D214A,B,D	1142
	5122 Profits of fiscal monopolies	D214-7.96e	D214J	1143
	5123 Customs/import duties	D2121-7.93	D2121; D2122A,B	1151
	5124 On exports	D213-7.95a	D214K	1152-4
	5125 On investment goods			
	5126 On specific services	D2122-7.94c; D214-7.96c	D2122E; D214E,F,G; D29F	1144; 1156
	5127 Other taxes on international trade and transactions	D2122-7.94d D29-7.95b D29-7.97g D59-8.64d	D2122F; D29D; D59E	1153 1155-6
	5128 Other taxes on specific goods and services			1146
	5130 Unallocable as between 5110 and 5120			
	5200 Taxes on use of goods			
	5210 Recurrent taxes			
	5211 Motor vehicle taxes households	D59-8.64c	D59D	11451
	5212 Motor vehicles taxes others	D29-7.97d	D214D; D29B	11451
	5213 Other recurrent taxes	D29-7.97c,d,f D59-8.64c	D29B,E,F;D59 D	11452
	5220 Non-recurrent taxes			
	5300 Unallocable as between 5100 and 5200			
6000	Other taxes			
	6100 Paid solely by business			
	6200 Paid by other than business, or unidentifiable	D59-8.64a,b	D59B,C	1162

88. These comparisons represent those that would be expected to apply in the majority of cases. However in practice some flexibility should be used in their application. This is because in particular cases, countries can adopt varying approaches to the classification of revenues in National Accounts.

K. Attribution of tax revenues by sub-sectors of general government

89. The OECD classification requires a breakdown of tax revenues by sub-sectors of government. The definition of each sub-sector and the criteria to be used to attribute tax revenues between these sub-sectors are set out below. They follow the guidance of the 2008 SNA and GFSM2001.

Sub-sectors of general government to be identified

a) Central government

90. The central government sub-sector includes all governmental departments, offices, establishments and other bodies which are agencies or instruments of the central authority whose competence extends over the whole territory, with the exception of the administration of social security funds.Central government therefore has the authority to impose taxes on all resident and non-resident units engaged in economic activities within the country.

b) State, provincial or regional government

91. This sub-sector consists of intermediate units of government exercising a competence at a level below that of central government. It includes all such units operating independently of central government in a part of a country's territory encompassing a number of smaller localities, with the exception of the administration of social security funds. In unitary countries, regional governments may be considered to have a separate existence where they have substantial autonomy to raise a significant proportion of their revenues from sources within their control and their officers are independent of external administrative control in the actual operation of the unit's activities.

92. At present, federal countries comprise the majority of cases where revenues attributed to intermediate units of government are identified separately. Spain is the only unitary country in this position. In the remaining unitary countries, regional revenues are included with those of local governments.

c) Local government

93. This sub-sector includes all other units of government exercising an independent competence in part of the territory of a country, with the exception of the administration of social security funds. It encompasses various urban and/or rural jurisdictions (e.g. local authorities, municipalities, cities, boroughs, districts).

d) Social security funds

94. Social security funds form a separate sub-sector of general government. The social security sub-sector is defined in the 2008 SNA by the following extracts from paragraphs 4.124 to 4.126 and 4.147:

"Social security schemes are social insurance schemes covering the community as a whole or large section of the community that are imposed and controlled by government units. The schemes cover a wide variety of programmes, providing benefits in cash or in kind for old age, invalidity or death, survivors, sickness and maternity, work injury, unemployment, family allowance, health care, etc. There is not necessarily a direct link between the amount of the contribution paid by an individual and the benefits he or she may receive." (Paragraph 4.124).

"When social security schemes are separately organised from the other activities of government units and hold their assets and liabilities separately from the latter and engage in financial transactions on their own account they qualify as institutional units that are described as social security funds" (Paragraph 4.125).

"The amounts raised, and paid out, in social security contributions and benefits may be deliberately varied in order to achieve objectives of government policy that have no direct connection with the concept of social security as a scheme to provide social benefits to members of the community. They may be raised or lowered in order to influence the level of aggregate demand in the economy, for example. Nevertheless, so long as they remain separately constituted funds, they must be treated as separate institutional units in the SNA. (Paragraph 4.126)

"The social security funds sub-sector (of general government) consists of the social security funds operating at all levels of government. Such funds are social insurance schemes covering the community as a whole or large section of the community that are imposed by government units" (Paragraph 4.147).

95. This definition of social security funds is followed in the OECD classification with the two following exceptions which are excluded

- Schemes imposed by government and operated by bodies outside the general government sector, as defined in §3 of this manual; and
- Schemes to which all contributions are voluntary.

Supra-national Authorities

96. This sub-sector covers the revenue-raising operations of supra-national authorities within a country. In practice, the only relevant supra-national authority in the OECD area is that of the institutions of the European Union (EU). As from 1998, supra-national authorities are no longer included in the *Revenue Statistics*, to achieve consistency with the SNA definition of general government which excludes them. For example, income taxes and social security contributions collected by European Institutions and paid by European civil servants who are resident of EU member countries should not be included. However the specific levies paid by the member states of the EU continue to be included in total tax revenues and they are shown under this heading.

Criteria to be used for the attribution of tax revenues

97. When a government collects taxes and pays them over in whole or in part to other governments, it is necessary to determine whether the revenues should be considered to be those of the collecting government which it distributes to others as grants, or those of the beneficiary governments which the collecting government receives and passes on only as their agent. The criteria to be used in the attribution of revenues are set out in §98 to §101 which replicate paragraphs 3.70 to 3.73 from the 2008 SNA.

98. In general, a tax is attributed to the government unit that:

a) exercises the authority to impose the tax (either as a principal or through the delegated authority of the principal);

b) has final discretion to set and vary the rate of the tax.

99. Where an amount is collected by one government for and on behalf of another government, and the latter government has the authority to impose the tax, and set and vary its rate, then the former is acting as an agent for the latter and the tax is reassigned. Any amount retained by the collecting government as a collection charge should be treated as a payment for a service. Any other amount retained by the collecting government, such as under a tax-sharing arrangement, should be treated as a current grant. If the collecting government was delegated the authority to set and vary the rate, then the amount collected should be treated as tax revenue of this government.

100. Where different governments jointly and equally set the rate of a tax and jointly and equally decide on the distribution of the proceeds, with no individual government having ultimate overriding authority, then the tax revenues are attributed to each government according to its respective share of the proceeds. If an arrangement allows one government unit to exercise ultimate overriding authority, then all of the tax revenue is attributed to that unit.

101. There may also be the circumstance where a tax is imposed under the constitutional or other authority of one government, but other governments individually set the tax rate in their jurisdictions. The proceeds of the tax generated in each respective government's jurisdiction are attributed as tax revenues of that government.

Levies paid by member states of the European Union

102. The levies paid by the member states of the EU take the form:

- VAT own resources; and
- Specific levies which include:
  - *a)* custom duties and levies on agricultural goods (5123),
  - *b)* gross monetary compensation accounts (5123 if relating to imports and 5124 if relating to exports); and
  - *c)* Steel, coal, sugar and milk levies (5128).

103. The custom duties collected by member states on behalf of the EU are recorded

- on a gross of collection fee basis
- using figures adjusted so that duties are shown on a 'final destination' as opposed to a 'country of first entry' basis where such adjustments can be made. These adjustments concern in particular duties collected at important (sea) ports. Although the EU duties are collected by the authorities of the country of first entry, when possible these duties should be excluded from the revenue of the collecting country and be included in the revenue of the country of final destination.

This is the specific EU levy that most clearly conforms to the attribution criterion described in §96 above. Consequently as from 1998, these amounts are footnoted as a memorandum item to the EU member state country tables (in Part III) and no longer shown under heading 5123. However the figures are included in the total tax revenue figures on the top line for all the relevant years shown in the tables.

104. The VAT own resources, which are determined by applying a rate not exceeding 1% to an assessment basis specified in the Sixth Directive,[20] are more of a borderline case. They have some of the characteristics of a transfer (they are not derived from a clearly identifiable source of funds that are actually collected) and some of a tax (the amount of the transfer is determined by the receiving sub-sector of government). In this publication they are *not* shown as a tax of the European Union (but as a tax of the EU member states), though the amounts involved are footnoted in the tables contained in Part IV.

L. Provisional classification of revenues from bank levies and payments to deposit insurance and financial stability schemes

105. The OECD have adopted the following interim approach to reporting revenue from bank levies plus deposit insurance and stability fees for the 2012 edition of *OECD Revenue Statistics*; The amounts should be recorded under category 5126.

- Compulsory payments of stability fees, bank levies and deposit insurance should generally be treated as tax revenues where the payments are made to General Government and allocated to the governments' consolidated or general funds so that the Government is free to make immediate use of the money for the purposes that it chooses. This principle would apply regardless of whether the Government is promising to make payments to guarantee the banks' customer deposits in some future contingency.

- If the compulsory payments are made to general government and placed in funds that are earmarked to be entirely channelled back to the sector of the economy that comprises the companies that are subject to the payment, they would still generally be treated as tax revenues on the grounds that the funds would be available for the government and would reduce its budget deficit, the fee is unrequited for an individual entity and the amounts raised could be unrelated to any eventual pay out to depositors or expenditure on wider support for the financial sector.

- Payments to made to the smaller long-standing schemes for insuring 'retail' deposits, where the payment levels are consistent with the costs of insurance should be classified as fee for service.

- Any payments which involve governments realising the assets of a failed institution or receiving a priority claim on its assets in liquidation in order to fund payments of compensation to customers for their lost deposits would be treated as a fee for a service as opposed to tax revenues.

- Compulsory payments that are made to funds operated outside the government sector and non-state institutions backed by the deposit takers and all payments to voluntary schemes should not be treated as tax revenues.

Notes

1. All references to SNA are to the 2008 edition.

2. See section K of this guide for a discussion of the concept of agency capacity.

3. It is usually possible to identify amounts of social security contributions and payroll taxes, but not other taxes paid by government.

4. If, however, a levy which is considered as non-tax revenue by most countries is regarded as a tax – or raises substantial revenue – in one or more countries, the amounts collected are footnoted at the end of the relevant country tables, even though the amounts are not included in total tax revenues.

5. Names, however, can frequently be misleading. For example, though a passport fee would normally be considered a non-tax revenue, if a supplementary levy on passports (as is the case in Portugal) were imposed in order to raise substantial amounts of revenue relative to the cost of providing the passport, the levy would be regarded as a tax under 5200.

6. There are practical difficulties in operating the distinction made by 1993 SNA.

7. A more detailed explanation of this distinction can be found in the special feature, 'Current issues in reporting tax revenues', in the 2001 edition of the *Revenue Statistics*.

8. Sometimes the terms 'non-refundable' and 'refundable' are used, but it may be considered illogical to talk of 'refundable' when nothing has been paid.

9. A different treatment, however, is accorded to non-wastable tax credits under imputation systems of corporate income tax (§32–34).

10. This is not strictly a true tax expenditure in the formal sense. Such tax expenditures require identification of a benchmark tax system for each country or, preferably, a common international benchmark. In practice it has not been possible to reach agreement on a common international benchmark.

11. Unless based on the profit made on a sale, in which case they would be classified as capital gains taxes under 1120 or 1220.

12. In some countries the same legislation applies to both individual and corporate enterprises for particular taxes on income. However, the receipts from such taxes are usually allocable between individuals and enterprises and can therefore be shown in the appropriate sub-heading.

13. For example, "...sufficiently self-contained and independent that they behave in the same way as corporations....... (including) keeping a complete set of accounts" (2008SNA, section 4.44).

14. In Canada – a country also referred to as having an imputation system – the (wastable) tax credit for the shareholder is in respect of domestic corporation tax deemed to have been paid whether or not a corporation tax liability has arisen. As there is no integral connection between the corporation tax liability and the credit given against income tax under such systems, these credits for dividends are treated, along with other tax credits, on the lines described in §21.

15. This may also apply where a scheme for government employees existed prior to the introduction of a general social security scheme.

16. In the 2008 SNA these are regarded as capital transfers and not as taxes (see section G).

17. This is the system by which the European Union adjusts for differences between the exchange rates used to determine prices under the Common Market Agricultural Policy and actual exchange rates. Payments under the system may relate to imports or exports and where these amounts are

separately identifiable they are shown under the appropriate heading (5123 or 5124). In this Report, these amounts are shown gross (i.e. without deducting any subsidies paid out under the MCA system).

18. Transfers of profits of State lotteries are regarded as non-tax revenues (see also §64).

19. See §26(*c*) as regards this distinction.

20. At the Edinburgh Summit (1992) EU Member countries have decided to gradually reduce this percentage from 1.4 to 1, and to effectuate this reduction between years 1995 and 1999.During the period 1970–1983 this percentage also amounted to 1.

ANEXO A

Clasificación de impuestos y guía de interpretación de la OCDE

Índice

Página

Clasificación de impuestos de la OCDE

1000 *Impuestos sobre la renta, las utilidades y las ganancias de capital*

- 1100 Personas físicas
  - 1110 Renta y utilidades
  - 1120 Ganancias de capital
- 1200 Sociedades
  - 1210 Renta y utilidades
  - 1220 Ganancias de capital
- 1300 No clasificables entre 1100 y 1200

2000 *Contribuciones a la seguridad social*

- 2100 Empleados
- 2200 Empleadores
- 2300 Trabajadores por cuenta propia o no empleados
- 2400 No clasificables entre 2100, 2200 y 2300

3000 *Impuestos sobre la nómina y la fuerza de trabajo*

4000 *Impuestos sobre la propiedad*

- 4100 Impuestos recurrentes sobre la propiedad inmueble
  - 4110 Hogares
  - 4120 Otros
- 4200 Impuestos recurrentes sobre la riqueza neta
  - 4210 Personas físicas
  - 4220 Sociedades
- 4300 Impuestos sobre sucesiones, herencias y donaciones
  - 4310 Impuestos sobre sucesiones y herencias
  - 4320 Impuestos sobre donaciones
- 4400 Impuestos sobre transacciones financieras y de capital
- 4500 Otros impuestos no recurrentes sobre la propiedad
- 4600 Otros impuestos recurrentes sobre la propiedad

5000 *Impuestos sobre los bienes y servicios*

5100 Impuestos sobre la producción, venta y transmisión de bienes y prestación de servicios

5110 Impuestos generales

5111 Impuestos sobre el valor agregado

5112 Impuestos sobre las ventas

5113 Otros impuestos generales sobre los bienes y servicios

5120 Impuestos sobre bienes y servicios específicos

5121 Impuestos selectivos

5122 Utilidades de los monopolios fiscales

5123 Derechos de aduanas y otros derechos de importación

5124 Sobre las exportaciones

5125 Sobre los bienes de inversión

5126 Sobre servicios específicos

5127 Otros impuestos sobre el comercio y las transacciones internacionales

5128 Otros impuestos sobre bienes y servicios específicos

5130 No clasificables entre 5110 y 5120

5200 Impuestos sobre el uso de bienes y sobre el permiso para usar bienes y realizar actividades

5210 Impuestos recurrentes

5211 Sobre vehículos automotores: hogares

5212 Sobre vehículos automotores: otros

5213 Otros impuestos recurrentes

5220 Impuestos no recurrentes

5300 No clasificables entre 5100 y 5200

6000 *Otros impuestos*

6100 Pagados únicamente por empresas

6200 Pagados por otros distintos de las empresas o no identificables

Guía de Interpretación de la OCDE

A. Cobertura

Criterios generales

1. En la clasificación de la OCDE, el término "impuestos" se circunscribe exclusivamente a los pagos sin contraprestación efectuados al gobierno general. Los impuestos carecen de contraprestación en el sentido en que, normalmente, las prestaciones proporcionadas por el gobierno a los contribuyentes no guardan relación directa con los pagos realizados por estos.

2. El término "impuestos" no incluye las multas o sanciones pecuniarias no relacionadas con infracciones tributarias ni los préstamos obligatorios pagados al gobierno. La delimitación entre ingresos tributarios y no tributarios en relación con ciertas tasas y cargos se abordan en los §§ 9–13.

3. El gobierno general comprende la Administración central y los organismos que se hallan bajo su control efectivo, los gobiernos estatales y locales y sus respectivas administraciones, y ciertos regímenes de seguridad social y entidades gubernamentales autónomas, excluidas las empresas públicas. Esta definición del gobierno proviene del Sistema de Cuentas Nacionales (SCN) 2008;[1] en esa publicación, el sector del gobierno general y sus subsectores se hallan definidos en el capítulo 4, sección F, páginas 80-84 de la versión inglesa.

4. Los pagos obligatorios a autoridades supranacionales y a los organismos vinculados a ellas no se incluyen como impuestos desde 1998, con contadas excepciones; sin embargo, los derechos de aduana recaudados por los estados miembros de la Unión Europea en nombre de esta siguen registrándose como partidas informativas y se incluyen en los cuadros de países (parte III de la publicación *Revenue Statistics* de la OCDE), concretamente en la recaudación tributaria total del país en el que se cobran (véase el § 95). Por otra parte, en los países en los que la Iglesia forma parte del gobierno general, se computan los impuestos eclesiásticos, siempre que reúnan los criterios establecidos en el § 1. Además, habida cuenta de que los datos hacen referencia a las entradas que recibe el gobierno general, quedan excluidos los gravámenes abonados a órganos no gubernamentales, organismos de bienestar o regímenes de seguro social externos al gobierno general, y sindicatos u organizaciones profesionales, aun cuando dichos gravámenes sean obligatorios; sin embargo, los pagos obligatorios al gobierno general asignados a esos entes sí están incluidos aquí siempre que el gobierno no actúe como mero agente de estos.[2] Las utilidades de los monopolios fiscales se diferencian de las de otras empresas públicas, y se tratan como impuestos porque reflejan el ejercicio del poder tributario del Estado mediante el uso de prerrogativas monopolísticas (véanse los §§ 62–64), al igual que las utilidades percibidas por el gobierno por la compra y la venta de divisas a diferentes tipos de cambio (véase el § 70).

5. Los impuestos pagados por el gobierno (p. ej., contribuciones a la seguridad social e impuestos sobre la nómina pagados por el gobierno en su calidad de empleador, impuestos sobre el consumo en sus compras o impuestos sobre sus propiedades) no se han excluido de

los datos presentados. Sin embargo, cuando ha sido posible identificar las cantidades de ingreso implicadas,[3] se han mostrado en la parte III, sección C, de la publicación *Revenue Statistics* de la OCDE.

6. La relación entre esta clasificación y la del Sistema de Cuentas Nacionales (SCN) se aclara en los apartados H y J *infra.*; dado que estas dos clasificaciones no coinciden en todos sus aspectos, en ocasiones, los datos presentados en las cuentas nacionales se calculan o clasifican de forma diferente a lo establecido en la presente guía y, aunque esas y otras diferencias se han mencionado en determinados casos (p. ej., en los §§ 13 y 26), no ha sido posible hacer referencia a todas ellas. Por otra parte, pueden darse asimismo ciertas disparidades entre la presente clasificación y la empleada internamente por algunas administraciones nacionales (véase el § 10), por lo que quizá las estadísticas de la OCDE y las nacionales no siempre concuerden; sin embargo, es más que probable que esas diferencias sean mínimas en lo que a la cuantía de ingresos se refiere.

Contribuciones a la seguridad social

7. Las contribuciones obligatorias a la seguridad social, tal y como se definen en el § 35, abonadas al gobierno general, se tratan aquí como ingresos tributarios, ya que, al tratarse de pagos preceptivos al gobierno general, se asemejan claramente a los impuestos. No obstante, pueden diferir de otros impuestos por el hecho de que la recepción de prestaciones de la seguridad social depende, en numerosos países, de que se hayan aportado las debidas contribuciones, aunque la magnitud de dichas prestaciones no tiene por qué estar supeditada obligatoriamente al importe de las contribuciones. Al tratar las contribuciones sociales como impuestos, se obtiene un mayor grado de comparabilidad entre países, aunque se han consignado en una categoría separada para poder distinguirlas en cualquier análisis.

8. Por el contrario, las contribuciones a la seguridad social voluntarias o no pagaderas al gobierno general (véase el § 1) no se tratan como impuestos, aunque en ciertos países, tal y como se indica debidamente en cada caso en las notas que figuran al pie de los cuadros, plantea dificultades el eliminar tanto las contribuciones voluntarias como algunos pagos obligatorios al sector privado.

Tasas, cargos a usuarios y licencias

9. Aparte de las tasas por licencia de vehículos, universalmente consideradas como impuestos, no resulta fácil distinguir entre las tasas y cargos a usuarios que deben tratarse como impuestos y las que no, ya que, aunque toda tasa o cargo se impone en conexión con un servicio o una actividad específicos, la intensidad del vínculo entre el derecho cobrado y el servicio prestado puede variar considerablemente, al igual que puede hacerlo la relación entre la cuantía de la tasa y el costo que supone proporcionar el servicio en cuestión. En todo caso, cuando el beneficiario del servicio pague una tasa claramente relacionada con el costo que supone prestar un servicio, puede inferirse que el gravamen tiene contraprestación y, de acuerdo con la definición reseñada en el § 1, no se considerará como impuesto. En sentido contrario, puede estimarse que el gravamen "carece de contraprestación" cuando:

a) el cargo exceda con creces el costo que supone prestar el servicio;

b) el pagador o sujeto pasivo del gravamen no sea el beneficiario del servicio (p. ej., tasas recaudadas de los mataderos para financiar un servicio proporcionado a los titulares de explotaciones agropecuarias);

c) el gobierno no proporcione un servicio específico a cambio del pago del gravamen, aun y cuando se emita un permiso en beneficio del sujeto pasivo (p. ej., cuando el gobierno concede licencias de caza, pesca o tiro que no otorgan el derecho a usar una zona específica propiedad del gobierno);

d) los servicios beneficien únicamente a los pagadores del gravamen, pero las utilidades recibidas por cada persona no guarden necesariamente proporción con sus pagos (p. ej., el gravamen sobre la comercialización de la leche que recae en los criadores de ganado lechero y que se utiliza para fomentar el consumo de la leche).

10. Pese a las anteriores consideraciones, en ciertos casos excepcionales la aplicación de los criterios plasmados en el § 1 puede resultar particularmente compleja. La solución adoptada –dada la conveniencia de uniformidad internacional y las cantidades de ingreso relativamente bajas implicadas por lo general– ha consistido en seguir la práctica dominante en la mayoría de las administraciones, en lugar de permitir que cada país aplique su propia visión sobre si estos gravámenes deben considerarse como ingresos tributarios o no tributarios.[4]

11. Seguidamente, se ofrece una lista de las principales tasas y cargos en cuestión, y su tratamiento normal[5] en esta publicación:

Ingresos no tributarios:	tasas procesales, permisos de conducir, tasas portuarias, tasas por expedición de pasaportes, licencias de radio y televisión cuando las autoridades públicas proporcionan el servicio de difusión.
Impuestos de la partida 5200:	permiso para realizar actividades tales como distribución cinematográfica; caza, pesca o tiro; suministro de instalaciones para actividades recreativas o de ocio o juegos de azar; venta de bebidas alcohólicas o tabaco; posesión de animales domésticos o uso de vehículos automotores; derechos sobre la extracción.

12. En la práctica, puede que no siempre resulte posible aislar las entradas tributarias de las no tributarias cuando estas se registran conjuntamente. En ese caso, si se considera que la mayoría de las entradas proviene de ingresos no tributarios, se tratará el importe total como tal; de lo contrario, esas entradas del gobierno se incluirán y clasificarán según las normas recogidas en el § 28.

13. En relación con la delimitación de los ingresos tributarios y no tributarios, se observan las dos siguientes diferencias entre la clasificación de la OCDE y la del SCN:

- El SCN considera un cierto número de gravámenes como impuestos indirectos si los abonan las empresas y como ingresos no tributarios si los satisfacen los hogares, una distinción obviada en la presente clasificación a la hora diferenciar entre ingresos tributarios y no tributarios.[6]

- La práctica dominante en la mayoría de las administraciones tributarias de la OCDE, un criterio empleado ocasionalmente en la presente clasificación para distinguir entre ingresos tributarios y no tributarios, no resulta pertinente a efectos del SCN.

Regalías

14. Las regalías percibidas por el derecho a extraer petróleo o gas, o a explotar otros recursos minerales, se consideran normalmente ingresos no tributarios, ya que son rentas de la propiedad procedentes de tierras o recursos del gobierno.

Multas y sanciones pecuniarias

15. Las entradas procedentes de multas y sanciones pecuniarias impuestas por el incumplimiento de normas vinculadas a un impuesto determinado, así como los intereses devengados por los pagos adeudados en relación con ese impuesto, se registrarán junto con las entradas derivadas de dicho impuesto. Otros tipos de multas vinculadas a infracciones tributarias se clasificarán en la partida residual 6000. Las multas que no deriven de infracciones tributarias (p. ej., infracción de aparcamiento) o que no puedan vincularse a una infracción tributaria concreta no se tratan como impuestos.

B. Principios de registro

Criterio de devengo

16. Los datos recogidos en esta publicación relativos a los últimos años se han registrado predominantemente según el criterio de devengo, esto es, se han computado en el momento en que nace la obligación. En las notas que figuran al pie de los cuadros de países de la parte III del informe, se ofrece más información al respecto.

17. Sin embargo, los datos relativos a años anteriores han seguido registrándose principalmente según el criterio de caja, es decir, en el momento en que el gobierno recibió el pago. Por lo tanto, por ejemplo, los impuestos descontados por los empleadores en un año pero pagados al gobierno al año siguiente y los impuestos debidos un año pero liquidados el año después constan ambos en las entradas del segundo año. Las transacciones correctoras, tales como devoluciones, reembolsos y reintegros, se deducen de los ingresos brutos del periodo en que se realizan.

18. Los datos sobre ingresos tributarios se registran sin deducción de los gastos administrativos propios de la recaudación impositiva. De igual modo, cuando los recursos generados por un impuesto se emplean para subvencionar a miembros particulares de la comunidad, el subsidio no se descuenta del producto impositivo, aunque puede que el impuesto aparezca sin los subsidios en los registros nacionales de algunos países.

19. En lo que a los monopolios fiscales se refiere (5122), únicamente se incluye en los ingresos del gobierno el importe realmente transferido a este. Sin embargo, si cualquier gasto de los monopolios fiscales se considera gasto del gobierno (p. ej., gastos sociales emprendidos por los monopolios fiscales en beneficio del gobierno), se añadirán posteriormente con el fin de llegar a cifras de ingreso tributario (véase el § 62 *infra.*).

Distinción entre disposiciones tributarias y disposiciones relativas al gasto[7]

20. Dado que la presente publicación aborda únicamente la actividad del gobierno desde el punto de vista del ingreso, sin tener en cuenta los aspectos relacionados con el gasto, resulta preciso realizar una distinción entre las disposiciones que rigen estos dos elementos. Por lo general, no existe dificultad alguna en diferenciar ambos aspectos, ya que los gastos operan en un ámbito externo al sistema tributario y sus cuentas, y se rigen por una legislación separada de la impositiva. En los casos de difícil delimitación, se emplea el flujo de caja para distinguir entre disposiciones tributarias y disposiciones relativas al gasto. En la medida en que una disposición incida en el flujo de pagos tributarios del contribuyente al gobierno, se entenderá que reviste un carácter tributario y se tendrá en cuenta en los datos recogidos en esta publicación. Cualquier disposición que no afecte a ese flujo se reputará como relativa al gasto y no se tendrá en consideración en la información plasmada en la publicación.

21. Las desgravaciones, exenciones y deducciones tributarias sobre la base imponible afectan claramente a la cantidad transferida al gobierno y, por ende, se consideran disposiciones de naturaleza tributaria. En el extremo opuesto, los subsidios o exoneraciones que no compensen la obligación tributaria y que estén claramente desvinculados del proceso de evaluación, no reducen los ingresos tributarios consignados en esta publicación. De particular interés en este ámbito resultan los créditos fiscales, que son cantidades deducibles del impuesto liquidable (lo que los diferencia de las deducciones sobre la base imponible). Cabe distinguir dos tipos de créditos fiscales: los créditos fiscales no exigibles (a veces denominados desaprovechables), limitados al importe de la obligación tributaria y que, por ende, no pueden generar un pago de las autoridades al contribuyente; y los créditos fiscales exigibles (o no desaprovechables), que no están sometidos a dicho límite, de forma que toda cantidad que exceda la obligación tributaria puede abonarse al contribuyente.[8] Al igual que las desgravaciones, un crédito fiscal no exigible afecta claramente a la cantidad transferida al gobierno y, por ende, se considerará como tributario. La práctica seguida para los créditos fiscales exigibles[9] consiste en distinguir entre "el componente de gasto tributario"[10] que es la porción del crédito empleada en reducir o eliminar la obligación del contribuyente" y el "componente de transferencia", constituido por la parte que excede la obligación del contribuyente y que se paga a este. Al registrar los ingresos tributarios deberá restarse la parte equivalente al componente de gasto tributario, pero no la correspondiente al componente de transferencia. Además, las cantidades de ambos componentes deberán figurar como partidas informativas en los cuadros de países. Los países que no puedan diferenciar entre estos dos componentes deberán indicar si se ha restado de los ingresos tributarios el total de ellos y presentar las evaluaciones disponibles del valor que ambos representan. Para mayor información, consúltese la sección C de la parte I de la publicación *Revenue Statistics* de la OCDE, que examina el efecto de los diversos tratamientos de los créditos fiscales exigibles en la relación impuestos sobre PIB.

Calendario y ejercicio fiscal

22. Las autoridades nacionales cuyos ejercicios fiscales no coinciden con el año calendario deben presentar los datos, siempre que sea posible, sobre la base del año calendario, a fin de permitir el mayor grado posible de comparación con la información de otros países. Subsisten algunos países en los que los datos hacen referencia a los ejercicios fiscales; para ellos, los datos relativos al PIB utilizados en los cuadros comparativos corresponden igualmente a los ejercicios fiscales.

C. Criterios generales de clasificación

Principales criterios de clasificación

23. El desglose de las entradas fiscales en las diversas categorías (1000, 2000, 3000, 4000, 5000 y 6000) se rige en general por la base sobre la cual recae el impuesto: 1000, renta, utilidades y ganancias de capital; 2000 y 3000, remuneraciones, nómina o número de empleados (fuerza de trabajo); 4000, propiedad; 5000, bienes y servicios; 6000, bases múltiples, otras bases o bases no identificables. Cuando un impuesto se calcula sobre más de una base, las entradas que genera se distribuyen, en la medida de lo posible, entre las diversas categorías (véanse los §§ 28 y 78). Las categorías 4000 y 5000 no sólo cubren aquellos impuestos en los que la base tributaria está constituida por la propiedad, los bienes o los servicios en sí mismos, sino también ciertos impuestos afines; y así, por ejemplo, los impuestos sobre transmisiones patrimoniales se incluyen en la partida 4400,[11] y los impuestos sobre el uso de bienes y sobre el permiso para realizar actividades, en la 5200. En las categorías 4000 y 5000, se distingue en ocasiones entre impuestos recurrentes y no recurrentes: son impuestos recurrentes los que se recaudan a intervalos regulares (por lo general, anualmente), y no recurrentes, los que se imponen una sola vez (véanse los §§ 43-46, 49–50 y 76–77 para profundizar en las aplicaciones particulares de esta distinción).

24. La asignación de un impuesto a fines específicos no afecta a la clasificación de las entradas fiscales que genera. Sin embargo, tal y como se explica en el § 35 en relación con la clasificación de las contribuciones a la seguridad social, el hecho de que estas confieran un derecho a recibir prestaciones sociales es decisivo para la definición de la categoría 2000.

25. La forma en que se establece o recauda un impuesto (p.ej., mediante el uso de timbres) no afecta a su clasificación.

Clasificación de los contribuyentes

26. En ocasiones, se distingue entre diversas clases de contribuyentes. Esas distinciones dependen de cada impuesto.

a) Entre personas físicas y sociedades en relación con los impuestos sobre la renta y sobre la riqueza neta

La distinción básica aquí es que los impuestos sobre la renta de las sociedades (impuesto de sociedades), a diferencia de los impuestos sobre la renta de las personas físicas, gravan a la sociedad como entidad y no a sus propietarios, independientemente de las circunstancias personales de estos; la misma distinción se aplica a los impuestos sobre la riqueza neta de las sociedades y de las personas físicas. Los impuestos liquidados sobre las utilidades de las asociaciones y sobre la renta de las instituciones, tales como seguros de vida o fondos de pensiones, se clasifican siguiendo la misma regla, y así, se considerarán impuestos sobre las sociedades (1200) si se cargan a la asociación o institución como persona jurídica sin tener en cuenta las circunstancias personales de sus propietarios, o impuestos sobre las personas físicas en el caso contrario (1100). Por lo general, los impuestos aplicados a las sociedades y a las personas físicas se rigen por legislaciones diferentes.[12] La distinción realizada aquí entre personas físicas y sociedades no sigue la categorización por sectores entre hogares, empresas, etcétera, del Sistema de Cuentas Nacionales para las cuentas de ingresos y desembolsos. La clasificación del SCN requiere que ciertas empresas no constituidas en sociedad[13] se excluyan del sector de los hogares y vengan a sumarse a las empresas no financieras y las instituciones financieras. Sin embargo, el impuesto sobre las utilidades de esos negocios no siempre puede separarse del impuesto sobre la renta de sus propietarios o, como mucho, puede deslindarse sólo arbitrariamente. Por ello, no se ha intentado reproducir aquí esa separación, y la totalidad del impuesto sobre la renta de las personas físicas se ha recogido en un solo bloque, independientemente de la naturaleza del ingreso imponible.

b) Entre hogares y otros en relación con los impuestos sobre la propiedad inmueble

Esta distinción es la misma que la adoptada por el SCN para las cuentas de gasto del consumo final de los hogares y de producción. Se trata pues de diferenciar a los hogares como consumidores (esto es, excluidas las empresas no constituidas en sociedad), por una parte, y a los productores, por otra. Los impuestos sobre las viviendas ocupadas por los hogares, tanto a cargo de los propietarios-ocupantes como de los arrendatarios o de los arrendadores, se incluyen en los hogares, lo que coincide con la diferenciación que suele hacerse comúnmente entre los impuestos sobre la propiedad doméstica y los impuestos sobre la propiedad empresarial. No obstante, algunos países no se hallan en situación de operar esta distinción.

c) Entre hogares y otros en relación con las licencias de vehículos automotores

Se distingue aquí entre los hogares como consumidores, por una parte, y los productores, por otra, al igual que en las cuentas de gasto del consumo final de los hogares y de producción del SCN.

d) Entre empresas y otros en relación con los impuestos residuales (6000)

La distinción es la misma que en c), esta vez, entre los productores, por una parte, y los hogares como consumidores, por otra. Los impuestos recogidos en la categoría 6000 bien porque gravan más de una base tributaria, o bien porque su base no entra dentro del ámbito de ninguna de las categorías anteriores pero es identificable como imponible sobre los productores, y no sobre los hogares, se incluyen en "empresas". El resto de los impuestos de la categoría 6000 se imputan a "otros" o "no identificables"

Recargos

27. Las entradas procedentes de recargos relacionados con impuestos particulares se clasifican por lo general en base al impuesto correspondiente, ya sea el recargo temporal o no. Pero si el recargo posee una característica que lo califica para ser clasificada en una categoría diferente de la lista de la OCDE, las entradas generadas por el recargo se recogen en dicha categoría, separadas de las del correspondiente impuesto.

Entradas tributarias no identificables y partidas residuales

28. En un cierto número de casos, no logra determinarse que los impuestos pertenezcan enteramente a una categoría o partida de la clasificación de la OCDE y, en esos casos, se aplican las siguientes pautas:

a) Se conoce la categoría, pero no la forma de distribuir las entradas entre las diversas subdivisiones: las entradas se clasifican en la correspondiente partida o subpartida residual (1300, 2400, 4520, 4600, 5130, 5300 o 6200).

b) Se sabe que la mayor parte de las entradas procedentes de un grupo de impuestos (normalmente, impuestos locales) proviene de impuestos de una categoría o una partida particulares, pero algunos de los impuestos del grupo cuya cuantía no puede determinarse con exactitud pueden clasificarse en otras categorías o partidas: las entradas se consignan en la categoría o partida a la que pertenezca la mayoría de ellas.

c) No puede identificarse ni la categoría ni la partida correspondiente al impuesto (normalmente, local): el impuesto se incorpora a la partida 6200, a menos que se conozca que se trata de un impuesto sobre las empresas, en cuyo caso se incluye en la partida 6100.

D. Comentarios sobre ítems de la lista

1000 – *Impuestos sobre la renta, las utilidades y las ganancias de capital*

29. Esta categoría cubre los impuestos aplicados a la renta o a las utilidades netas (esto es, la renta bruta menos las deducciones permitidas) de las personas físicas y las sociedades, así como los impuestos a los que se someten las ganancias de capital de esos mismos sujetos pasivos, y las ganancias obtenidas en juegos de azar.

30. Se incluyen en esta categoría:

a) los impuestos que gravan predominantemente la renta o las utilidades, aunque recaigan parcialmente sobre otras bases; los impuestos aplicados a varias bases que no sean mayoritariamente la renta o las utilidades se clasifican de acuerdo con los principios establecidos en los §§ 28 y 78;

b) los impuestos sobre la propiedad aplicados a un ingreso presunto o estimado como parte de un impuesto sobre la renta (véase el § 43(*a*), (*c*) y (*d*));

c) los pagos obligatorios al fondo de contribuciones de la seguridad social impuestos sobre la renta que no confieran un derecho a prestaciones sociales; si esas contribuciones otorgan derecho a prestaciones sociales, se incluyen en la categoría 2000 (véase el § 35);

d) el producto de los sistemas integrados de impuestos sobre la renta de régimen cedular se clasifican como un todo en esta categoría, aunque algunos de los impuestos cedulares puedan basarse en la renta bruta y no tener en cuenta las circunstancias personales del contribuyente.

31. La principal división de esta categoría se efectúa entre los gravámenes a personas físicas (1100) y aquellos a sociedades (1200). A su vez, en cada partida, se separa entre impuestos sobre la renta y las utilidades (1110 y 1210) e impuestos sobre las ganancias de capital (1120 y 1220). Si algunas entradas no pueden atribuirse pertinentemente a la partida 1100 o a la 1200, o si no puede realizarse esta distinción en la práctica (p. ej., por falta de datos fiables sobre los receptores de los pagos de los que se deducen los impuestos con retención en la fuente), las entradas se incorporan a la partida 1300 como "no clasificables".

Tratamiento de los créditos fiscales en los sistemas de imputación

32. En los sistemas de imputación del impuesto de sociedades, los accionistas están exentos, total o parcialmente, de responder en concepto del impuesto sobre la renta por los dividendos abonados por la compañía a partir de la renta o de las utilidades sometidas al impuesto de sociedades. En los países con este sistema,[14] una parte del impuesto sobre las

utilidades de la sociedad está disponible para exonerar a los accionistas de su propia obligación tributaria. La exoneración del accionista reviste la forma de un crédito fiscal, cuyo importe puede ser inferior, igual o superior al pasivo tributario total del accionista. Si el crédito fiscal excede al pasivo tributario, puede que ese exceso sea pagadero al accionista. Dado que este tipo de crédito fiscal es parte integrante del sistema de imputación del impuesto sobre la renta de las sociedades, cualquier pago a los accionistas se trata como devolución tributaria, y no como gasto (compárese con el tratamiento de otros créditos fiscales descrito en el § 21).

33. Puesto que en los sistemas de imputación el crédito fiscal (incluso cuando excede la obligación tributaria) debe considerarse como disposición tributaria, se plantea la cuestión de determinar si deberá deducirse de las entradas en concepto de impuesto sobre la renta de las personas físicas (1110) o de las entradas atribuibles al impuesto sobre la renta de las sociedades (1210). En este informe, la cantidad total pagada a título del impuesto sobre la renta de las sociedades se recoge en la subpartida 1210, y el impuesto no imputado en la subpartida 1110. Por lo tanto, la cuantía total del crédito se resta de esta última subpartida, tanto si el crédito da lugar a una reducción de la obligación tributaria por renta personal, como si se realiza un reembolso porque el crédito fiscal excede el pasivo tributario por este concepto. (No obstante, si los créditos fiscales se deducen del impuesto de sociedades por dividendos repartidos a otras sociedades, las correspondientes cantidades se descuentan de las entradas registradas en la subpartida 1210.)

1120 y 1220 – *Impuestos sobre las ganancias de capital*

34. Como su nombre indica, estas subpartidas engloban los impuestos sobre las ganancias de capital, ya de las personas físicas (1120), ya de las sociedades (1220), siempre que las entradas procedentes de estos impuestos puedan identificarse por separado. Ese no es el caso en numerosos países, y las entradas de estos impuestos se clasifican junto con las del impuesto sobre la renta. La subpartida 1120 contiene asimismo los impuestos sobre las ganancias obtenidas en juegos de azar.

2000 – *Contribuciones a la seguridad social*

35. Entran en esta categoría todos los pagos obligatorios que confieran un derecho a recibir una prestación social futura (contingente). Esos pagos suelen estar asignados al financiamiento de prestaciones sociales y, a menudo, se pagan a las instituciones del gobierno general que proporcionan dichas prestaciones. Sin embargo, esa asignación no forma parte de la definición de las contribuciones a la seguridad social y no es necesaria para que un impuesto sea clasificado en esta categoría, pero, para que un impuesto se incluya aquí, sí será preciso que confiera un derecho. Y así, los gravámenes sobre la renta o la nómina asignados a los fondos de seguridad social pero que no confieran el derecho a recibir prestaciones sociales quedan excluidos de la presente categoría y se registran bien entre los impuestos sobre la renta de las personas físicas (1100), bien junto con los impuestos sobre la nómina y la fuerza de trabajo (3000). Los impuestos que reposen sobre otras bases, como los bienes y servicios, no se consignarán aquí aunque estén asignados a prestaciones de la seguridad social, sino que se catalogarán según sus respectivas bases, ya que por lo general no otorgarán derecho alguno a prestaciones sociales.

36. Entre otras, se incluirán aquí las contribuciones a los siguientes tipos de prestaciones de la seguridad social: prestaciones y suplementos por seguro de desempleo; prestaciones por accidente, lesión o enfermedad; pensiones por jubilación, invalidez y supervivencia; ayudas familiares; reembolsos de gastos médicos u hospitalarios o prestación de servicios médicos u

hospitalarios. Las contribuciones pueden recaudarse tanto de los empleados como de los empleadores.

37. Las contribuciones pueden tener como base bien las remuneraciones o la nómina ("sobre la base de la nómina"), bien la renta neta tras deducciones y exenciones por circunstancias personales ("sobre la base del impuesto sobre la renta"), y el producto de ambas bases deberá identificarse separadamente en la medida de lo posible. Cuando las contribuciones al régimen general de la seguridad social se basen en la nómina, pero las de grupos particulares (tales como los trabajadores por cuenta propia) no puedan evaluarse en función de esta base y se emplee en ese caso la renta neta como una aproximación de las remuneraciones brutas, las entradas seguirán clasificándose sobre la base de la nómina. En principio, esta categoría excluye las contribuciones voluntarias aportadas a los regímenes de seguridad social, que, cuando sea posible identificarlas de forma separada, se recogerán en la partida informativa sobre el financiamiento de las prestaciones sociales; sin embargo, en la práctica, estas aportaciones no siempre pueden desvincularse de las contribuciones obligatorias, en cuyo caso se incluirán igualmente en esta categoría.

38. Las contribuciones a los regímenes de seguro social no vinculados a instituciones del gobierno general, así como las aportaciones a otros tipos de sistemas de seguro, tales como planes de previsión o planes de pensiones, mutualidades u otros planes de ahorro, no se consideran contribuciones a la seguridad social. Los planes de previsión son acuerdos por los que las contribuciones de cada empleado y la parte correspondiente del empleador en nombre de aquél se conservan en una cuenta separada que genera interés, de la que pueden retirarse en circunstancias específicas. Por su parte, los planes de pensiones son regímenes organizados separadamente, negociados entres empleados y empleadores, que conllevan disposiciones sobre diversas contribuciones y prestaciones, a veces más directamente vinculadas a los niveles salariales y a la duración del servicio que en otros esquemas sociales. Cuando las contribuciones a esos regímenes son obligatorias o cuasiobligatorias (p. ej., en virtud de un acuerdo con sindicatos u organizaciones profesionales), se hacen constar en la partida informativa (véase la parte III, sección B, de la publicación *Revenue Statistics* de la OCDE).

39. Las contribuciones de los empleados del gobierno y de este con respecto a sus empleados a los regímenes de seguridad social incluidos en el gobierno general se clasifican en esta categoría. También se consideran impuestos las contribuciones de los empleados del gobierno a regímenes diferentes que puedan reputarse sustitutivos de los regímenes generales de seguridad social.[15] Por el contrario, cuando un régimen diferente no pueda considerarse sustitutivo de uno general y haya sido negociado entre el gobierno, en su papel de empleador, y sus empleados, no se estimará como régimen de seguridad social y, por lo tanto, las contribuciones a él no se tendrán como impuestos, aunque el régimen haya sido instaurado por la legislación.

40. Esta categoría excluye las contribuciones "imputadas", que corresponden a las prestaciones sociales pagadas directamente por los empleadores a sus empleados, antiguos empleados o personas a cargo de estos (p. ej., cuando los empleadores están legalmente obligados a correr con las prestaciones por enfermedad durante cierto tiempo).

41. Las contribuciones se dividen en tres partidas principales –empleados (2100), empleadores (2200) y trabajadores por cuenta propia o no empleados (2300)– y se subdividen posteriormente en función de la base que gravan. A efectos de la presente publicación, se entiende por empleados todas las personas contratadas en actividades de unidades empresariales, órganos gubernamentales, instituciones privadas sin ánimo de lucro

u otro tipo de empleo remunerado, con excepción de los dueños de empresas no constituidas en sociedad y de los miembros no remunerados de sus familias. También se consideran empleados los miembros de las Fuerzas Armadas, independientemente de la duración y del tipo de su servicio, siempre que coticen a regímenes de la seguridad social. Por su parte, las contribuciones de los empleadores se definen como las aportaciones que estos realizan por cuenta de sus empleados a los sistemas de seguridad social. Si los empleados o los empleadores tienen la obligación de continuar cotizando a la seguridad social en el caso de desempleo de un empleado, esas contribuciones se muestran en las partidas 2100 y 2200, respectivamente, siempre que los datos lo permitan. En consecuencia, la partida 2300 queda reservada a las contribuciones abonadas por los trabajadores por cuenta propia y por quienes no se hallan incluidos en la población activa (p. ej., incapacitados o jubilados).

3000 – *Impuestos sobre la nómina y la fuerza de trabajo*

42. Esta categoría cubre los impuestos satisfechos por los empleadores, los empleados o los trabajadores por cuenta propia, ya como una proporción de la nómina, ya como una cantidad fija por persona, que no confieren derecho a prestaciones sociales. Como ejemplos de impuestos integrados en esta categoría, cabe citar la aportación al seguro nacional del Reino Unido (introducido en 1977), el impuesto sobre la nómina de Suecia (1969–1979) o la contribución al fondo de equiparación de la carga familiar e impuesto comunitario de Austria.

4000 – *Impuestos sobre la propiedad*

43. Esta categoría engloba los impuestos, recurrentes y no recurrentes, sobre el uso, la titularidad o la transmisión de la propiedad, lo que incluye impuestos sobre la propiedad inmueble y la riqueza neta, sobre el cambio de titularidad en la propiedad por herencia o donación, y sobre transacciones financieras y de capital. Quedan excluidas de esta categoría los siguientes tipos de impuestos:

a) los impuestos sobre las ganancias de capital procedentes de la venta de propiedad (1120 o 1220);

b) los impuestos sobre el uso de bienes y sobre el permiso para usar bienes o realizar actividades (5200): véase el § 73;

c) los impuestos sobre los bienes inmuebles gravados sobre la base de un ingreso neto presunto que tiene en cuenta las circunstancias personales del contribuyente: se clasifican como impuestos sobre la renta junto con los impuestos sobre la renta y sobre las ganancias de capital derivadas de la propiedad (1100);

d) los impuestos sobre el uso de la propiedad con fines residenciales, tanto si debe responder del impuesto el propietario como el arrendatario, siempre que la cantidad debida tenga en cuenta las circunstancias personales del usuario (ingresos, personas a cargo, etcétera): se integran en los impuestos sobre la renta (1100);

e) los impuestos sobre los edificios con una densidad máxima superior a la permitida; sobre la ampliación, construcción o modificación de ciertos edificios más allá de un valor umbral; y sobre la construcción de edificios: todos ellos se integran en los impuestos sobre el permiso para realizar actividades (5200);

f) los impuestos sobre el uso de la propiedad propia para fines comerciales especiales, tales como la venta de bebidas alcohólicas, tabaco o carne, o para la explotación de tierras (p. ej., impuestos sobre la extracción en Estados Unidos): se integran en los impuestos sobre el permiso para realizar actividades (5200).

4100 – *Impuestos recurrentes sobre la propiedad inmueble*

44. Esta partida comprende los impuestos con que se grava de forma regular el uso o la titularidad de bienes inmuebles.

- Estos impuestos gravan las tierras y los edificios.
- Pueden consistir en un porcentaje del valor tasado de una propiedad, basado a su vez en un ingreso por alquiler hipotético, en el precio de venta, en un rendimiento capitalizado o en otras características de la propiedad inmueble (por ejemplo, el tamaño o la ubicación) de las que quepa inferir un alquiler o un valor de capital hipotéticos.
- Estos impuestos pueden aplicarse a los propietarios, a los arrendatarios o a ambos. También pueden pagarse de un nivel de gobierno a otro en relación con los bienes bajo jurisdicción de este último.
- Para la evaluación de estos impuestos, no se tienen en cuenta las deudas y, en ese sentido, difieren de los impuestos sobre la riqueza neta.

45. Los impuestos recurrentes sobre la propiedad inmueble se subdividen a su vez en los pagados por los hogares (4110) y los abonados por otros sujetos pasivos (4120), de acuerdo con los criterios establecidos en el § 26(*b*) *supra*.

4200 – *Impuestos recurrentes sobre la riqueza neta*

46. Esta partida abarca los impuestos con que se grava periódicamente (por lo general, anualmente) la riqueza neta, esto es, los impuestos sobre un amplio abanico de bienes muebles e inmuebles, descontadas sus deudas. Esta partida se subdivide a su vez en los impuestos pagados por las personas físicas (4210) y los abonados por las sociedades (4220), de acuerdo con los criterios establecidos en el § 26(*a*) *supra*. Si existen cifras separadas para las entradas correspondientes a pagos realizados por instituciones, se añaden a la subpartida de las sociedades.

4300 – *Impuestos sobre sucesiones, herencias y donaciones*

47. Esta partida se divide entre impuestos sobre sucesiones o herencias (4310) e impuestos sobre donaciones (4320).[16] Los impuestos sobre sucesiones gravan el valor total de la sucesión o del caudal hereditario, mientras los impuestos sobre herencias se aplican a las cuotas recibidas por los causahabientes individualmente considerados o en función de la relación de estos con el difunto.

4400 – *Impuestos sobre transacciones financieras y de capital*

48. Esta partida incluye, entre otros, los impuestos sobre la emisión, transmisión, compra y venta de valores, sobre los cheques, y sobre transacciones legales específicas, tales como la validación de contratos o la venta de bienes inmuebles. La partida no incluye:

a) los impuestos sobre el uso de bienes y sobre el permiso para realizar ciertas actividades (5200);

b) las tasas abonadas en concepto de costos procesales o expedición de actas de nacimiento, matrimonio o defunción, que suelen considerarse como ingresos no tributarios (véase el § 9);

c) los impuestos sobre ganancias de capital (1000);

d) los impuestos recurrentes sobre la propiedad inmueble (4100);

e) los impuestos recurrentes sobre la riqueza neta (4200);

f) otros impuestos no recurrentes sobre la propiedad o la riqueza (4500).

4500 – *Otros impuestos no recurrentes sobre la propiedad*[16]

49. Esta partida cubre los gravámenes sobre la propiedad que, a diferencia de los impuestos recurrentes, se recaudan una sola vez. Se divide en impuestos no recurrentes sobre la riqueza neta (4510) y otros impuestos no recurrentes sobre la propiedad (4520). La subpartida 4510 contiene los impuestos que se recaudan a fin de hacer frente a gastos excepcionales o de redistribuir la riqueza. Por su parte, la subpartida 4520 comprende los impuestos que gravan los incrementos de valor de la tierra, debido, por ejemplo, a permisos para su desarrollo concedidos por el gobierno general o a la provisión por parte de este de instalaciones locales adicionales; cualesquiera impuestos sobre la reevaluación del capital; y aquellos impuestos gravados una sola vez sobre determinados tipos de propiedad.

4600 – *Otros impuestos recurrentes sobre la propiedad*

50. Aunque este tipo de impuestos rara vez se dan en los países miembros de la OCDE, esta partida incluye los impuestos sobre bienes tales como ganado bovino, joyas, ventanas y otros signos externos de riqueza.

5000 – *Impuestos sobre los bienes y servicios*

51. Se incluyen en esta categoría todos los impuestos y derechos sobre la producción, extracción, venta, transmisión, arrendamiento y entrega de bienes, así como sobre la prestación de servicios (5100), y también los impuestos aplicados al uso de bienes y al permiso para usar bienes o realizar actividades (5200). Por lo tanto, esta categoría comprende:

a) los impuestos acumulativos de etapas múltiples;

b) los impuestos generales sobre las ventas aplicados, ya sea en la fabricación/producción, ya sea en la venta al por mayor o al por menor;

c) los impuestos sobre el valor agregado;

d) los impuestos selectivos;

e) los impuestos sobre las importaciones y exportaciones de bienes;

f) los impuestos sobre el uso de bienes y sobre el permiso para usar bienes o realizar ciertas actividades;

g) los impuestos sobre la extracción, el procesamiento o la producción de minerales y otros productos.

52. Los casos de difícil delimitación entre esta categoría y la categoría 4000 (impuestos sobre la propiedad) o la partida 6100 (otros impuestos pagados únicamente por empresas) se tratan en los §§ 43, 48 y 75. La partida 5300 y la subpartida 5130, ambas residuales, incluyen, respectivamente, las entradas tributarias que no hayan podido clasificarse entre las partidas 5100 y 5200 o entre las subpartidas 5110 y 5120.

5100 – *Impuestos sobre la producción, venta, transmisión, arrendamiento y entrega de bienes, y la prestación de servicios*

53. Esta partida comprende todos los impuestos aplicados a transacciones de bienes y servicios por las características intrínsecas de estos (p. ej., valor, peso del tabaco, graduación de las bebidas alcohólicas, etcétera) a diferencia de los impuestos determinados por el uso de bienes o por el permiso para usar bienes o realizar actividades, que entran dentro del ámbito de la partida 5200.

5110 – *Impuestos generales*

54. En esta subpartida, se incluyen todos los impuestos, aparte de los derechos de importación y exportación (5123 y 5124, respectivamente), que gravan la producción, el arrendamiento, la transmisión, la entrega o la venta de un amplio abanico de bienes o la prestación de una gran variedad de servicios, independientemente de que sean de producción nacional o importados, o de la etapa de producción o de distribución en la que recaigan. Por ende, comprende los impuestos sobre el valor agregado, los impuestos sobre las ventas y los impuestos acumulativos de etapas múltiples. A las entradas brutas generadas, se añaden las entradas por ajustes fronterizos en concepto de esos impuestos cuando se importan bienes, y se restan las devoluciones de dichos impuestos cuando se exportan bienes. Esta subpartida se divide a su vez en los epígrafes 5111, impuestos sobre el valor agregado; 5112, impuestos sobre las ventas; y 5113, otros impuestos generales sobre los bienes y servicios.

55. Suelen plantearse dificultades de delimitación entre esta subpartida y la dedicada a los impuestos sobre bienes y servicios específicos (5120) cuando los impuestos se aplican a un gran número de bienes, como, por ejemplo, en el caso del impuesto sobre las compras del Reino Unido (abolido en 1973) o el impuesto sobre mercancías de Japón (abolido en 1988). De acuerdo con las respectivas perspectivas nacionales, el antiguo impuesto sobre las compras británico se ha clasificado como impuesto general (5112), mientras el desaparecido impuesto sobre mercancías japonés se ha incluido entre los impuestos selectivos (5121).

5111 – *Impuestos sobre el valor agregado*

56. Todos los impuestos generales al consumo cargados sobre el valor agregado entran dentro de este epígrafe, independientemente del método de deducción y de las etapas en las que recaiga el impuesto. En la práctica, todos los países de la OCDE con este tipo de impuestos permiten que todos los intermediarios, excepto el consumidor final, se deduzcan inmediatamente los impuestos sobre las compras e imponen tributación en todas las etapas. Para algunos países, puede que se incluyan en este epígrafe otros impuestos, tales como los aplicados sobre actividades financieras y de seguros, o bien porque las entradas que generan no pueden identificarse separadamente de las procedentes del impuesto sobre el valor agregado, o bien porque se considera que forman parte de este último, aunque esos mismos impuestos puedan clasificarse diferentemente en terceros países (p. ej., como impuestos sobre servicios específicos (5126) o impuestos sobre transacciones financieras y de capital (4400).

5112 – *Impuestos sobre las ventas*

57. Se clasifican aquí todos los impuestos generales aplicados a una sola etapa, ya sea en la fabricación/producción, o en la venta al por mayor o al por menor.

5113 – *Otros impuestos generales sobre los bienes y servicios*

58. Este epígrafe comprende los impuestos acumulativos de etapas múltiples (también conocidos como "impuestos en cascada"), en los que el impuesto se aplica cada vez que se

realiza una transacción sin deducción del valor del impuesto pagado sobre los insumos, así como los impuestos generales al consumo cuando estos combinan elementos de los impuestos sobre el valor agregado, sobre las ventas o en cascada.

5120 – *Impuestos sobre bienes y servicios específicos*

59. Se incluyen en esta subpartida los impuestos selectivos, las utilidades generadas y transferidas por los monopolios fiscales, y los derechos de aduana y otros derechos de importación, así como los impuestos sobre las exportaciones, las transacciones de divisas, los bienes de inversión y las apuestas, y los impuestos especiales sobre los servicios que no formen parte de uno de los impuestos generales de la subpartida 5110.

5121 – *Impuestos selectivos*

60. Los impuestos selectivos son impuestos que se aplican a productos particulares o a un abanico limitado de productos, que no pueden clasificarse ni en 5110 (impuestos generales) ni en 5123 (derechos de aduana y otros derechos de importación) ni en 5124 (impuestos sobre las exportaciones). Pueden imponerse en cualquier etapa de la producción o la distribución, y suelen determinarse por referencia al peso, la graduación o la cantidad del producto, aunque, en ocasiones, también en función del valor de éste. Se incluyen, por lo tanto, en este epígrafe, los impuestos especiales sobre, por ejemplo, el azúcar, la remolacha, los fósforos o el chocolate; los impuestos a tasas impositivas variables sobre una cierta gama de bienes; y los impuestos que gravan en la mayoría de los países los productos derivados del tabaco, las bebidas alcohólicas, y los aceites de hidrocarburos y otras fuentes de energía.

61. Los impuestos selectivos se distinguen de:

a) los impuestos generales (5110): abordado en los §§ 54 y 55;

b) los derechos de aduana y otros derechos de importación (5123): si un impuesto recaudado principalmente sobre los bienes importados también se aplica, o podría aplicarse, de conformidad con la misma ley que establece el impuesto, a bienes comparables producidos en el país, las entradas de dicho impuesto se clasifican como impuestos selectivos (5121); este principio rige incluso cuando no existan productos nacionales comparables ni la posibilidad de que se produzcan (véase el § 65);

c) los impuestos sobre servicios específicos (5126): el problema se plantea en relación con los impuestos sobre la electricidad, el gas y la energía, que se consideran impuestos sobre los bienes y se incluyen en el epígrafe 5121.

5122 – *Utilidades de los monopolios fiscales*

62. Este epígrafe comprende la parte de las utilidades de los monopolios fiscales transferida al gobierno general o usada para financiar gastos considerados como gastos del gobierno (véase el § 19). Las cantidades implicadas se registran cuando se transfieren al gobierno general o cuando se usan para gastos considerados como gastos del gobierno.

63. Los monopolios fiscales reflejan el ejercicio del poder tributario del gobierno mediante el uso de prerrogativas monopolísticas. Se trata de empresas públicas no financieras que ejercen un monopolio, en la mayoría de los casos sobre la producción o la distribución de tabaco, bebidas alcohólicas, sal, fósforos, cartas de juego, productos derivados del petróleo y productos agrícolas (es decir, sobre el tipo de productos susceptibles de estar sometidos, alternativa o adicionalmente, a los impuestos selectivos del epígrafe 5121), con el fin de recaudar ingresos para el gobierno que en otros países se obtienen gravando las operaciones que sobre dichos bienes efectúan las unidades empresariales privadas. El monopolio del

gobierno puede intervenir en la etapa de producción o, en el caso de los establecimientos de licores propiedad del gobierno o bajo control de éste, en la etapa de distribución.

64. Cabe distinguir los monopolios fiscales de los servicios públicos, tales como el transporte ferroviario, la electricidad, los servicios de correos y otras comunicaciones, que pueden gozar también de una posición monopolística o cuasimonopolística, pero cuyo fin primero suele ser la prestación de servicios básicos y no la obtención de ingresos para el gobierno; las transferencias de esas otras empresas públicas al gobierno se consideran ingresos no tributarios. El concepto tradicional de monopolio fiscal no llega a abarcar las loterías estatales, cuyas utilidades se consideran, en consecuencia, ingresos no tributarios. Las utilidades de los monopolios fiscales se han separado de las de los monopolios de importación y exportación (5127) transferidas de juntas de comercialización u otras empresas dedicadas al comercio internacional.

5123 – *Derechos de aduana y otros derechos de importación*

65. Se incluyen aquí los impuestos, derechos de timbre y sobrecargas limitados por ley a los productos importados, así como los gravámenes sobre los productos agrícolas importados impuestos en los países miembros de la Unión Europea y las cantidades satisfechas por algunos de esos países a tenor del sistema de montantes compensatorios monetarios (MCM).[17] Desde 1998, los derechos de aduana recaudados por los Estados miembros de la Unión Europea en nombre de ésta ya no se registran en este epígrafe en los cuadros de países (parte III de la publicación *Revenue Statistics* de la OCDE). Quedan excluidos aquí los impuestos recaudados de las importaciones como parte de un impuesto general sobre los bienes y servicios, así como los impuestos selectivos aplicables tanto a bienes importados como a bienes de producción nacional.

5124 – *Impuestos sobre las exportaciones*

66. En los años 1970, los derechos de exportación se aplicaban en Australia, Canadá y Portugal como una medida de carácter regular, y en Finlandia se han utilizado con fines contracíclicos. Algunos países miembros de la Unión Europea pagan un gravamen sobre las exportaciones, en el marco del sistema MCM (véase la nota a pie de página 18 en el § 65). Cuando las cantidades recaudadas son identificables, se integran en este epígrafe, que no incluye, sin embargo, las devoluciones de impuestos generales al consumo, de impuestos selectivos o de derechos de aduana sobre los bienes exportados, que se deducirán de las entradas brutas de 5110, 5121 o 5123, según corresponda.

5125 – *Impuestos sobre los bienes de inversión*

67. Este epígrafe cubre los impuestos sobre los bienes de inversión, tales como la maquinaria. Estos impuestos pueden cargarse por un cierto número de años o temporalmente con fines contracíclicos. No se incluyen aquí aquellos impuestos sobre los insumos industriales que recaen también en los consumidores (p. ej., el impuesto sobre la energía en Suecia, que se clasifica en 5121).

5126 – *Impuestos sobre servicios específicos*

68. Todos los impuestos sobre el pago por servicios específicos, tales como los impuestos sobre las primas de seguro, los servicios bancarios, los juegos de azar y las apuestas (p. ej., carreras de caballos, quinielas de fútbol, lotería), el transporte, las actividades recreativas o de ocio, los restaurantes y la publicidad, entran dentro de este epígrafe. También se clasifican aquí los impuestos sobre el ingreso bruto de las empresas que prestan el servicio (p. ej., primas de seguro o apuestas brutas recibidas por una empresa). Los ingresos tributarios procedentes de gravámenes bancarios y pagos a sistemas de seguro de depósitos y

de estabilidad financiera se han incluido provisionalmente en este epígrafe para la edición de 2012. La clasificación detallada figura en el Anexo A.

69. Se excluyen de este epígrafe:

a) los impuestos sobre servicios que formen parte de un impuesto general sobre los bienes y servicios (5110);

b) los impuestos sobre la electricidad, el gas y la energía (5121, impuestos selectivos);

c) los impuestos sobre las ganancias de las personas físicas en los juegos de azar (1120, impuestos sobre las ganancias de capital de las personas físicas o de las empresas no constituidas en sociedad) y los impuestos fijos sobre la transferencia de loterías privadas o sobre el permiso para crear loterías (5200);[18]

d) los impuestos sobre los cheques y sobre la emisión, transmisión o compra y venta de valores (4400, impuestos sobre transacciones financieras y de capital).

5127 – *Otros impuestos sobre el comercio y las transacciones internacionales*

70. Este epígrafe abarca los ingresos percibidos por el gobierno por la compra y la venta de divisas a diferentes tipos de cambio. Cuando el gobierno ejerce poderes monopolísticos para obtener un margen entre los precios de compra y de venta de divisas superior al que sería necesario para cubrir los costos administrativos, el ingreso generado constituye un gravamen obligatorio impuesto en proporciones indeterminadas tanto sobre el comprador como sobre el vendedor de divisas. Es un equivalente común de los derechos de importación y exportación cargados en un sistema con tipo de cambio único o de un impuesto sobre la compraventa de divisas. Al igual que las utilidades de los monopolios fiscales o de los monopolios de importación y exportación transferidas al gobierno, representa el ejercicio de las prerrogativas monopolísticas con fines fiscales y, por lo tanto, se incluye en los ingresos tributarios.

71. El epígrafe engloba asimismo las utilidades de los monopolios de importación y exportación, que, sin embargo, son inexistentes en los países de la OCDE; los impuestos sobre la compraventa de divisas; y cualesquiera otros impuestos que recaigan sobre el comercio o las transacciones internacionales.

5128 – *Otros impuestos sobre bienes y servicios específicos*

72. Este epígrafe incluye los impuestos sobre la extracción de minerales, combustibles fósiles y otros recursos agotables de yacimientos de propieddad privada o de otro nivel de gobierno, así como cualesquiera otras entradas no identificables procedentes de impuestos sobre bienes y servicios específicos. Los impuestos sobre la extracción de recursos agotables suelen traducirse en un importe fijo por cantidad o peso, pero también pueden adoptar un valor porcentual. Los impuestos se registran en el momento de extracción de los recursos. Los pagos por extracción de recursos agotables de yacimientos propiedad de la unidad de gobierno que recibe el pago se clasifican como alquiler.

5200 – *Impuestos sobre el uso de bienes y sobre el permiso para usar bienes o realizar actividades*

73. Esta partida incluye los impuestos aplicados al uso de bienes a diferencia de los impuestos sobre los propios bienes. Al contrario que los impuestos de este último tipo (registrados en la partida 5100), los impuestos considerados aquí no se basan en el valor de los bienes, sino que suelen revestir la forma de importes fijos. Los impuestos sobre el permiso para usar bienes o realizar actividades entran asimismo en esta partida, como, por

ejemplo, los impuestos sobre la contaminación que no se basan en el valor de bienes particulares. En ocasiones, resulta complejo distinguir entre cargos obligatorios a los usuarios y tasas de licencia que se consideran como impuestos y aquellos que quedan excluidos por reputarse como ingresos no tributarios; los criterios de deslinde empleados se explican en los §§ 9 y 10.

74. Aunque el título de esta partida menciona el "uso" de bienes, es posible que sea el registro de la propiedad, y no el uso, lo que dé lugar a la obligación tributaria, y que los impuestos contenidos aquí se apliquen más al hecho de ser titular de ciertos animales o bienes (p. ej., caballos de carreras, perros y vehículos automotores) que al uso que se hace de ellos, o que recaigan incluso en bienes inutilizables (p. ej., vehículos automotores o armas inservibles).

75. Se plantean casos de difícil delimitación con respecto a:

a) los impuestos sobre el permiso para realizar actividades empresariales que parten de una base combinada de renta, nómina o volumen de ventas, que se clasifican de acuerdo con las normas del § 78;

b) los impuestos sobre la propiedad o el uso de la propiedad de las partidas 4100, 4200 y 4600; la partida 4100 se dedica exclusivamente a los impuestos sobre la titularidad o la posesión de bienes inmuebles y, a diferencia de los impuestos de la partida 5200, recaen siempre sobre el valor de la propiedad; los impuestos sobre la riqueza neta (4200) y otros impuestos recurrentes sobre la propiedad (4600) se circunscriben al hecho de ser titular de propiedades, y no al uso de activos; se aplican a grupos de activos, y no a bienes particulares; y están en todo caso relacionados con el valor de los activos en cuestión.

5210 – *Impuestos recurrentes*

76. La principal característica de los impuestos consignados aquí es que se recaudan a intervalos regulares y se cobran por lo general según una cantidad fija. En términos de ingresos, el elemento más importante está constituido por los impuestos por licencia de vehículos, aunque también integran esta subpartida los impuestos sobre los permisos de caza, pesca o tiro o sobre la venta de ciertos productos, así como los impuestos sobre la propiedad de animales domésticos y sobre la prestación de ciertos servicios siempre que estos reúnan los criterios establecidos en los §§ 9 y 10. Los epígrafes en que se divide la partida 5210 son: los impuestos sobre vehículos automotores pagados por los hogares (5211) y los satisfechos por otros sujetos pasivos (5212);[19] por su parte, el epígrafe 5213 abarca las licencias a propietarios de animales domésticos y los cargos a usuarios por el permiso de realizar actividades, tales como la venta de carne o de bebidas alcohólica cuando los gravámenes se imponen de forma recurrente, así como las licencias generales periódicas de caza, pesca y tiro cuando el derecho a emprender esas actividades no se otorga como parte de una transacción comercial normal (p. ej., la concesión de la licencia no implica el derecho a usar una zona específica propiedad del gobierno).

5220 – *Impuestos no recurrentes*

77. Se incluyen aquí los impuestos no recurrentes aplicados sobre el uso de bienes y sobre el permiso para utilizar bienes o realizar actividades, así como los impuestos aplicados cada vez que se utilizan los bienes.

- Entran en esta subpartida los impuestos sobre la emisión o liberación en el medio ambiente de gases y líquidos nocivos y otras sustancias peligrosas. Los pagos por permisos negociables de emisión expedidos por los gobiernos en el marco de programas de límites máximos y comercio de emisiones deberán registrarse aquí en la fecha en que se produzcan las emisiones. No se computarán ingresos por los permisos que los gobiernos expidan a título gratuito.

- El registro según el criterio de devengo implica que habrá una diferencia temporal entre el momento en que el gobierno reciba el pago por los permisos y el momento en que se produzca la emisión. En las cuentas nacionales, esta diferencia genera un pasivo para el gobierno durante ese periodo.
- Se excluirán los pagos efectuados por la recogida y eliminación de desechos o sustancias nocivas por parte de los poderes públicos, ya que constituyen una venta de servicios a las empresas.

78. También se incluyen aquí otros impuestos que entren dentro del ámbito de aplicación de la partida 5200 y que no se recauden recurrentemente. Por lo tanto, quedarán comprendidos los pagos únicos por permisos para la venta de alcohol o tabaco o para la creación de centros de apuestas, siempre que cumplan los criterios de los §§ 9 y 10.

6000 – *Otros impuestos*

79. Esta categoría recoge los impuestos que reposan en una o varias bases diferentes de las descritas en las categorías 1000, 3000, 4000 y 5000, o en bases que no puedan considerarse predominantemente las mismas que las incluidas en esas categorías. En relación con los impuestos de base múltiple, si es posible estimar las entradas relacionadas con cada base (p. ej., el impuesto *Gewerbesteuer* en Alemania y Austria), las cantidades desglosadas se repartirán en las correspondientes categorías. Si no pueden calcularse los valores por separado, pero se sabe que la mayoría de las entradas proceden de una base determinada, el total de estas se atribuirán de acuerdo con dicha base. Si no puede seguirse ninguno de estos procedimientos, las entradas se clasificarán aquí. Las diversas partidas de esta categoría podrán incluir asimismo el producto de impuestos que los gobiernos no puedan identificar o aislar (véase el § 28). Se incorporan asimismo aquí las multas y sanciones pecuniarias pagadas por el incumplimiento de normas tributarias, pero no imputables a una categoría particular de impuestos (véase el § 15). Esta categoría se subdivide entre los impuestos pagados completa o principalmente por las empresas (6100) y los abonados por otros sujetos pasivos (6200).

E. Conciliación con las cuentas nacionales

80. Esta sección de los cuadros reconcilia el cálculo de la recaudación tributaria total realizado por la OCDE y el total de todos los impuestos y contribuciones sociales pagados al gobierno general tal y como figuran en el registro de las cuentas nacionales de cada país. Cuando el país es miembro de la Unión Europea (UE), la comparación se establece entre el cálculo de la recaudación tributaria total realizado por la OCDE y la suma de los ingresos tributarios y contribuciones sociales registrado en la combinación del gobierno general y de las instituciones de los sectores de la UE de las cuentas nacionales.

F. Partida informativa sobre el financiamiento de las prestaciones sociales

81. A la vista de la variedad de relaciones entre la tributación y las contribuciones a la seguridad social y de los casos mencionados en los §§ 35–41, se ha previsto una partida informativa que recopile todos los pagos asignados a las prestaciones tipo de la seguridad social, aparte de los pagos voluntarios al sector privado. Los datos se presentan de la forma siguiente (véase la parte III, sección B, de la publicación *Revenue Statistics* de la OCDE):

a) Impuestos de la categoría 2000.

b) Impuestos asignados a las prestaciones de la seguridad social.

c) Contribuciones voluntarias al gobierno.

d) Contribuciones obligatorias al sector privado.

Los §§ 35–41 ofrecen las debidas orientaciones para efectuar el desglose entre las rúbricas (*a*) a (*d*).

G. Partida informativa sobre impuestos identificables pagados por el gobierno

82. Los impuestos identificables realmente pagados por el gobierno se presentan en una partida informativa, desglosados según las principales categorías de la clasificación de impuestos de la OCDE. En la vasta mayoría de los países, sólo pueden identificarse las contribuciones a la seguridad social y los impuestos sobre la nómina satisfechos por el gobierno, que, sin embargo, suelen ser los gravámenes más importantes liquidados por los gobiernos (véase la parte III, sección C, de la publicación *Revenue Statistics* de la OCDE).

H. Relación de la clasificación de impuestos de la OCDE con el Sistema de Cuentas Nacionales

83. El Sistema de Cuentas Nacionales (SCN) pretende proporcionar un marco coherente para registrar y presentar los principales flujos relacionados con la producción, el consumo, la acumulación y las transacciones con el exterior de una determinada zona económica, por lo general, un país o una región destacada de un país, y, en este sentido, los ingresos del gobierno constituyen una importante parte de las transacciones registradas en todo sistema de cuentas nacionales. En agosto de 2009, la versión final del SCN 2008 se publicó conjuntamente por cinco organizaciones internacionales: la Organización de las Naciones Unidas, el Fondo Monetario Internacional, la Unión Europea, la Organización para la Cooperación y el Desarrollo Económicos, y el Banco Mundial. La publicación está diseñada para ser empleada en países con economías de mercado, sea cual sea su estadio de desarrollo económico, así como en países en transición hacia economías de mercado. Las principales partes del marco conceptual y las definiciones de los diversos sectores económicos del SCN se han plasmado en la clasificación de impuestos de la OCDE.

84. Sin embargo, existen ciertas diferencias, reseñadas seguidamente, entre la clasificación de impuestos de la OCDE y los conceptos del SCN, debidas a que la finalidad de la clasificación de la OCDE consiste en lograr la máxima desagregación posible de los datos estadísticos en relación con lo que, por lo general, las Administraciones tributarias consideran como impuestos. Y así:

a) la OCDE incluye las contribuciones a la seguridad social en la recaudación tributaria total (véanse los §§ 7 y 8 *supra.*);

b) los puntos de vista sobre la calificación de algunos gravámenes y tasas como impuestos son diferentes (§§ 9 y 10 *supra.*);

c) la OCDE excluye los impuestos imputados o los subsidios procedentes de la aplicación de múltiples tipos de cambio oficiales;

d) los créditos fiscales exigibles se tratan de forma diferente.

85. Tal y como se ha apuntado en los §§ 1 y 2, las categorías 1000 a 6000 de la lista de impuestos de la OCDE cubren todos los pagos sin contraprestación al gobierno general, aparte de las multas y los préstamos obligatorios. Esos pagos sin contraprestación, incluidas las multas pero excluidos los préstamos obligatorios, pueden obtenerse añadiendo los siguientes valores del SCN 2008:

- impuestos sobre el valor agregado (D211);
- impuestos y derechos sobre las importaciones, IVA no incluido (D212);
- impuestos sobre las exportaciones (D213);
- impuestos sobre los productos, IVA e impuestos sobre las importaciones y exportaciones no incluidos (D214);
- otros impuestos sobre la producción (D29);
- impuestos sobre la renta (D51);
- otros impuestos corrientes (D59);
- contribuciones sociales (D61), excluidas las contribuciones voluntarias;
- impuestos sobre el capital (D91).

I. Relación de la clasificación de impuestos de la OCDE con el sistema de estadísticas de finanzas públicas del Fondo Monetario Internacional

86. La cobertura y la valoración de los ingresos tributarios en el sistema de estadísticas de finanzas públicas (EFP) y en el SCN 2008 son muy similares. Por lo tanto, a excepción del tratamiento dado a los créditos fiscales exigibles, las diferencias entre la clasificación de la OCDE y la del SCN 2008 (véase el § 84 *supra.*) son de aplicación igualmente al sistema de EFP. Además, el Fondo Monetario Internacional (FMI) escinde la categoría única 5000 de la OCDE en dos categorías distintas dedicadas a los impuestos nacionales sobre bienes y servicios (114) y a los impuestos sobre el comercio y las transacciones internacionales (115). Esto refleja el hecho de que, mientras estos últimos impuestos suelen generar insignificantes cantidades de ingresos en la zona de la OCDE, ese no es el caso en la mayoría de los países no pertenecientes a la Organización.

J. Comparación de la clasificación de impuestos de la OCDE con otras clasificaciones internacionales

87. El cuadro siguiente recoge una comparación ítem por ítem entre la clasificación de impuestos de la OCDE y las clasificaciones empleadas en:

i) el Sistema de Cuentas Nacionales (SCN 2008);
ii) el Sistema Europeo de Cuentas (SEC 1995);
iii) el *Manual de estadísticas de finanzas públicas* del FMI (MEFP 2001).

88. Estas comparaciones representan equivalencias que podrán aplicarse en la mayoría de los casos. Con todo, deberán emplearse con cierta flexibilidad, ya que, en casos particulares, los países pueden adoptar enfoques diferentes para la clasificación de los ingresos en las cuentas nacionales.

	Clasificación de la OCDE	SCN 2008	SEC 1995	MEFP 2001
1000	Impuestos sobre la renta, las utilidades y las ganancias de capital			
	1100 Personas físicas			
	1110 Renta/utilidades	D51-8.61a	D51A	1111
	1120 Ganancias de capital	D51-8.61c,d	D51C,D	1111
	1200 Sociedades			
	1210 Renta/utilidades	D51-8.61b	D51B	1112
	1220 Ganancias de capital	D51-8.61c	D51C	1112
	1300 No clasificables entre 1100 y 1200			1113
2000	Contribuciones a la seguridad social			
	2100 Empleados	D613-8.85	D61111	1211
	2200 Empleadores	D611-8.83	D61121	1212
	2300 Trabajadores por cuenta propia o no empleados	D613-8.85	D61131	1213
	2400 No clasificables entre 2100, 2200 y 2300			1214
3000	Impuestos sobre la nómina y la fuerza de trabajo	D29-7.97a	D29C	112
4000	Impuestos sobre la propiedad			
	4100 Impuestos recurrentes sobre la propiedad inmueble			
	4110 Hogares	D59-8.63a	D59A	1131
	4120 Otros	D29-7.97b	D29A	1131
	4200 Impuestos recurrentes sobre la riqueza neta			
	4210 Personas físicas	D59-8.63b	D59A	1132
	4220 Sociedades	D59-8.63b	D59A	1132
	4300 Impuestos sobre sucesiones, herencias y donaciones			
	4310 Impuestos sobre sucesiones y herencias	D91-10.207b	D91A	1133
	4320 Impuestos sobre donaciones	D91-10.207b	D91A	1133
	4400 Impuestos sobre transacciones financieras y de capital	D59-7.96d; D29-7.97e	D214B,C	1134:1161
	4500 Otros impuestos no recurrentes sobre la propiedad	D91-10.207a	D91B	1135
	4600 Otros impuestos recurrentes sobre la propiedad	D59-8.63c	D59A	1136
5000	Impuestos sobre los bienes y servicios			
	5100 Impuestos sobre la producción, venta y transmisión de bienesy prestación de servicios			
	5110 Impuestos generales			
	5111 Impuestos sobre el valor agregado	D211-7.89	D211; D29G	11411
	5112 Impuestos sobre las ventas	D2122-7.94a; D214-7.96a	D2122D; D214I	11412
	5113 Otros impuestos generales sobre los bienes y servicios	D214-7.96a	D214I	11413
	5120 Impuestos sobre bienes y servicios específicos			
	5121Impuestos selectivos	D2122-7.94b; D214-7.96b	D2122C; D214A,B,D	1142
	5122 Utilidades de los monopolios fiscales	D214-7.65e	D214J	1143
	5123 Derechos de aduanas y otros derechos de importación	D2121-7.93	D2121; D2122A,B	1151
	5124 Sobre las exportaciones	D213-7.95a	D214K	1152-4
	5125 Sobre los bienes de inversión			
	5126 Sobre servicios específicos	D2122-7.94c; D214-7.96c	D2122E; D214E,F,G; D29F	1144;1156
	5127 Otros impuestos sobre el comercio y las transacciones internacionales	D2122-7.94d D29-7.95b D29-7.97g D59-8.64d	D2122F; D29D; D59E	1153 1155-6
	5128 Otros impuestos sobre bienes y servicios específicos			1146
	5130 No clasificables entre 5110 y 5120			
	5200 Impuestos sobre el uso de bienes y sobre el permiso para usar bienes y realizar actividades			
	5210 Impuestos recurrentes			
	5211 Sobre vehículos automotores: hogares	D59-8.64c	D59D	11451
	5212 Sobre vehículos automotores: otros	D29-7.97d	D214D; D29B	11451
	5213 Otros impuestos recurrentes	D29-7.97c,d,f D59-8.64c	D29B,E,F; D59D	11452
	5220 Impuestos no recurrentes			
	5300 No clasificables entre 5100 y 5200			
6000	Otros impuestos			
	6100 Pagados únicamente por empresas			
	6200 Pagados por otros distintos de las empresas o no identificables	D59-8.64a,b	D59B,C	1162

K. Atribución de ingresos tributarios por subsectores del gobierno general

89. La clasificación de la OCDE requiere un desglose de los ingresos tributarios por subsectores del gobierno general. Seguidamente, se establecen la definición de cada subsector y los criterios que deben emplearse para atribuir los ingresos tributarios entre ellos, que siguen las orientaciones del SCN 2008 y del MEFP 2001.

Identificación de los subsectores del gobierno general

a) Gobierno central

90. El subsector del gobierno central incluye todos los departamentos, oficinas y establecimientos del gobierno, así como otros órganos que constituyen organismos o instrumentos de la autoridad central, cuya competencia se extiende a todo el territorio, con excepción de la administración de los fondos de seguridad social. En consecuencia, el gobierno central tiene la facultad de someter a tributación a todas las unidades residentes y no residentes que emprendan actividades económicas en el país.

b) Gobierno estatal, provincial o regional

91. Este subsector está compuesto por unidades intermedias del gobierno que ejercen su competencia a un nivel inferior al del gobierno central. Incluye a todas las unidades que operan independientemente del gobierno central en una parte del territorio de un país que engloba numerosas pequeñas localidades, con la excepción de la administración de los fondos de seguridad social. En los países unitarios, puede considerarse que los gobiernos regionales tienen una existencia separada, en la que cuentan con la suficiente autonomía como para recaudar sus ingresos de fuentes bajo su control, y sus funcionarios son independientes del control administrativo externo en el ejercicio de las actividades de la unidad.

92. En la actualidad, los países federales representan la mayoría de los casos en los que los ingresos atribuidos a unidades intermedias del gobierno se identifican de forma separada. España es el único país unitario en ese caso; en el resto de los países unitarios, los ingresos regionales se computan junto con los de los gobiernos locales.

c) Gobierno local

93. Este subsector incluye todas las demás unidades del gobierno que ejercen una competencia independiente en parte del territorio de un país, con excepción de la administración de los fondos de seguridad social. Engloba varios entes urbanos o rurales (p. ej., autoridades locales, municipios, ciudades, delegaciones, distritos).

d) Fondos de seguridad social

94. Los fondos de seguridad social forman un subsector separado del gobierno general. El SCN 2008 define el subsector de la seguridad social según lo expuesto en sus puntos 4.124 a 4.126 y 4.147, citados seguidamente:

"Los regímenes de seguridad social son sistemas de seguros sociales que cubren a la comunidad en su conjunto o a amplios sectores de la misma, y que son impuestos y controlados por unidades del gobierno. Los sistemas abarcan una gran variedad de programas, y ofrecen prestaciones en dinero o en especie por vejez, invalidez o muerte, supervivencia, enfermedad y maternidad, accidentes de trabajo, desempleo, ayudas familiares, asistencia sanitaria, etc. No existe necesariamente una relación directa entre la cuantía de la contribución pagada por un individuo y las prestaciones que este pueda recibir." (4.124)

"Cuando los sistemas de seguridad social se organizan por separado de las demás actividades de las unidades del gobierno, mantienen sus activos y pasivos separados de estas últimas, y realizan operaciones financieras por cuenta propia, se califican de unidades institucionales, que reciben el nombre de fondos de seguridad social." (4.125)

"Las cantidades recaudadas y pagadas por contribuciones y prestaciones de la seguridad social pueden modificarse deliberadamente con el fin de alcanzar determinados objetivos de la política del gobierno que no tengan relación directa con el concepto de la seguridad social como sistema destinado a ofrecer prestaciones sociales a los miembros de la comunidad. Pueden aumentarse o disminuirse, por ejemplo, con el fin de influir en el nivel de la demanda agregada de la economía. No obstante, mientras se mantengan como fondos constituidos por separado, han de ser tratados, en el SCN, como unidades institucionales diferentes." (4.126)

"El subsector de los fondos de seguridad social [del gobierno general] está conformado por los fondos de seguridad social que operan en todos los niveles del gobierno. Dichos fondos son sistemas de seguros sociales que cubren a la comunidad en su conjunto o a amplios sectores de la misma, y que son impuestos por unidades del gobierno." (4.147)

95. La clasificación de la OCDE sigue esta definición de los fondos de seguridad social con las dos siguientes excepciones, por las se excluyen:

- los sistemas impuestos por el gobierno pero administrados por órganos externos al sector del gobierno general, tal y como se ha definido en el § 3 de este manual, y
- los sistemas en los que todas las contribuciones son voluntarias.

Autoridades supranacionales

96. Este subsector engloba las operaciones de recaudación fiscal de autoridades supranacionales dentro de un país. En la práctica, la única autoridad supranacional que cabe tener en cuenta en la zona de la OCDE es la que conforman las instituciones de la Unión Europea (UE). Desde 1998, las autoridades supranacionales no se incluyen en *Revenue Statistics*, a fin de ser coherentes con la definición que el SCN da del gobierno general, que las excluye. Por ejemplo, los impuestos sobre la renta y las contribuciones a la seguridad social recaudados por instituciones europeas y pagados a empleados públicos europeos que residen en países miembros de la OCDE no deberían incluirse. Pese a todo, ciertos gravámenes específicos pagados por los Estados miembros de la UE siguen incorporándose a la recaudación tributaria total y, en ese caso, se muestran bajo esta denominación.

Criterios de atribución de los ingresos tributarios

97. Cuando un gobierno recauda impuestos y los transfiere, en todo o en parte, a otros gobiernos, es necesario determinar si esos ingresos se imputarán al gobierno recaudador que los distribuye a otros en forma de donaciones, o si se atribuirán a los gobiernos beneficiarios para los que el gobierno recaudador actúa como mero agente, recibiendo el producto de los impuestos y transfiriéndolos posteriormente. Los criterios de atribución de los ingresos se establecen en los §§ 98–102 siguientes, y siguen lo dispuesto en los puntos 3.70 a 3.73 del SCN 2008.

98. Por regla general, un impuesto se atribuye a la unidad de gobierno que:

a) ejerce la facultad de aplicar el impuesto (como entidad principal o a través de la autoridad delegada por la entidad principal), y

b) puede a su discreción establecer y modificar la tasa del impuesto.

99. Cuando un gobierno recauda impuestos para y en nombre de otro, y este último tiene la facultad de aplicar el impuesto y establecer y modificar su tasa impositiva, entonces el gobierno recaudador actúa como agente de este, y el impuesto se reasigna. Cualquier cantidad retenida por el gobierno recaudador como cargo por la recaudación deberá tratarse como pago por un servicio. Cualquier otra cantidad retenida por el gobierno recaudador, por ejemplo, en el marco de un arreglo de coparticipación de impuestos, deberá tratarse como una donación corriente. Si se delegó al gobierno recaudador la autoridad para establecer y modificar la tasa impositiva entonces las cantidades recaudadas deberán tratarse como ingresos tributarios de este gobierno.

100. Cuando diferentes gobiernos establecen conjuntamente y por igual la tasa de un impuesto y el uso de los recursos, sin que ninguno de ellos tengan la autoridad final y exclusiva, entonces los ingresos tributarios se atribuyen a cada gobierno según la proporción de recursos que le corresponda; si el acuerdo permite a una unidad del gobierno ejercer el control final y exclusivo, entonces todos los ingresos tributarios se atribuirán a dicha unidad.

101. También puede ocurrir que un gobierno tenga la autoridad constitucional o de otra índole de aplicar un impuesto, pero que otros gobiernos establezcan individualmente la tasa de ese impuesto en sus jurisdicciones; los recursos generados por el impuesto en cuestión en la jurisdicción de cada gobierno se atribuirán como ingresos tributarios a los respectivos gobiernos.

Gravámenes satisfechos por los Estados miembros de la Unión Europea

102. Los gravámenes satisfechos por los Estados miembros de la Unión Europea (UE) revisten la forma de:

- recursos propios por IVA, y
- gravámenes específicos, entre los que se incluyen:
  - *a)* derechos de aduana y gravámenes sobre los bienes agrícolas (5123),
  - *b)* montantes compensatorios monetarios brutos (5123 en relación con las importaciones y 5124 en relación con las exportaciones), y
  - *c)* gravámenes sobre el acero, el carbón, el azúcar y la leche (5128).

103. Los derechos de aduana recaudados por los Estados miembros de la UE en nombre de esta se registran de la siguiente forma:

- sobre la base de un coeficiente de recaudación bruta;
- ajustando los resultados, siempre que sea posible, de forma que esos derechos se muestren en relación con una base de "destino final", por oposición a la base de "país de primera entrada"; estos ajustes atañen particularmente a los derechos colectados en importantes puertos (marítimos); aunque los derechos de la UE se perciben por las

autoridades del país de primera entrada, siempre que sea posible cabrá excluir esos derechos del ingreso del país recaudador e incluirlos en el ingreso del país de destino final.

Este es el gravamen específico de la UE que más claramente se ciñe al criterio de atribución consignado en el § 97. En consecuencia, desde 1998, las cantidades en relación con este gravamen se registran como partida informativa en los cuadros de países de los Estados miembros de la UE (en la parte III de la publicación *Revenue Statistics* de la OCDE) y no se integran ya en el epígrafe 5123. Sin embargo, se incluyen en las cifras de recaudación tributaria total de la línea superior para los años correspondientes mostrados en los cuadros.

104. En cuanto a los recursos propios por IVA, que se determinan aplicando una tasa no superior al 1 por ciento a una base cuya evaluación viene dada en la Sexta Directiva,[20] se trata ciertamente de un caso de más difícil delimitación, ya que estos recursos reúnen ciertas características de una transferencia (no nacen de una fuente claramente identificable de fondos realmente recaudados) y ciertas otras de un impuesto (la cantidad de la transferencia viene determinada por el subsector del gobierno receptor). En esta publicación, *no* se consideran un impuesto de la Unión Europea (sino un impuesto de los Estados miembros), aunque las cantidades implicadas se indican al pie de los cuadros de la parte IV de la publicación *Revenue Statistics* de la OCDE.

L. Clasificación provisional de los ingresos tributarios procedentes de gravámenes bancarios y pagos a sistemas de seguro de depósitos y de estabilidad financiera

105. La OCDE ha adoptado el siguiente enfoque provisional para el registro de los ingresos procedentes de gravámenes bancarios, así como de seguro de depósitos y tasas de estabilidad para la edición 2012 de la publicación *Revenue Statistics* de la OCDE. Los importes deberán consignarse en el epígrafe 5126.

- Los pagos obligatorios de tasas de estabilidad, gravámenes bancarios y primas de seguro de depósitos se tratarán por lo general como ingresos tributarios cuando se abonen al gobierno general y se asignen a los fondos consolidados o generales de este, de forma que el gobierno pueda utilizar libre e inmediatamente el dinero para los fines que elija. Este principio se aplicará independientemente de que el gobierno prometa revertir esos pagos para garantizar los depósitos de los clientes de los bancos en caso de necesidad futura.
- Si los pagos obligatorios se abonan al gobierno general y se destinan a fondos afectados exclusivamente a volver al sector de la economía que engloba a las sociedades sujetas a dichos pagos, éstos seguirán considerándose ingresos tributarios dado que los fondos estarán disponibles para el gobierno y podrán reducir su déficit presupuestario, que la tasa no conlleva contraprestación para una entidad individual y que las cantidades recaudadas no tienen relación con cualquier pago posterior a los depositantes o cualquier gasto realizado como medio de respaldo más amplio al sector financiero.
- Se clasificarán como tasa por servicio los pagos que deban aportarse a sistemas permanentes más reducidos para garantizar los depósitos de "particulares" cuando los niveles de pago concuerden con el coste del seguro.
- También se clasificarán como tasa por servicio, y no como ingreso tributario, los pagos que impliquen que el gobierno ejecute los activos de una institución en quiebra o tenga un derecho prioritario sobre la liquidación de activos de esta con objeto de financiar los pagos de compensación a los clientes por la pérdida de sus depósitos.

No se tratarán como ingresos tributarios los pagos obligatorios destinados a fondos externos al sector de gobierno y a instituciones no estatales respaldadas por los tomadores de depósitos, ni los pagos hechos a sistemas voluntarios.

Notas

1. Todas las referencias al SCN deberán entenderse hechas a la edición de 2008.

2. Véase el apartado K de la presente guía para el análisis del concepto de agente.

3. Por lo general, es posible identificar la cuantía de las contribuciones a la seguridad social y de los impuestos sobre la nómina, pero no otros impuestos asumidos por el gobierno.

4. Sin embargo, si un gravamen considerado como ingreso no tributario en la mayoría de los países se califica de tributario –o permite recaudar sustanciales ingresos– en uno o más países, las entradas en concepto de dicho gravamen se indican en las notas que figuran al pie de los cuadros de países, pero no se incluyen en la recaudación tributaria total.

5. Obsérvese, no obstante, que los nombres pueden dar lugar a confusión. Por ejemplo, aunque una tasa sobre los pasaportes se trataría normalmente como ingreso no tributario, si se impone un gravamen suplementario sobre los pasaportes (como en el caso de Portugal) con el fin de conseguir un ingreso sustancialmente mayor que el costo que supone proporcionar el pasaporte, dicho gravamen deberá considerarse como un impuesto sobre el uso de bienes (5200).

6. Existen ciertas dificultades prácticas para llevar a cabo la distinción operada por el SCN 1993.

7. Para una explicación más detallada de esta distinción, consúltese el estudio especial sobre cuestiones de actualidad en relación con el registro de los ingresos tributarios *Current issues in reporting tax revenues*, en la edición 2001 de *Revenue Statistics*.

8. En ocasiones, se emplean asimismo los términos "no reembolsable" y "reembolsable", pero puede parecer ilógico hablar de "reembolsable" cuando no se ha pagado nada.

9. Con la excepción del diferente tratamiento dado a los créditos fiscales exigibles en los sistemas de imputación del impuesto sobre sociedades (§§ 32–34).

10. No se trata aquí de verdaderos gastos tributarios en sentido formal, ya que tales gastos requieren que se identifique un sistema tributario de referencia para cada país o, mejor si cabe, una referencia internacional común y, en la práctica, no se ha logrado acuerdo sobre esta última.

11. A menos que se basen en la plusvalía obtenida con la venta, en cuyo caso se clasificarían como impuestos sobre las ganancias de capital, en las subpartidas 1120 o 1220.

12. Con todo, algunos países aplican la misma legislación a ambos en impuestos particulares sobre la renta, aunque las entradas procedentes de dichos impuestos suelen ser fácilmente atribuibles a uno u otro caso y pueden, por lo tanto, consignarse en la debida partida.

13. Por ejemplo, "[...] que son suficientemente autónomas e independientes y se comportan como si fueran sociedades [...] (incluido en el hecho de llevar) conjuntos completos de cuentas" (SCN 2008, 4.44).

14. En Canadá, país en el que se considera que rige un sistema de imputación, el crédito fiscal (no exigible) para el accionista nace en relación con el impuesto nacional sobre sociedades que se reputa haber pagado, tanto si ha surgido una obligación tributaria para la sociedad como si no. Habida cuenta de que no existe una conexión íntegra entre la obligación tributaria de la sociedad y el crédito concedido en relación con el impuesto sobre la renta en esos sistemas, los créditos por dividendos se tratan, junto con otros créditos fiscales, según lo descrito en el § 21.

15. Esto puede darse, por ejemplo, cuando ya existía un régimen para los empleados del gobierno previo a la introducción de un régimen general de seguridad social.

16. En el SCN 2008, se consideran transferencias de capital y no impuestos (véase el apartado G).

17. Mediante este sistema, la Unión Europea ajusta las diferencias entre los tipos de cambio empleados para determinar los precios de la política agrícola común (PAC) y los tipos de cambio reales. Los pagos realizados en este sistema pueden estar relacionados con importaciones o exportaciones y, cuando ha sido posible identificar por separado las respectivas cantidades, se han mostrado en el correspondiente epígrafe (5123 o 5124). En el presente informe, esas cantidades se han consignado en valores brutos (esto es, sin deducir ningún subsidio otorgado en el marco del sistema MCM).

18. Las transferencias de las utilidades de las loterías del Estado se consideran ingresos no tributarios (véase el § 64).

19. Véase el § 26(*c*) en relación con esta distinción.

20. En la Cumbre de Edimburgo (1992), los países miembros de la UE decidieron reducir paulatinamente este porcentaje del 1.4 al 1, entre los años 1995 y 1999. Durante el periodo 1970-1983, este porcentaje también fue de 1.

ORGANISATION FOR ECONOMIC CO-OPERATION AND DEVELOPMENT

The OECD is a unique forum where governments work together to address the economic, social and environmental challenges of globalisation. The OECD is also at the forefront of efforts to understand and to help governments respond to new developments and concerns, such as corporate governance, the information economy and the challenges of an ageing population. The Organisation provides a setting where governments can compare policy experiences, seek answers to common problems, identify good practice and work to co-ordinate domestic and international policies.

The OECD member countries are: Australia, Austria, Belgium, Canada, Chile, the Czech Republic, Denmark, Estonia, Finland, France, Germany, Greece, Hungary, Iceland, Ireland, Israel, Italy, Japan, Korea, Luxembourg, Mexico, the Netherlands, New Zealand, Norway, Poland, Portugal, the Slovak Republic, Slovenia, Spain, Sweden, Switzerland, Turkey, the United Kingdom and the United States. The European Union takes part in the work of the OECD.

OECD Publishing disseminates widely the results of the Organisation's statistics gathering and research on economic, social and environmental issues, as well as the conventions, guidelines and standards agreed by its members.

CENTRE FOR TAX POLICY AND ADMINISTRATION

The Centre for Tax Policy and Administration (CTPA) is the focal point for the OECD's work on taxation. The Centre provides technical expertise and support to the Committee on Fiscal Affairs and examines all aspects of taxation other than macro-fiscal policy. Its work covers international and domestic tax issues, direct and indirect taxes, tax policy and tax administration. CTPA also carries out an extensive global programme of dialogue between OECD and non-OECD tax officials through events held annually on the full range of OECD work, bringing together over 100 non-OECD economies. For information on the Centre for Tax Policy and Administration, please visit *www.oecd.org/tax*

OECD DEVELOPMENT CENTRE

The OECD Development Centre was established in 1962 as an independent platform for knowledge sharing and policy dialogue between OECD member countries and developing economies, allowing these countries to interact on an equal footing. Currently, 18 non-OECD countries are full members of the Centre's Governing Board. The Centre draws attention to emerging systemic issues likely to have an impact on global development and more specific development challenges faced by today's emerging and developing countries. It uses evidence-based analysis and strategic partnerships to help countries formulate innovative policy solutions to the global challenges of development. For more information on the Centre and its members, please see *www.oecd.org/dev*

ECONOMIC COMMISSION FOR LATIN AMERICA AND THE CARIBBEAN (ECLAC)

ECLAC is one of the five regional commissions of the United Nations. ECLAC was founded in 1948 for the purpose of contributing to the economic development of Latin America and the Caribbean, coordinating actions to promote that development and reinforcing economic ties among the region's countries and with other nations of the world.

Over the years, the institution's in-depth analysis of the region has taken the form of two main lines of action: economic and social research and the provision of technical cooperation to Governments. The Commission's ongoing concern for growth, technical progress, social justice and democracy has characterized the integral approach towards development that now forms part of the legacy of its rich intellectual tradition.

The 33 countries of Latin America and the Caribbean are member States of ECLAC, together with the United States, Canada, and several European and Asian countries that have historical, economic or cultural ties with the region. The Commission thus has a total of 44 member States. In addition, eight non independent Caribbean territories hold the status of associate members.

INTER-AMERICAN CENTER OF TAX ADMINISTRATIONS (CIAT IN SPANISH)

CIAT is an international public organization with a non-profit aim, which promotes international cooperation and the exchange of experiences and information related to tax administrations. It also delivers technical assistance services, studies and training.

It was founded in 1967 as an initiative of American countries to serve as a permanent forum to address the issues and concerns, first, of tax administrators, and then, of the tax administrations. Currently CIAT has 38 member countries and associate member countries from 4 continents: 31 countries of the Americas, 5 European countries, 1 African country and 1 Asian country.

CIAT is governed by a General Assembly consisting of representatives of member countries, an Executive Council composed of one President and 8 Council members, and an Executive Secretariat in charge of daily management, whose headquarters are in Panama City, Republic of Panama.

OECD PUBLISHING, 2, rue André-Pascal, 75775 PARIS CEDEX 16
(23 2014 01 3 P) ISBN 978-92-64-20793-6 – No. 61106 2014-01